P⁶
80

# Military Institutions and the Sociology of War

# SAGE SERIES ON ARMED FORCES AND SOCIETY

---

## INTER-UNIVERSITY SEMINAR ON ARMED FORCES AND SOCIETY

**Morris Janowitz,** *University of Chicago*
Chairman and Series Editor

**Charles C. Moskos, Jr.,** *Northwestern University*
Associate Chairman and Series Editor

**Sam C. Sarkesian,** *Loyola University*
Executive Secretary

*Also in this series:*

HANDBOOK OF MILITARY INSTITUTIONS
**Edited by Roger W. Little**

MILITARY PROFESSIONALIZATION AND POLITICAL POWER
**by Bengt Abrahamsson**

# Military Institutions and the Sociology of War

*A REVIEW OF THE LITERATURE*
*WITH ANNOTATED BIBLIOGRAPHY*

KURT LANG

SAGE PUBLICATIONS

Beverly Hills / London

*For information address:*

SAGE PUBLICATIONS, INC.
275 South Beverly Drive
Beverly Hills, California 90212

SAGE PUBLICATIONS LTD
St George's House / 44 Hatton Garden
London E C 1

Printed in the United State of America

International Standard Book Number 0-8039-0120-8

Library of Congress Catalog Card No. 72-162436

First Printing

# CONTENTS

## PREFACE

The text and the bibliography that follows it attempt to present an overview of the sociological literature on military affairs, that is to say of military sociology. This field as defined in Chapter 1 includes all those situations and structures where the element of organized violence constitutes a major and legitimate preoccupation—be it as a readily available means to some shared objective or as a potential last resort against attacks on the social order.

What is or is not sociological among the variety of orientations and approaches to this subject matter is far more difficult to specify. The countless hours I have spent trying to formulate explicit criteria leave me less than convinced of the virtues of being consistent. On this point as on others, readers will inevitably form their own judgments.

Quite obviously neither the disciplinary affiliation of an author, nor the journal in which he publishes is a very sound way of marking off military sociology from other writings on the subject. Though I have in all probability tended to favor the things written by sociologists and published in the regular sociological journals, the number of such entries amounts to less than half of the bibliography. Nonsociologists—i.e. political scientists, social historians, psychologists, and some military men—have gradually begun incorporating sociological concepts into their analyses. Others have systematically illuminated some military subject in ways that no sociologist can afford to ignore. Hence, I have no doubt stretched the boundaries on those topics that interest me in particular and on others on which information of any kind has been scarce.

Three types of writing were excluded as a matter of principle. The first is that of a clearly tendentious nature. Not the conclusions, but the type of analysis that leads toward some preconceived position, whatever it may be, is what limits the value such writing has for sociologists. A second type consists of the numerous policy studies conducted under various rubrics, like national security, strategic studies, or even peace research. Although some of them have made important contributions, the majority are highly topical. Finally there are the codifications of military experience into doctrines.

Although much can be learned from such men as Clausewitz, Jomini, Herman Kahn, Mao Tse-Tung, Che Guevara, Beaufré, and others like them, the sociologist should consider these writings on strategy and on military affairs primarily as data inviting analysis and not as the result of such analysis.

I have to the best of my ability covered the significant sociological literature from all countries and all theoretical perspectives. If American items nevertheless seem to predominate, this has several reasons, one of them the high sociological output in the United States over several decades. Others have nothing to do with this circumstance. The author, since he was himself trained in American sociology, inevitably has acquired some preconceptions that may not be shared by everyone else. Also his greater familiarity with the American literature and his inability to read languages other than English, German, and French—putting much literature beyond his reach—is a deficiency for which even the most generous aid from colleagues in other countries who drew his attention to representative works there could not fully compensate. Finally it has become evident to him that in some countries what we would call military sociology is published mostly, if at all, in reports whose circulation is restricted. As this type of publication could not possibly have been covered for all countries, it was covered for none.

The various in-house reports, certain types of government reports, most dissertations, and privately circulating drafts of unpublished papers are not usually obtainable through normal library channels. They have not been listed because to do so would be of little help to the person seeking an introduction to the field. One can also assume that those of more than passing interest and/or declassified will eventually find their way into the published professional literature. This decision unfortunately exacts its price. The inevitable time lag between the completion of any manuscript and its appearance in print means that this bibliography like others, of course, will be on the way towards obsolescence even before it is published. Its coverage of the literature goes only through the first half of 1970, and the limits of my attention span make it likely that the number of omissions for the last few months will be greater than for earlier years.

The actual treatment of the literature in the text is in some respects independent of the bibliographical listings. References in the text are merely illustrative of what seemed to me important concepts and propositions. Sources have been cited as they came to mind with no effort to be exhaustive. Moreover the headings and sequence differ from those in the bibliography as I found it too difficult to write with any degree of continuity while retaining a division that was meant to be discrete.

In the bibliography books, monographs, articles, and so forth are listed by author under headings they seemed best to fit with some cross listing of those that clearly cut across these artificial boundaries. Collections with diverse contributions from several authors are listed under the name of the editor with separate entries for individual articles by author whenever the importance of the item or the diversity of subjects treated between the covers of a single volume seemed to warrant it. Journal titles appear in their entirety throughout except for the following abbreviations in English-language publications:

| | |
|---|---|
| A. = Annals | P. = Proceedings |
| B. = Bulletin | Q. = Quarterly |
| J. = Journal | R. = Review |
| M. = Monograph | |

Annotations have also been used to supplement the descriptions of content given by the subject heading and the title alone. When a book has several editions, only the most recent is shown.

Special acknowledgment is due to Morris Janowitz and to the Inter-University Seminar on Armed Forces and Society which he founded and has piloted for many years. His prodding and encouragement as well as some financial aid through the seminar have helped this enterprise along. Among others generous with advice and assistance, I would like to mention in particular Bengt Abrahamsson, Dario Canton, M. D. Feld, Jacques van Doorn, and Jerzy Wiatr. A small grant-in-aid from the Graduate School of the State University of New York at Stony Brook provided for some extra hours of student assistance sorely needed to obtain missing information and to correct the errors that unavoidably show up only in the last minute. No such assistance, however competent and conscientiously given, can, of course, substitute for the compiler's own familiarity with the literature and with libraries. Where this turns out to have been deficient, he can only beg indulgence from those authors who may feel they have been offended against and invites them to submit whatever information would make a new edition more complete and more accurate.

*Kurt Lang*

Stony Brook, New York

# Military Institutions and the Sociology of War

# Chapter 1

# INTRODUCTION

## Scope and Definition

The subject matter of military sociology is best defined by reference to organized violence. All those situations and structures in which this element constitutes a major and legitimate preoccupation—whether as a readily available means to achieve some social objective or as a potential last resort—are within its scope. However offensive the persistence of brute force in human affairs may be to civilian sensibilities one is compelled to recognize that all societies, including those most "civilized," have certain institutionalized arrangements for developing and maintaining the capability to inflict, deter, and absorb physical violence when and if this should become necessary or advantageous. Recourse to armed force looms as an ever present possibility in the external relations between sovereign social units particularly in disputes that touch vital interests and threaten security. Hence, calculations of military strength are clearly a major component in the foreign policies of all states. Even those small nations whose limited resources cannot support armed forces at a level adequate to secure their territorial boundaries and whose moves within the interstate system depend on the tolerance and/or protective shield of the larger powers maintain some kind of military establishment to symbolize their sovereign status. In general military activities are directed against external and internal "enemies" that attack, or are perceived as attacking, the constituted power of the society.

The criterion of "violent means" places the field of military sociology within a more inclusive sociology of conflict, but sporadic outbursts of violence and conflict between individuals or groups insofar as the element of organization is lacking are not military phenomena. For intergroup violence to assume a military character, the claims of both parties in a conflict to belligerent status must be at least tacitly recognized by one another. Accordingly military sociology focuses on the permanent structures indispensable to the conduct of organized warfare. That military formations often have considerable impact on a society even when they are not involved in active hostilities is easily recognized. Not only can they double as internal security forces, but their bayonets and machine guns can be used to shore up a ruling group without a popular mandate. In still other instances members of the armed forces have intervened against constituted authority to advance their own interests. The military's possession of the instruments of violence places in its hands social and economic resources that must always be reckoned with. The characteristics of military men as a social type, the way military institutions operate and maintain themselves, as well as their role in domestic politics and in the interstate system are all matters of evident sociological concern.

This review of the literature is organized into five subdivisions, each of which identifies a particular focus of interest in the military: the military profession, military organizations, military systems, civil-military relations, and war and warfare.

*1. The Profession of Arms.* The military in most narrow terms constitutes a group whose members are dedicated to the martial arts as a lifetime pursuit. Today this identifies the professional officer for whom service in the armed forces represents a full career commitment rather than a part-time avocation or the fulfillment of a contractual or compulsory obligation. Recruitment, professional socialization, and career mobility are basically influenced by the fact that the military profession can be practiced only by members of the armed forces. In other words military professionals are not just specialists in the management of violence; they are also officers in an organization and subject to discipline in applying their expertise. The norms of behavior that professional officers accept as valid and the content of military ideology mirror a specific subculture. To the extent that participation in this subculture results in a unique point of view, a cluster of attitudes sometimes referred to as the "military mind," the various elements that form this outlook must be related to the nature of military expertise and to the milieu in which officers perform their duties.

*2. Military Organizations.* Armed forces, especially modern ones, are complex organizations. As such they have certain features associated with civilian bureaucracies of comparable size and complexity, but differ from these organizations insofar as they are structurally adapted to fulfill a unique, primary function. Military organizations are focally oriented toward the battle field. To be sure, the introduction of long-range nuclear weapons has changed priorities. The dominant mission and major preoccupation of the military in the most advanced countries, the superpowers in particular, has shifted away from violence aimed at the destruction of enemy forces to the development of a threat system designed as a deterrent. Yet the latter will not be credible unless the armed forces are prepared and capable of doing battle. Hence, combat readiness remains the critical measure of organizational effectiveness and military authority structure, managerial practices, work organization, and other internal arrangements continue to incorporate this rationale, even in units with no combat assignments.

*3. Military Systems.* Military activities in their totality make up an institutional system functionally integrated with the society at large. Exchanges and transfers of all sorts continually take place between the military and the civilian sector. From this perspective the military can be viewed as a complex system whose requirements for manpower and resources must be met. The effectiveness of a military system depends, on the one hand, on the nature and magnitude of military needs and, on the other, on the ease with which resources, skill, status, and power can be transferred between one sector and another without causing serious imbalances in either. Crucial to this perspective is the relation of armed forces to their social base.

*4. Civil-Military Relations.* Civil-military conflict and accommodation are elements in an emerging social order. To the extent that one focuses on the influence of military men in the social, ideological, and political domain or, conversely, on the extent of "civilian control" over broad policy and specific practices within the military, the issue is one of normative rather than functional integration. Traditions, ideologies, and institutional mechanisms for reaching accommodation may soften or exacerbate conflicts endemic in the divergent outlooks of the two groups. A major source of potential conflict lies in the relations between military leaders and their governments. Yet civil-military relations, though a natural topic for the political sociologist, are not confined to the governmental level. The attitudes of uniformed men and the civilian population toward one another, the work relations that form in specific contexts, and the political alliances between military and civilian groups help determine what influence the armed forces will exert not only in politics but also on social life generally.

5. *War and Warfare.* The study of war and warfare takes us into the area of violent intergroup conflict. Sociologists have naturally addressed themselves to the social causes, functions, and consequences of war as well as to the diverse forms it will take under different social conditions. However, the patterns of violence constitute collective behavior and as such merit attention not only in their own right, but also for whatever their study can contribute to our understanding of the dynamics of conflict. The processes that lead to the outbreak, intensification, and termination of hostilities have analogies in other conflicts that are pursued by less violent means.

In delineating the field of military sociology, I have explicitly rejected the notion that military sociology is essentially an applied discipline, its prime concern as defined by Hutchinson (17) the application of behaviorial science to problems of direct concern to military management. Despite some monumental contributions derived from this type of research (for example, 309, 405, 437, and 473), much of the work conducted by the services themselves, concerned as it is with testing, diagnosing, evaluating specific programs and practices, and so forth remains too particularistic to shed much light on basic sociological problems.

It is also essential to make a distinction between sociologists *of* the military and those working *in* the military or *for* the military, i.e., as their client. The former have full freedom in their choice of subject matter. They will select whatever they think will contribute to sociological knowledge. Hence, they are far more likely to question in their work the basic assumptions behind the military ethos and behind military activities—as for example, the viability of force in international relations, the domination of some associations by ex-officers, or the traditions and doctrines taken for granted within the military—than their peers in the employ, directly or indirectly, of the military. The work of the latter is nearly always responsive in some way or other to the needs of the military usually as perceived by nonsociologists. Perhaps this is only as it should be. The point is, however, that with the monitoring of the internal military environment becoming a more and more routine operation, sociologists in the military are being redirected toward area study and the type of political and strategic analysis which are adjuncts to normal intelligence operations. To this extent many sociologists in the U.S. military have ceased in any way to function as "military sociologists" as here defined.

Finally it should be pointed out that the activities of the police in quelling an internal disturbance, those of "civil defense," those of irregulars, or even those of armed brigands engaged in organized forage also involve perspectives that are to some extent military. As a rule these are not treated as military sociology, however. Yet propositions derived from the study of the military could be tested or certainly clarified with respect to these kindred structures and situations in which the element of organized violence is similarly present though in a different way.

## General Overview

The persistence of organized violence as an element in the relations between states and also to some degree in internal politics has been the subject of much thought and moral recrimination, but has until recently received only scant attention from empirically minded social scientists. This neglect is attributed to the discovery of social structure during the 19th century which, as Speier (1064) has pointed out, diverted concern away from violence. In place of threats to physical safety, the most elementary form of risk, the vulnerabilities and deprivations related to social position have commanded the greatest share of attention. Concern over the effects of economic insecurity and of exclusion from the full rights of citizenship led to the development of a sociology of class conflict, of economic exploitation, of poverty, and of minorities, all of them significant social concerns, long before a sociology of the military gained status as a distinct field.

To the extent that violence by individuals lay outside the framework of social norms, it could be treated as a manifestation of irrationality, as an individual or group pathology, and as a form of deviance. But violence acclaimed as a legitimate instrument of national policies could not so easily be discounted. The meliorative orientation typical of sociologists inclined them towards an anti-militarist position from which war was viewed as a throwback to primitive barbarism and military institutions as anachronisms. Despite the increasing mechanization of warfare and the wholesale adoption by the armed forces of the most advanced technology, many sociologists held military and industrial societies to be founded on two entirely different principles with modes of social and political life of the two antithetical to one another.

The theorem positing an irreconcilable contradiction between military activity predicated on brute force and inherently peaceful industrial pursuits based on the division of labor is heir to a long and respectable tradition going back at least as far as Adam Ferguson's *Essay on the History of Civil Society* published in 1767. The distinction was sharpened by St. Simon and taken over by the Social Darwinists in whose sociological system it occupied a critical place. To primordial warfare were attributed the original amalgamations out of which arose society, the state, and other institutions of social control. In this formulation the significance of violent struggle is largely relegated to the past and believed to be progressively diminishing. Thus, Herbert Spencer (507) who more than any other social theorist is closely identified with Social Darwinism firmly held that industrial competition being more efficient would inevitably replace earlier forms of struggle.

Evolutionary notions of this sort were shared by even the most extreme advocates of the 19th century conflict school. According to Gumplovicz (1016) deadly hatred among the races which had once led to slaughter was being transmuted with the advance of history into slavery and economic exploitation. His student, Ratzenhofer, similarly discerned the gradual and progressive replacement of the "conflict state" by the "culture state." It is from Ratzenhofer's work that William G. Sumner (1041) derived the view that war served to consolidate a group and that its major historical consequence lay in the extension of the area within which peace and order prevailed.

The treatment these writers give to war and military activity are primarily expressions of their image of society not based on empirical research and it is toward the premises underlying these theories that the critics of Social Darwinism directed their fire. As the numerous illustrations amassed by the Russian anarchist Prince Peter Kropotkin were to show, spontaneous cooperation was far more important even in animal and primitive societies than either conflict or competition.[1] Contrariwise, Werner Sombart (626), generally viewed as a spokesman for German nationalist interest, attempted to demonstrate in a monograph published in 1913 the compatibility of war with capitalist development. Sombart based his argument on observations limited to Central Europe in the 16th and

17th centuries and his critics concede their partial validity. Yet his general thesis meets stern rejection by John U. Nef (1248) who not only takes Sombart to task for his complete failure to understand the spirit on which industrial civilization was founded, but charges him with a deliberately one-sided use of historical evidence which leaves entirely out of account the setbacks resulting from the destructive effects of the Thirty Year War.

The costs and losses incurred in war are focal in several works written before World War I. The content of *La guerre et ses bienfaits prétendus* by the French sociologist Jacques Novicow (1250) is clearly indicated by its title. Special mention should also be made of a multivolume work by an industrialist turned social critic whose warnings anticipated in many respects the strategic considerations with which we have become fully familiar during the nuclear era. Jean de Bloch (1149a) turned his attention to the destructive power of the weapons in existence at the turn of the century and to the high cost of maintaining armies in the field. In the war of the future, he concluded, there could no longer be any victors; all would lose alike. War had therefore become "impossible." The prediction, its sound logical basis notwithstanding, appears to have been somewhat premature; yet its tone is surprisingly similar to that of the prophets of atomic holocaust with which our era has become fully familiar.

The unleashing of organized violence on an unprecedented scale in the years 1914 to 1918 brought such destruction and social disorganization as to leave little doubt that armed conflict had not been superseded by less violent forms of struggle. And the improved statistical records available offered a chance to detail the effects of war with far greater accuracy than had ever before been possible. The Carnegie Endowment for International Peace project on *The Economic and Social History of the World War* (34) under the general editorship of James T. Shotwell sponsored about 150 monographs, each detailing how some aspect of the economy or society had been affected by the war in one or more of twenty-one countries. None of the monographs sought explicitly to contribute to the sociological study of war, but this assessment of war "damages" covers a wide range of sociologically relevant materials, among them the demographic consequences of war, its effect on public health, on crime, on income distribution, as well as problems relating to prisoners of war, population movements, and refugees.

Some of these materials were incorporated into the sociological analyses of war that appeared during the interwar period. A major tome was the *Soziologie des Krieges* by Steinmetz (1040), a vastly expanded version of his earlier *Philospohie des Krieges* which had appeared in 1908. Steinmetz continued to take a Social Darwinist position, hailing war as the mechanism par excellence for testing the national will. He did not believe that the destructive power of weapons was very relevant for the character of a war; a nation always had the option of surrendering even before the first shot. There were other works in this tradition (see 1017), but they were counterbalanced by those where the pacifist tradition of the author was clearly evident. The treatise of Cornejo (1005) is a good example of the latter; also the writings of Norman Angell who had considerable popular impact, and other nonsociologists. None of the studies written in the aftermath of World War I seem in retrospect to have had much influence on military sociology as it subsequently developed, whatever their point of view.

Of significant influence, however, was the group that formed at the University of Chicago in the mid-thirties around two political scientists, Harold D. Lasswell and Quincy Wright. Their approach was thoroughly empirical, and Wright's two volumes (1049) are still a major work on the sociology of war. Soon afterwards with World War II looming on the horizon, a group of refugee scholars at the New School for Social Research formed an interdisciplinary faculty and a seminar. Some of the papers presented there were published as *War in Our Time* (1262).

Another line of inquiry developed around the time-honored theme that pervasive militarism at home and imperialist ventures abroad served certain class interests. St. Simon, to cite one of the main precursors of modern sociology, had seen standing armies as the main obstacle to progress, and the critics of imperialism—socialists and others—believed imperialism to be a reactionary, if not an outright diabolical, social force. Guided by this assumption, sociologists set out to document how feudal archaisms, class bias, and social snobbery so rampant among professional officers of "modern" and even republican nations ensured the social dominance of groups whose power was waning and who rarely possessed the superior virtues and competence on which their claims to superior status were based. Hamon's inquiry into the psychology of the professional military (179) published in 1895 is formulated in sociological terms, but his incrimination of the officers' devotion to patriotism draws almost exclusively on journalistic accounts so that in the end the essay itself is not much more than a journalistic tract. Later studies not only provided more systematic documentation, but also surpassed this level of conceptualization. For example the class discrimination practiced in the German Imperial officer corps was the subject of several articles in the 1920's; one by Endres (174) and another by Kehr (703) represent significant contributions to the understanding of the officers' ideology in relation to the social structure of the German army.

Much wider in scope than the above is Schumpeter's classic essay on the sociology of imperialism (1063) where, writing after World War I, he endeavors systematically to link the military and imperialist expansionism. Using the same logic that had led him in his explanation of economic growth to identify the innovating entrepreneur as the carrier of economic development, he pointed in this essay to the machine of warriors as the driving force behind military ventures. "Created by the wars that required it, the machine now creates the wars it requires" (p. 25). It is Schumpeter's thesis that capitalism did not create this military machine, but since it existed was ready to capitalize on whatever adventures the warriors that had survived in its midst were prone to seek.

In this connection another distinction commends itself. It is the one between what is "military" in a strict sense of being related to the preparation for and the conduct of war and the phenomenon called "militarism." The latter as defined by Vagts (102) refers to the vast array of attitudes, sentiments, and ceremonial practices through which the ideological belief in the superiority of everything military to anything civilian is cultivated and continuously reaffirmed. Others (for example 707 and 818) have emphasized instead the unwarranted intrusion of military men into other realms.

Militarism in either of the above senses has little to do with either military capability or efficiency in military operations; often it actually leads to the very obverse result. Interest in militarism tends to preempt the field of military sociology to the degree that disillusionment with and organized opposition to the armed forces and their role in society are widely prevalent. The obviously disastrous policies that had culminated in the outbreak of World War I with its apparently senseless slaughter of men could only underscore the irrationality of the militant enthusiasm with which countries embarked on this course. War sentiment and the unwarranted exaltation of the military are far more tempered today than they were at the turn of the century. Following the ravages of World War I apprehensiveness over impending war gradually led people to question what was so often presented as inexorable military necessity.

Although military influence on policy and politics are significant facets of militarism, they are by no means the only ones. If it is true that war is too serious a business to be left in the hands of military men, the same can be said with regard to other matters to which the conventional military wisdom provided ready answers. World War I revealed dramatically, as other wars had before, the inadequacies of traditional orientations regarding military discipline and troop leadership. These had always been exclusively under the direction of the military, and it must be recognized that some military men despite professional and class biases exhibited considerable acuity in analyzing the interplay between material and moral, i.e., social, factors in war, the direction of war, the nature of military leadership, and the factors in combat effectiveness. One illustration of this is the work of Colonel Ardant du Picq, who in his *Battle Studies* (423) developed generalizations based on 19th-century wars that in many ways anticipate sociological propositions subsequently rediscovered by social scientists once they turned their attention to the behavior of troops in combat and in captivity. A sizeable body of literature on this topic was produced during and after World War I, most of it by medical specialists including psychologists (447).[2] Although the rigor with which these studies were conducted fell far short of present-day standards, they nevertheless amounted in their totality to a damning indictment of the traditional philosophy of military leadership and manpower management, an indictment that was dramatically underscored by the susceptibility of returning soldiers, even in victorious nations, to the political ferment of the 1920's. The lessons implicit in frontline experience were most systematically exploited in a book published in Germany in 1922. In it Dr. Kurt Hesse (326) who had seen combat service set forth systematically the ways in which combat leadership would have to be adapted to the new realities of warfare.

As methodology in the behavioral sciences advanced in the interwar years, officials gradually recognized that techniques useful in studying other areas could yield similar returns for military management. Here, too, the Germans appear to have been pace-setters. The Reichswehr of the 1920's, drastically curtailed in size and therefore faced with a surfeit of volunteers, sought optimal utilization of what manpower it could draw upon. By incorporating psychological tests and group interviews into its selection procedures, it sought to improve the qualifications of military personnel and, as a prerequisite for future expansion, to identify those with special leadership potential. Initially sociologists had little to do with these innovations. The first major step toward their full involvement came in the United States where the Army Research Branch, formed in 1941 and headed by an academic sociologist, conducted attitude surveys among servicemen to locate and diagnose morale problems that would inevitably arise during rapid mobilization. Sociologists in this group were the first to be employed explicitly as sociologists by any branch of the U.S. government. Work conducted by the Tavistock Institute in Britain during World War II was in many ways similar, but conducted on a smaller scale and somewhat more psychological in orientation. The process toward greater involvement has become irreversible. In the years since, various kinds of behavioral science investigations have become routine adjuncts of managerial procedures.

The studies of the U.S. Army Research Branch, the major findings of which were summarized and interpreted in several volumes commonly known as *The American Soldier* (309 and 473), touched on many matters beyond the scope of its mission as initially defined. Their data on army promotion, on military leadership, on combat performance, and several other topics provide bench marks that no subsequent inquiries could ignore. Important contributions to the sociology of military organization also accrued from other World War II activities adjunct to military operations. I am referring to publications based on the surveys of German soldiers taken prisoner by U.S. troops conducted by the Psychological Warfare Board (437); the reports of S.L.A. Marshall, a military historian charged with the investigation of incidents where ground combat troops had performed poorly or even panicked (431); and observations of the behavior of troops by psychiatrists (427). The above certainly have entered the mainstream of sociological literature. The collective picture they offered of the significance of interpersonal relations and group cohesion for performance under fire has been substantiated as well as refined in subsequent research.

The growth of sociology in the United States by World War II is also manifest in the number of young professionals and graduate students called into military service. Although their wartime duties, more likely than not, had absolutely no relationship to professional training, many brought their sociological sensitivity and analytic skills to bear on whatever new experiences their assignments opened to them. The July 1946 issue of the *American Journal of Sociology*, entitled "Human Behavior in Military Society" (50) is made up entirely of articles by those recently separated from the armed forces. Many of the articles in this issue, as in other issues of sociological journals in the immediate postwar period, offer interpretations based on participant observation about the essential character of military social structure either as a bureaucracy (209, 251, and 261) or in contrast with civilian life (201, 202, 204, and 212, for example). There are in addition discussions of specific aspects of the military milieu, such as ceremonialism (172, 385), soldiers' language (391), rites de passage (354), rumor (388), and morality (280).

The military milieu had thus attained legitimate status as a subject of sociological inquiry. One of the main stimuli to further development came from the armed services. Intent on finding the key to morale and effectiveness through research, they began to invest heavily in a variety of sociological, group psychological, and psychiatric studies. Other countries followed bit by bit the course set by the United States and Britain in conducting research as a normal adjunct to managerial operations. Summaries of some of the inquiries typically conducted by the various centers and institutes serving the armed forces can be found in Hall (14) and in Bowers (4) for the United States, in Vial (27) and in Chandessais (7) for Germany, and in Solomon (368) for Canada. The NATO symposium edited by Geldard (53) provides some insight into the similarities and differences of focus within the countries of the Western alliance. Inquiries of an essentially similar nature are also conducted by the military of Soviet bloc nations. (See, for example, 1 and 52.)

Not that these studies failed to touch on basic sociological issues, but there was some tendency, as Hall (14) points out in his review of the American work in the first postwar decade, to conceive the problem in narrow terms with an emphasis on factors subject to manipulation and without full acknowledgment of the various indirect ramifications. Insights to be gained from this kind of military sociology are consequently limited. Michaels (970) made a similar criticism of U.S. military operations research. Part of the problem arises from the natural sensitivity all organizations have with the close scrutiny of their operations by outsiders. In the case of the military, this sensitivity was, and still is, all too readily legitimated by national security considerations. Access to pertinent information is often denied unless the military acts as the sponsor and sees its particular interests served by the inquiry, while the data so collected are often placed in the category of classified information. These restrictions, though becoming less stringent in some regards, make it more difficult to test propositions cross nationally and to use such replicative studies to develop a body of cumulative knowledge.

As long as war aims and policy goals enjoyed full popular support, as they generally did in World War II, sociologists were apt to view civil-military relations primarily in terms of adaptations forced on citizen soldiers by the exigencies of a military life tolerated by civilian leaders. The prolonged cold war changed all this. Policy issues which had always been the province of political scientists came to the fore again. Interest revived in the implications of maintaining a large-scale permanent military establishment. It inspired studies of the legal and administrative structure of civil-military relations and of specific decision-making episodes. Most of these were historical and descriptive, including the Twentieth Century Fund studies of decisions in the area of military policy (955), noteworthy for the care with which they detailed the various steps in the policy process.

Although sociologists initially ceded this area to political scientists, a fusion of perspectives is taking place. The latter are progressively incorporating explicitly sociological perspectives into their political studies of civil-military relations. One of the first post-war books of this genre is Huntington's study on *The Soldier and the State* (657), which appeared in 1957. His discussion of the legal and administrative framework within which modern nations adjust policy and strategy contains a brief treatment of the sociological character of the officer profession including its ethos and ideology. Huntington also offers a set of propositions that relate military political power, military professionalism, and the prevailing ideology to balance and equilibrium in civil-military relations. *The Professional Soldier* by Janowitz (88) which appeared two years after the Huntington study takes as its central topic the changing character of the military profession. This volume presents a detailed and partly quantitative social and political profile of the American military; social background, career patterns, and professional subculture are invoked to explain policy commitments and ideological divergences as they exist within the military leadership nucleus, i.e., the small body of powerful officers who play a major role in the formation of policy.

Sociological studies of the professional military in other nations are becoming available. These studies differ both in their main focus and methods, but all address themselves to the same kind of problem. The second and enlarged editions of Demeter's work (72) depicts the structural transformation of the German officer corps over a period of 300 years. A volume edited by Girardet (76) contains several studies of French officers that deal with changes occurring during the period of "decolonization." The book by Busquets Bragulat (68) on the professional officer in Spain parallels Janowitz's work on the American soldier in several respects, while the monograph by Ochoa de Eguileor and Beltran (190) is largely a study of social and political attitudes among officers in Argentina. These studies address themselves to structure; some, like the article on the Finnish military elite by Krekola (93) and that on the Irish army by Jackson (181), set out especially to test some of Janowitz's hypotheses. All of them are more than social history.

Whether in the hands of sociologists or of historians and political scientists, the case study method when used by itself has obvious limitations. Nowhere is this more evident than in the attempt to develop a theory of civil-military relations. Every case seems to suggest new variables and contingent influences with the actual number used highly dependent on the sensitivity and analytic style of the investigator. In any event, paradigms based on a single case have a way of escaping the legitimate bounds imposed by the actual data.

Hence, the thrust of research toward comparative analysis. In terms of the scope of material it attempts to cover, *Military Organization and Society* by Andreski (482), the first edition of which appeared in 1954, was certainly a significant step forward, but like some earlier studies on army and society, such as the book by Katherine Chorley (751), the procedure is to amass historical illustrations in support of stated propositions. In this regard, it is not in any rigorous sense either inductive or a test of a hypothesis. To a degree the same criticism applies to Finer's more recent book on the role of the military in politics (764). Unlike his predecessors he was, however, able to draw on postwar experience with military takeovers in nations just freed from foreign domination. Attempts at broad theoretical synthesis are to be found in essays by Edinger (925), Shils (674), Aron (638), Janowitz (660), Bobrow (485), Ronneberger (672), and Lissak (853). These relate the structural characteristics of the armed forces to the role they are likely to play in the policy process or in the economic, political, and social development of emerging nations. Intensive comparisons among countries sharing an essentially similar tradition can likewise be useful. Thus Rudolf and

Rudolf (819) have compared India and Pakistan, Haddad (777) four Near Eastern nations, Janowitz (87) the countries of modern Europe, McAlister (802), Putnam (867), and others the countries of Latin America. The focus in most of these comparative studies is on political intervention by the military. In fact, the bulk of the work in current academic journals deals with the military in the new nations and the underdeveloped parts of the world.

Any parochialism in military sociology is in large measure a legacy of the way research efforts were launched during World War II when the use of behavioral scientists in psychological warfare, strategic intelligence, morale and personnel management was a direct response to military needs. This made the field suspect. Parochialism would not have been overcome to the degree that it has without the existence of a forum where sociologists interested in research on the military could meet in a nonmilitary setting and share their concerns. Such a forum was created by Morris Janowitz in the Inter-University Seminar on Military Organization organized in the mid-fifties at the University of Michigan. The research contained in *The New Military* (55) indicates the range of interests among the participants. The name of the seminar was subsequently changed to Inter-University Seminar on Armed Forces and Society, and this group became the nucleus for the similarly designated working group of the International Sociological Association. The two volumes entitled *Armed Forces and Society* (61), and *Military Profession and Military Regimes* (62), both edited by Van Doorn, contain a selection of papers presented at two conferences. In this way the work on the military by academic sociologists has not only found a place within sociology but also become familiar to military men. The international group has directed some efforts toward encouraging the release of research reports from the various armed forces so as to promote comparative study.

That military sociology has gained acceptance as a recognized specialty within sociology is further documented by the increasingly frequent appearance of articles under this rubric in such bibliographical sources as the *Sociological Abstracts* and by the inclusion of chapters on the military, written by sociologists, in compendia of research (4, 14, 23, 28, 206, and 245). The precedent set by the postwar issue of the *American Journal of Sociology* was repeated several times in the 1960's, when issues of major sociological journals were almost wholly given over to military sociology. The latest of these, a special issue of the *Kölner Zeitschrift für Soziologie* (56), brings together the work of German and American sociologists.

The availability of a relevant body of empirical materials has naturally spawned efforts to summarize and synthesize the field (see Section I.1 of the bibliography). Most of these efforts have fallen far short in their coverage of the total range of sociological interests in military phenomena. The little book which Janowitz first prepared for the American Sociological Association in 1959 was revised with Roger Little and appeared in a second edition six years later (18). Its main focus is on the military establishment as a social system responsive to social and technological change. The International Sociological Association with the support of UNESCO subsequently also sponsored a bibliographical and trend report on military sociology in which the literature is systematically reviewed but not evaluated (20). The present summary is in fact an extensive revision of that report.

Despite the availability of an increasing body of research material, the interest and number of academic offerings in military sociology outside the educational institutions of the armed forces is still quite paltry. Perhaps this has something to do with the lack of conventional texts and other reading materials. Although the first introduction to military sociology, written by Wiatr (29), appeared in 1960, both this text and what appears to be a revised edition (30) were published under the imprimatur of the Polish ministry of defense and not as accessible as they would have been had editions in other languages been available. There is available a Spanish text written by an Argentine general (22). The only English language text is the one co-authored by Coates and Pellegrin (8), the former a retired U.S. colonel. Perhaps because it was published privately, it has only enjoyed a limited distribution. All this, however, is merely symptomatic of the reluctance of sociologists to face up to the realities of the military presence. Testimony on the relatively modest amount of work currently being done on the subject can be obtained from a perusal of headings in the *International Social Science Bibliography: Sociology*. It contains subheadings for such institutional systems as education, medicine, and law but not for the military. In fact, the number of entries listed in the index under such terms as war, military, and army is far larger in the political science than in sociology volumes of the bibliography. It is unlikely that this state of affairs will persist for very much longer. The "new" sociology is, among other things, an indication that the role played by power and brute force clamors for recognition. Hopefully this will be translated into the kind of analysis that is at once objective and revealing. The work so far is at least a start.

## NOTES

1. P. A. Kropotkin, *Mutual Aid as a Factor in Evolution*. New York: McClure, Phillips, 1902. The more recent work by the naturalist and ethologist, Konrad Lorenz, offers a far more balanced account of the way aggression functions in the animal world to distribute members of the same species and how it is redirected and inhibited in the interest of social solidarity. See K. Lorenz, *On Aggression*. New York: Harcourt, Brace & World, 1966. Unfortunately his theories have received a rather dogmatic extension in the work of R. Ardrey, *The Territorial Imperative: a Personal Inquiry into the Animal Origins of Property and Nations*. London: Collins, 1967.

2. See, for example, A. Gemelli. *Il nostro soldato; saggi di psichologia militare* [Our soldier: cases in military psychology]. Milan: F. Treves, 1917; A. L. Vischer. *Barbed Wire Disease: a Psychological Study of the Prisoner of War*. London: J. Bale, Sons & Danielsson, 1919.

Chapter 2:

# THE PROFESSION OF ARMS

In the modern world the management of the armed forces is usually entrusted to a group of men who consider themselves professional officers and who exhibit many of the characteristics that are the hallmark of professional bodies everywhere. Huntington (657) offers a succinct discussion of the military as a profession. The professional military, according to Huntington, lays claim to a distinct field of expertise: the management of violence. It furthermore subscribes to a concept of professional responsibility; officers apply their specialized military knowledge in their capacity as public servants. Finally, the professional military has a corporate identity. The unique customs, codes, traditions, and lore that are part of the military way of life, the clubs and associations officers belong to, the uniforms and insignia they wear—all of these tend to set them apart from other officials. Professional military officers are a world unto themselves.

*Professionalization.* Andreski (482) cites two conditions which encourage professionalism—a concept he never quite defines. The first exists when the skills necessary for martial activity "can be acquired only by protracted and continuous training . . . with which normal economic activities cannot be reconciled"; the second when war waged in distant theatres impedes communication and contact between the people and their army (p. 34). Both conditions do contribute to the isolation of the military from society, but the second in particular seems just as likely to promote military formations not under the management of professionals. Mercenaries, to be sure, are soldiers by vocation; they will fight for pay and booty and without necessarily embracing the idea of professional service. Nor need they develop a core of esoteric knowledge. The point is that skill in such things as the use of fire arms, the handling of horses, of ships, of planes, etc., has to be acquired and maintained through practice, but such proficiency differs from the kind of expertise that goes into strategic and operational planning, into the organization and training of a force, and into its direction in combat. Only the latter is the unique acquisition of the military professional. All too often such expertise has been conspicuously lacking in armies whose officers were selectively recruited on the basis of their elite connections, including aristocratic origin. The concern of an officer corps, thusly recruited, about its traditional privileges tended to make the standing armies of absolutism inhospitable to reforms designed to improve the level of skill and military effectiveness, even when members of the aristocracy were themselves prime movers behind these efforts (102). Wherever military activities are the exclusive prerogative of an estate or of a caste of warriors, as they were for example in ancient India (685), professionalization is apt to be blocked rather than advanced.

Although warfare is a time-honored pursuit and military institutions are largely crescive, it does not follow that the military constitutes the "oldest profession," at least not in any strict sociological sense. On the contrary, professionalization of the officer corps is a relatively recent development brought about by the twin forces of industrial development and modern nationalism. The new technology and the more complex forms of organization that corresponded to it have progressively raised the level of skill required to direct troops in battle; these and other activities related to the management of armed forces could no longer be performed simply as an honorific avocation. Thus, officership ceased to be a part-time pursuit and became a life-time career. Meanwhile with the emergence of new political forces, armies whose officers were tied to the sovereign by an oath of personal fealty increasingly took on the character of a national military establishment whose officers, even more than the men they led, were responsive to patriotic appeals. To be sure, some ingredients of the old status honor did survive in the codes of professional officers, but their meaning and significance changed once they became assimilated and subordinate to more inclusive notions of duty to people and nation.

The development of professionalism is a major theme in many book-length historical studies of officers in particular nations, such as Chalmin (70), Colby (71), Demeter (72), Girardet (77), Gorlitz (78), Kitchen (90), de La Gorce (793), Lewis (95), and—for Western Europe generally—Vagts (102). Also, many of the more general surveys of armed forces and military institutions focus on this topic (see for example 8, 18, 648, and 784). Certainly the concept of professionalism provides a useful framework for the analysis of many aspects of the military ethos and of officer behavior, including how willing they are to limit their political role to expert advice on strictly military issues. The latter is, in fact, the focus of Huntington's *The Soldier and the State* which, as already pointed out, discusses why the military should be treated as a profession. That book and many of the case studies listed in Part V of the bibliography emphasize civil-military relations. They should be consulted by those who are primarily interested in the patterns of conflict and accommodation between soldiers and their governments. In this section we are concerned with developments internal to the military.

Professionalism, as that term is understood by sociologists, was gradually imposed on the officer corps of most European nations. The internal impetus came primarily, as we have said, from advances in weapons technology. The claims by persons of high social standing to elevated rank solely on that basis could no longer be sustained. Because they did not produce a sufficiently qualified military leadership, it became necessary to evolve new criteria of eligibility and rank. Yet the change did not occur all at once. Not only are traditional and modern elements normally fused within the professional military ethos, but different individuals and different units often give remarkably different emphases to each. Thus, there was the long drawn-out tug of war during the period of British naval ascendancy between the "seaman commanders" who were essentially mariners and craftsmen and worked their way up by degree as they gained the experience to command and the "gentlemen commanders" whose training was casual and who were granted their rank largely because of their social standing. The naval profession was born when the rivalry was finally resolved in favor of the seamen (74; see also 95). Likewise in the various land armies, criteria of demonstrated competence for promotion to higher rank were themselves established only against strong opposition (96). Wherever in the military traditionalist officers were entrenched, they tended to cultivate all kinds of feudal archaisms (75 and 102). That they continued to do so long after their disutility had become fully evident is demonstrated by the tenacity with which officers resisted replacement of the horse cavalry by motorized infantry (246). In many European countries a few guard regiments, usually those stationed near the capital, remained the privileged preserve of aristocratic officers up to the beginning of World War I and sometimes even longer. A limited number of officer positions in these regiments were available for purchase by sons of wealthy families. The existence of such discrimination in Imperial Germany where the majority of middle class officers had to content themselves with less desirable assignments, such as a provincial garrison town, is fully documented by Endres (174). Similar tendencies prevailed in other countries. The armed forces nearly everywhere contained enclaves for officers who, whether or not of aristocratic birth, above all were "gentlemen." One sees this, for example, in the lower social class background of officers in the British colonial forces compared with those in the Home Army (132). Class background continues to play a role in India (110) whose armed forces have taken over much of the British tradition.

The demand for talent has always been greater in the more technical branches. Hence, some of the ablest young men have always been drawn to engineering, artillery, and transport where performance could more easily compensate for the lack of a requisite family background. This has in fact been true of nearly every newly formed branch. For example aristocratic traditions never held sway in the German navy—a significant force only toward the end of the nineteenth century—to the degree they did in the army (73), and the air arms nearly everywhere have opened new opportunities. Van Riper and Umwalla (138) note that even in the U.S. armed forces a technical career provides unusual opportunity for those with rare skills but often without the requisite service academy backgrounds.

It also stands to reason that the more technological branches led the way in upgrading the expertise of their officers through education. Schools of artillery and engineering had been set up by each of the major continental powers—France, Russia, and Prussia— as well as Great Britain by the middle of the eighteenth century (106). To be sure, the curriculum in these schools remained primarily technical, and since at that time these branches did not enjoy the prestige that is nowadays associated with a technological image, a career in them could be held against an officer when he came up for promotion for the higher levels of command. It was from such beginnings, however, that the role of military expertise gradually gained full recognition.

To a degree, of course, technical knowledge has always played a part im military operations, only this was not the basis on which officers qualified. At the root of the various conflicts and divisions are two divergent role models: the "heroic" and the "managerial" Janowitz (88) calls them. Until not too long ago, the heroic and personal element associated with troop command formed the dominant part of the image of what an officer was. Although troop command continues to occupy an important place among the functions officers perform and such assignments, especially in combat, are still eagerly sought by many officers hoping to advance, because they remain a means for judging leadership potential, the military manager has displaced the troop leader as the model of success at the highest ranks.

The new role model takes account of the growing organizational complexity and internal diversity of armed forces. It has become institutionalized in a general staff of which the German version founded in the middle of the nineteenth century has been the prototype (247). Although that organizational innovation has broken the path for most other armies to follow, traditionalist resistance was strong everywhere and forced many a compromise, even in Germany, as a result of which some of the older forms were retained along with the new. Thus, the Imperial German Army entered World War I with still an essentially dual structure: the highest commands were reserved for the scions of royal houses, while the general staff corps retained collective responsibility for the actual tasks of military management (78 and 755). This arrangement was a source of considerable strain within the German command, but a new military leadership adequate to the new demands could not be developed without the complete structural transformation of the officer corps. Appropriate criteria had somehow to be worked out or the old ones accordingly modified. How this has recently taken place in the German army is the topic of an interesting monograph by Model (128).

Many problems remain. In Germany the dominance of the land forces among the nucleus of professionally trained managers interfered with the evolution in World War II of a concept of combined operations adequate to the new realities (247). The army elite was unable to divest itself of the overriding strategic importance of ground combat, a notion that had been implanted in them early in their professional career. Residues can be found everywhere. Thus, the promotion system of the U.S. Navy remains formally geared to what is "normal" for officers of the line, retaining an established principle while allowing for considerable flexibility in the selection of other categories of officers for promotion. Officer rotation, too, acquires a new meaning under the changed circumstances. This practice, originally intended to weed out those not suited for troop command, has become an institutional device for exposing potential military managers to a broad range of experience through which they can acquire the perspective essential for the duties they will have to assume at the highest levels of command responsibility.

Not all these changes in role apply equally throughout the entire profession. Hence, strains and dilemmas will arise that, unless resolved by the profession as a whole, the individual officers have to learn somehow to tolerate. Insofar as neither adaptation nor resolution results, cleavages within the military are apt to multiply. These cleavages will not be confined to those who cling to tradition versus those others more responsive to new requirements, but they will also divide the advocates of different solutions.

*Recruitment.* Historically, common soldiers were commoners led by their social superiors. Officers, it was assumed, had to be "born" to command. The shift, in the apt phrase by Janowitz (88), "from ascription to achievement," which exemplifies the growth of professionalism is indexed by the shift in the social origins of officers. The general trend, though far from universal, is still unmistakable: a preponderance of the aristocratic component diminished everywhere and sons of middle class families joined the officer ranks. (See 68, 87, 88, 92, 93, 103, 123 and others.) The rate of change has accelerated since the turn of the century with lower and lower middle class persons qualifying more readily so long as they have the requisite education. In terms of social origin, officers at all ranks are somewhat more representative of the general population nowadays than they once were. This leveling effect has been somewhat less apparent in the highest ranks since recruitment into top positions is usually from within the organization. Even so, the family connections many top ranking officers still have with other elites seem nowadays to play a smaller role in their rise.

The social origins of officers have been a matter of considerable concern largely as a clue to the military's attitudes on social and political matters. Political leaders have viewed the democratization of officer recruitment as a means of ensuring the loyalty of the armed forces, especially during periods of political instability. In some countries, among them France during the nineteenth century and Russia following the revolution, this became an issue to which governmental policy addressed itself. A republican regime had to have a commoner officer contingent to offset the monarchist sentiments shared by most aristocrats; a socialist or communist regime felt it imperative to increase the number of "proletarians" within the officer corps. Thus, Wiatr (141) has suggested that once bourgeois elements are eliminated in an initial purge and socialist institutions are well-rooted, the social composition of the officer corps is no longer any issue. Kolkowicz (182 and 183) states that the Soviet army, despite its revolutionary origins, has become fully professionalized; the only vestige of this past is the demand for indisputable allegiance to a single political party by which it is rigidly controlled. Intercohort changes in the military elite in China since the revolution are systematically documented in an article by Whitson (140).

What needs to be recognized is this: the development of professionalism is by no means a direct consequence of democratization of the officer recruitment base, nor is such democratization a prerequisite of professionalization. In general, however, the two developments have tended to coincide. In Germany, for example, the upgrading of the education and training of officers was achieved through internal reform, led by men who wanted to maximize the effectiveness of the armed forces but were themselves aristocrats and monarchists. In the Soviet Union the drive to improve the qualifications of officers in the Red Army not only led to the recall of many former Czarist officers, but also restored the numerical preponderance of the middle class (691). Data on officer origins in socialist Eastern Europe are gradually becoming available (104 and 115). The observation by the late C. Wright Mills that "social origins and early background are less important to the character of the professional military man than to any other social type" (946, p. 192; see also 87, 650, and 802), made with regard to the "American power elite," would seem to hold true only for those relatively modern establishments in which indoctrination is specifically shaped to inculcate in every officer a professional attitude to be reinforced by subsequent service experiences.

Universalistic standards for entry into and for advancement within the military open the officer career to all on an equal basis. Yet, even where this principle is strictly adhered to, the military, like every profession, is never entirely representative of the male adult population. The trend toward more representative recruitment is limited by two factors. On the one hand, socially conditioned disabilities limit career opportunities of many people; on the other, social valuations of the officer career as unattractive keep many who could easily qualify from seeking a commission and still others called to active duty against their will from extending their obligatory service beyond the minimal tour. These two factors result in selective recruitment even where no other social barriers are imposed.

The main obstacle to full "democratization" of officer origins today lies in the unequal availability of the minimum academic education that has become the standard for a commission in an increasing number of nations. The new prerequisites for the general education of officers are not normally waived except under unusual circumstances, as in wartime when the demand for officers suddenly increases and noncommissioned officers who have proven their ability to lead troops in battle are offered reserve commissions. In the United States in the 1960's almost all officers, including those commissioned from the ranks, are college graduates (580, 581); those in other industrially advanced countries have equivalent schooling (544). Such education usually qualifies a person for commission after only a relatively brief course in training. It is the indispensable base for continuing education and broadening as an officer advances in his career (106 and 124).

If these requirements stack the cards in favor of the middle classes, this bias can be partly offset by arranging to educate prospective officers at public expense. Most countries, even those where advanced education remains the privilege of the more well-to-do, have military schools and service academies geared to the production of professional officer material with military training provided in conjunction with an academic education. Obviously admission policies and practices in these institutions can modify the impact of educational requirements. They are the determining influence on the social composition of the professional military when such schools are the main source of new officers.

To the extent that sons of officers receive preferential admission to these schools, the tendency toward self-recruitment, present in all professions, is enhanced. In Imperial Germany state-supported preparatory schools—the notorious cadet houses—compensated the impoverished postfeudal nobility for their economic disabilities by opening to them secure careers as officers (72 and 102). During the same period in France, the armed forces were mandated to fill a certain proportion of officer vacancies by promoting men from the ranks. In this way ascriptive and plutocratic factors were somewhat de-emphasized and, depending on the size of the intake from this source, the officer corps democratized with respect to its social origins (70, 77, and 735). Military fathers with the financial means could still send their sons to the prestigious military colleges—i.e., les grandes écoles—to preserve the family tradition, but they did so in inadequate numbers. Hence, although the proportion of French officers whose fathers were career military rose sharply in the period after 1945, the sons of NCO's given the chance to rise, rather than sons from a traditional military family, account for much of the rise (118). In the United States, by contrast, admission into the service academies has become more openly competitive, notwithstanding some preferential treatment still given to sons of officers and those with political connections. Only those with academic potential as measured by tests can qualify. Meanwhile the needs of the services have far outstripped the capacity of the academies and the traditional private military schools to supply regular officers. The number of regular officers directly commissioned from college or from civilian life has become several times as large as the number who are academy graduates.

Geographical and social isolation promote occupational endogamy, and many sons of officers who opt for a military career simply are carrying on the family tradition. The extent of self-recruitment, as opposed to external recruitment, varies considerably among different levels and components in the military. It varies also in relation to the expansion or contraction of opportunities. From all appearances occupational inheritance within the military is higher than among other professions. For example, somewhat fewer students in American schools of medicine and schools of law had fathers who were physicians or lawyers than students at the U.S. Military Academy at West Point had fathers who were military men.[1] There does appear to have been an increase in the number of West Point students who are following in the footsteps of their officer fathers (154), but this trend, if it continues, may be a function of the larger number of men in the population who have or will have at one time served in the military.

The amount of occupational continuity within the military elite is likely to exceed that within comparable civilian elites. Warner and his associates (139) collected data as part of a larger study of the U.S. federal executive on both the fathers and grandfathers of all incumbents in such positions in the 1950's, so that this study actually spans three generations. Military officers in the first generation were much more likely to have passed on this occupation to their sons than the nonmilitary grandfathers of the military and civilian executives studied. Over all, however, the amount of self-recruitment into the military elite was low—some 8.5 percent— but still higher than self-recruitment into the top echelons of civilian federal service. The role of family tradition is likewise strongly apparent in the unusually high self-recruitment rate among the elite of the reconstituted Bundeswehr. Thirty-seven percent of those whose father's occupation was known had officer fathers. By contrast, twelve percent of the top ranking civil servants were sons of civil servants while eight percent of the German professors were sons of professors (107).

As a general rule the importance of family tradition increases when social and political changes cause sharp reductions in the size of the military and in the attractiveness for the general population of a military career. Thus, the effect of the marked social bias in officer recruitment in Imperial Germany was strengthened through selective retention in the officer corps during the Republic. The Reichswehr actually become slightly more aristocratic; the rest of the society less so. The proportion of aristocrats who applied for and received a commission into the army during the Weimar period was actually slightly higher than it had been just before World War I (72, 511, and 755). A recent study of the entrants into the various French officer academies by Michelat and Thomas (156) suggests that the strongly motivated officer has a "traditionalist" family background, as measured by such objective indices as number of children, father's occupation, and religious orientation. The authors think this recruitment pattern is characteristic of armies during a period of decolonialization before a new technological image of the military has fully diffused.

The choice of an occupation for those who have alternatives is based on comparative evaluations of career possibilities. Men with some education but of humble origin have often found the security and potential for advancement in a military career attractive when compared to their chances in other fields where lack of wealth and elite connections may be a greater handicap. In many industrially underdeveloped countries, the comparative appeal of a military career is especially seductive because opportunity in other professions is severely limited. Insofar as the armed forces in such areas are relatively unencumbered by a tradition of ascriptive recruitment, a military career represents a major avenue of mobility for men of modest but not usually depressed origins (648, 740, 755, 784, and others), but the relative attractiveness of this alternative evidently declines as industrialization increases the number of alternatives. The progressive rationalization of all phases of life, including a de-emphasis of the heroic dimension in the military image, also strips the military career of much of its traditional glamor. Thus, a national sample of American adults and teenagers in ranking occupations by prestige rated the officer below the traditional professions though higher than the school teacher. Such rankings have considerable stability;[2] and the order is generally replicated in countries at comparable phases of industrial development as Wiatr (142) shows. However, one reversal he found in socialist Poland—school teachers held in higher esteem than military officers—leads him to speculate about what effects the different priority of goals in noncapitalist countries might have on these judgments.

Further analysis makes it evident that these prestige rankings express more than differences in economic remuneration. It was found in one study that Japanese high school students rated the officer career far higher on economic grounds than in terms of either desirability or prestige (558). Studies of the motivations of officer applicants also find that economic remuneration is not usually the prime consideration in their occupational choice (146, 156, and 158). Neither do the satisfactions and inadequacies experienced by officers in various assignments (121 and 127) or by comparison with civilian managers at comparable levels (228 and 235), insofar as one can gauge this from officer self-ratings on particular instruments, center on a single element. To want to be an officer entails being attracted to a certain professional style and mode of life.

*Commitment and Assimilation.* The milieu into which a person is born influences his life chances; his family of origin provides anticipatory socialization. The impact of family background persists beyond the initial career choice even though its influence on the person's subsequent career operates only in conjunction with other factors. To begin with, the granting of a regular commission has always presupposed, at least in theory, a full commitment to the military as a career. The assumption accords poorly with the contemporary reality when an increasing number of officers leave the service at the first opportunity or as soon as they become eligible for retirement benefits in order to pursue careers outside the military.

The whole question of lateral mobility, mostly away from the military and into civilian employment, has occasioned a good deal of comment lately but so far only a limited number of systematic investigations. Articles like those of Coates (114) and of Fränden (117) as well as the book by Coates and Pellegrin (8) are still based on a relative paucity of data. Among those studies available the one by Zald and Simon (143) is of special interest. The expressed intentions of a sample of U.S. officers on active duty to remain or to separate from the service are subjected to multivariate analysis. Education emerges as a key variable related to commitment to continued military service. Those with college degrees and, by implication with skill and status transferable to other spheres, most often declared themselves decided to separate once they were free to make that choice. This same intention is expressed much less frequently by officers whose limited educational attainments limited their job prospects on the civilian labor market. Apparently the desire to remain does not usually express a positive commitment to the military, such as the realization of a lifelong ambition. Insofar as the lack of appealing alternatives is the determining factor, the military represents a "weak" career choice.

Given these circumstances the primary function of the main service academies is to provide a core of firmly committed professional officers. The entrants are to begin with usually highly screened, and beyond that the severe military discipline under which they complete their extended course of study subjects their motivations to a severe test. Because of this and because of their superior opportunities to advance in the military, the commitments of academy graduates to a military career tend to be much stronger than that of other officers (148). Yet the resignation rates among this group, too, show the influence of background. According to an unpublished self-study of its graduates by the U.S. Military Academy at West Point, the sons of officers are less likely than others to resign.

Social background is related also to preferences for a particular career field. That this reflects more than the vagaries of opportunity is brought out in a study of students at naval officer academies in France (156). Wanting to be an officer and a commander, together with a special interest in the social responsibilities and human relations activities associated with the officer role, was found to carry more weight among candidates from families with a "traditional orientation." Like the men who have been the mainstay of the naval profession in the past, a disproportionate number came from large families where the father either had followed a military career himself or was an industrial manager or a member of one of the free professions. This motivational pattern was also more prevalent among officer candidates who had received their prior education in military or private schools. The attraction of the technical side of the officer role was far greater by comparison among officer candidates who had entered the officer academies from the public schools and who as a rule came from smaller families and a more modest background. In this study, unfortunately, the influence of each of the indicators used to infer a "traditional background"—like having a military father—was not examined apart from that of the rest. This was done by Lovell (154) in his study of socialization at West Point in the course of which he also touched on the role model held by freshmen there. Within this population the sons of officers were more likely than the rest to emphasize the "managerial" as opposed to the traditional "heroic" elements in the officer role. The apparent contradiction between the two findings may be explained by the fact that the U.S. military had not engaged as recently as had the French in overseas operations at the time the study was conducted. The emphasis had already shifted toward deterrence.

These differences attributable to background are noteworthy because it is rather widely taken for granted that indoctrination in military schools and service experiences are remarkably effective in casting recruits into a uniform mold. Making soldiers out of men means implicitly and explicitly to eradicate the orientations they bring with them in the service. The efficacy of the indoctrination procedures in this regard has, however, seldom been empirically demonstrated. Even sociological accounts written by those who have undergone officer training are often colored by felt isolation and humiliations from superiors (see, for example, 162). To be sure, the pressure to accommodate is very considerable, but excessively heavy pressure may have adverse effects on motivation and actually interfere with the assimilation of professional norms. It is necessary to study not only the treatment to which officer candidates are subjected but also its effects.

Dornbusch (148) concludes from his personal recollections that the status deprivations he and others encountered as cadets in the U.S. Coast Guard Academy had a positive impact: the officer status to which cadets aspired became more valued as they prepared on receiving their commissions to adopt disparaging attitudes and behavior toward those of lesser status. The general validity of his conclusion may be limited, however, inasmuch as these officer cadets entered military service while their country was at war and few among them had ever personally envisioned a military career.

According to a panel study by Lammers (152, 153) of officer candidates at the Dutch Naval College adjustment to life at the institution improved more than did their commitment to the Navy; the latter was in large measure a function of background and attitudes at time of entry, i.e., a consequence of anticipatory socialization. Moreover, commitment to the Navy had far greater impact on assimilation of Navy culture than on adjustment to life at the College. Still another study, this one of a Swedish reserve officer academy, failed to find that the course of training added in any way to the appeal of a career as professional officer (160).

The Lammers study is of special interest since it systematically compares the process of socialization among midshipmen seeking a regular commission and others taking a much briefer course of training to qualify them as officers in the Naval Reserve. Differences between the two groups were marked. From the beginning, midshipmen scored higher in their acceptance of Navy culture than did reserve officer trainees, and the environment in which the former moved further strengthened their assimilative dispositions. Midshipmen not only confined any outside contacts pretty much to the families of naval officers living nearby, but the atmosphere prevailing at the Naval College meant that affiliative tendencies within the academy reinforced assimilation. Only among midshipmen, not among reserve officer trainees, was the correlation between commitment to a career in the Navy and acceptance of naval culture contingent on a person's popularity within the total group. From this it appears that a generally popular midshipman, if he very much wanted to become an officer, was impelled toward accepting the viewpoint of the Navy in order to maintain his standing with classmates. This suggests that a midshipman strongly committed to the Navy could resist assimilating certain Navy viewpoints but only by forsaking popularity. A quite different situation prevailed among reserve officer trainees. Wanting to be an officer and accepting Navy culture generally went together regardless of the individual's popularity within the total group. The correlation between the two depended rather on a trainee's subgroup affiliations. This suggests in turn that for the reserve officer trainee the pressure toward assimilation of Navy ways was a direct consequence of his motivation. Any social reinforcement towards assimilation came primarily from his close associates rather than from the group as a whole.

Where military ways are alien and externally imposed, young officer trainees will form their own subculture regardless of their career motivations. American cadets in aviation training were found to have an "authoritarian" image of the officer leader. Still, asked at the start and end of their training to name the persons they preferred as leaders, their nominations showed a clear shift away from the more authoritarian toward the less authoritarian among their peers (327). The authoritarianism (F-scale) measure has also been used to tap the attitudes of the cadets themselves. By the end of their military aviation training, a similar group of cadets were found by Campbell and McCormack (358) to have scored lower on an authoritarian scale than they had during a pretraining interview. Randell (160) used a population in a reserve officer school which he matched with a group of high school seniors in order to test a number of propositions about the impact of the organizational environment. The high rate of interaction in the officer school, so he reasoned, would produce uniformity in the images officer candidates had of various occupational roles, including that of the military officer. Although on three of the four occupations, the images of the officer trainees did indeed converge somewhat, one does not quite know what to make of the one exception: no such effect was recorded with regard to the image of the typical officer. Perhaps the particular test—the Osgood semantic differential—is not sufficiently sensitive for measuring the kind of changes to be expected in the military setting and a different instrument should have been used. This is, in fact, the explanation Campbell and McCormack advanced for the decrement in authoritarian scores.

From differences in the strategic perspectives subscribed to by members of the freshman and senior class at West Point as observed by Lovell (154), one gains the impression that extended study at one of the main officer academies does, as one would expect, promote agreement on some matters of central concern to the profession. General professional orientations and strategic perspectives in the freshman class were clearly related to family background with sons of officers already conforming to what was clearly the norm in the senior class. By the fourth year at the academy, the influence of background on these subjects had largely disappeared. Cadets from other than military families apparently had come to accept the viewpoints prevailing there. More important, the slight shift away from the "heroic" and toward a "managerial" role model as cadets move ahead in the academy seemed to occur together with a much stronger shift in branch preferences toward infantry and artillery where, despite the poor technological images of these branches, opportunities for advancement were clearly better. In terms of the cadets' expressed interest, however, the appeal of technical career fields did not decline, but rather was supplemented by a steady growth of interest within the student body in careers characterized by interpersonal activity. Thus, academy experience fosters attitudes among its students that are generally consistent with the activities and roles most can be expected to assume during their careers as officers.

Professional socialization is a continuous process. As an officer advances, he must develop the appropriate skills and perspectives necessary for higher management or lose out in the competition for promotion. Those in high rank generally score lower on authoritarian ideology (358) and dogmatism (349). If these tests measure what they purport to measure, the lower scores may reflect the premium placed on formal education and innovative ability at top echelons. Among other things officers must shed their service viewpoints (180) and learn to assume responsibility for policy decisions.

*Career Mobility.* A successful military career leads to positions at the highest levels of military command and management. Being a graduate of one of the elitist military schools improves an officer's career prospects. This is true in one way or other just about everywhere. In the United States the rank distribution among such graduates is far more favorable than among the officer corps as a whole, and this holds true even when reserve officers serving on contractual tours are not included. They clearly dominate the general officer ranks despite the fact that they account for only a small proportion of the total officer intake (88, 135, and 138). The formidable advantage they enjoy in the competition for promotion is the joint product of several circumstances. Academy graduates are to begin with more committed than others to an officer career; still, their concentration at upper ranks is not solely a consequence of selective retention. They are usually carefully screened for both ability and motivation, and associational ties and friendships formed as students can be translated into preferred assignments. Considering all these interwoven factors, the more rapid rise of academy graduates takes on a deeper sociological significance: it maintains the structural integrity of the profession. Despite the overlap of military and civilian skills paralleling the growing complexity of the techno-logical base, the service academies still promulgate an ideology that sees the military as a distinctive "calling." Thus, Segal (135, 136) interprets this "bias" in selection as a response to the broadening of the officer recruitment base and the growing number of civilians involved in military activities at many levels. These, he believes, require a new emphasis on "militariness."

Convincing as his interpretation may be, the case for it rests entirely on quantitative changes observed among the American military in the post-World War II era, a period of such rapid expansion in the country's standing forces that its armed forces encountered some difficulty in procuring a sufficent number of qualified officers. The number of officers available for promotion to the executive level, as well as the distribution of abilities among them, always influences the composition of the cadres of general (flag) officers, and comparisons among the services reflect this fact. As Segal himself notes, the trend toward higher saturation of the top ranks with academy graduates was apparent only in the Army and Navy. In the Air Force where the number of academy graduates within the cohorts available for promotion was scarce during this period, their number within the elite actually suffered a decline. The Marine Corps was another exception. Perhaps the structural autonomy and esprit de corps of this service suffice to ensure that those selected to high rank possess the appropriate "military" orientation regardless of the source through which they were initially recruited. There are, in other words, alternative mechanisms for achieving the same results. Such mechanisms may gain in importance as the military shifts emphasis toward continuing education and career development. Thus, the German military had been able to absorb a large periphery of officers by formally identifying general staff service as a distinct career line for grooming young officers for high command. Most other armies, including the Bundeswehr, have shied from making so sharp a distinction. However, the progression of steps and sequence of assignments have undergone considerable formalization. The U.S. military has what it calls "career management" plans to guide individual officers into patterns consistent with service needs (580, 581). High proficiency ratings, greatly needed skills, and an appropriate pattern of assignments can help an officer make up for the initial disability of not having an academy education.

In their article, "Military Careers at the Executive Level," Van Riper and Umwalla (138) point to the importance of a career in "operations" either by itself or in conjunction with some other single type of service experience for the achievement of general or flag rank in the United States. The early dispositions of academy cadets toward primary combat and combat related areas manifest among students at West Point are thus reinforced by the promotion system. Officers with "operations" experience are more likely than others to "get ahead" regardless of where they were schooled and how they obtained their initial commission. But the increased importance in recent years of support activities (e.g. administration, supply, and technical services) has resulted in a larger number of openings in these areas. As a consequence officers in these career lines if they achieve general (flag) rank, apparently do so somewhat more rapidly than others; they nevertheless remain at some disadvantage in competing for the very highest grades.

The age at which an individual reaches a "leadership" position within an organization depends partly on the number of such positions available and on the age structure of the available pool of candidates. It therefore stands to reason that the expansion of the armed forces as during the war will bring younger leaders to the fore and the greater the rate of expansion, the younger the age at which officers achieve general rank (125). Yet other, more long-range factors are also at work. Studies by Vagts (137) and Lehman (122) point to a secular trend. With increasing bureaucratization of the officer career, top commanders in the twentieth century reached their position of eminence at a later age on the average than those holding similar commands in previous eras. However, their period of tenure was apt to be shorter; an officer was often forced to step down to make room for new blood. Particularly in periods of rapid technological change, the premium placed on experience declines; sometimes "experience" acquired in the past is a downright hindrance. Hence, opportunities do open for relatively youthful military leaders, thus counteracting somewhat the trend toward age-graded mobility.

These and other observations help us highlight Janowitz's notion (88) that entry into the inner nucleus of decision-makers, as opposed to the mere achievement of high rank in recognition for effective service, requires something beyond what is prescribed as normal for all. Such officers are often innovators who follow what he calls "adaptive" careers. They manage to be in step with the times by developing expertise with new weapons, pioneering with new tactics or procedures, or serving in a variety of quasi-political assignments that offer them special insight into the complexities of military policy decisions and contacts with the world with which they will deal. In this way the system provides for innovation within a formally prescribed framework. On the other hand too great a

specialization in some narrow technical area precludes the development of a broad perspective and is incompatible with the role of
military manager who is above all a "generalist."

*Ideology and Self-Image.* Despite the far-reaching changes ushered
in by advances in military technology, the professional military
retains its character as an insular community. Its separation from
civilian society is social as well as geographical. While Vagts (102),
Janowitz (88), Bouju and Thomas (111), and Kjellberg (91, 92) have
discussed the general manifestations and diminution of this phenomenon as it existed within the officer corps of several nations, the
findings from a small sample of British officers suggest that the social
contacts of the military, even those working at the highest staff
levels, are still more restricted than those of the civilian counterparts
in the ministry (130). The same situation prevails, according to
Garthoff (930), among the Soviet military. In some respects the
military can be likened to a religious order; its members dedicate
themselves to render service, not to God, but to the Nation. A similar
fusion of profession and organization, as van Doorn put it (103), is
also to be found within some other institutions, the church
especially, but also in the foreign service. Most comparisons deal with
the organizational aspects and, as far as I know, there is only one
study (98) in which a systematic comparison of the military with the
diplomatic corps has even been attempted. Sometimes another
organization is used as point of comparison for some particular
aspects. (See for example 136.)

The monopoly that the military claim over military expertise has
naturally thrust them in their capacity as technical advisors into
important policy roles. Since the military sense a strong identification between their own professional commitments and the national
interest, disputes inevitably arise over how much say they or civilians
should have over certain national security matters with the military
tending to insist, often unsuccessfully, that the responsibility they
shoulder should weigh heavily in the counsels, if not give them the
final word. Statesmen inevitably counter this pressure. As long as
some military can be found to support policy, they usually manage
to retain firm control. Nevertheless, the advice of the military,
insofar as it reflects sound technical knowledge, is difficult to ignore.
Its representatives will inevitably exert considerable influence on
policy as long as such knowledge is deemed exclusively their own and
not equally accessible to others.

The main threat to military professionalism in industrially advanced countries comes from developments that jeopardize this monopoly of expertise. Efforts to downgrade professional military judgment by making officers ideologically and/or politically subservient to party viewpoints are really an aspect of civil-military relations and have no place in the present discussion. Not so the challenge the military faces because of its dependence on the esoteric knowledge of other professions which is no longer confined to marginal areas but rather has come to pervade all facets of military policy. Both strategic and structural innovations today are normally founded on a depth and breadth of expert knowledge professional officers pursuing organizational careers are unlikely themselves to possess. For this reason Abrams (168) in an article on the "late" profession of arms calls the military a declining profession. The obituary may be premature, more applicable perhaps to Britain than to the superpowers, but there is no question that, notwithstanding the large number of officers with advanced academic degrees in fields covering the continuum of human knowledge, dependence on civilian expertise is increasing rather than diminishing. A new type of civilian military expert (965) has actually come into being and with regard to him most officers would probably echo the view of Robert N. Ginsburgh in an article in Foreign Affairs (177). Their activity and influence, he holds, are not only an unwarranted intrusion but actually undermine the foundations on which the professionalism of the military is founded. The military is most vulnerable where these civilians venture into the realm of strategy, long the special preserve of the officer corps. To counter the threat the military broadens the training given to officers as well as extends its preoccupation beyond the subjects and doctrines traditionally studied.

The doctrines in which military men are trained represent the codification of experience gained in past wars (1156). Conflicts waged in essentially similar fashion give the military a sense of continuity. Their ideology is based on an image of the battlefield. Therefore, the revolution in armaments exemplified above all by the discovery of nuclear power and the invention of intercontinental ballistic missiles has called for drastic revision of strategic concepts. Doctrines prevailing in the two superpowers, each of which possesses a significant nuclear arsenal and the capability for delivery, have taken an essentially similar turn (1161, 1280, and 1281). But this reorientation poses problems. As the whole world becomes a potential battlefield, the distinction between victory and defeat, once so clear-cut, is on the way toward obsolescence. Neither unconditional viability against every kind of possible attack in peacetime nor the decisive battle in wartime can remain the single absolute goal of military activity. For violence to be politically effective in the international arena today, it has to be carefully graduated. Consequently the military is confronted with the need to organize for many different goals, ranging from nuclear deterrence on the one side to coping with guerilla forces on the other. New challenges arise from complex arms control negotiations and from the demands to patrol areas of potential conflict with a minimum of force (55).

This ambiguity of goals has a number of consequences, positive as well as disruptive. On the negative side it contributes to the sense of alienation that many observers consider typical of the military in the modern world (167, 169, and 191). The alienation finds many diverse expressions. Among the French, for example, negotiating the army out of Algeria caused cumulative frustration to erupt (178). The crisis that followed divided the armed forces no less than the parties. On the positive side the pressure of reality has led to the search for new doctrines, sometimes hesitantly and unwillingly, but an exploration of new viewpoints nevertheless. In this connection Speier (1301) has discussed the unwillingness of the German elite in the 1950's to face up to the prospect of nuclear war. Yet the most basic internal debate still is the one first described by Janowitz in 1960 (88) between the adherents of "absolutist" doctrines where narrowly military considerations overruled all others and the "pragmatists" who judged the use of force in relation to other political means. The issue is by no means fully settled. It has, on the contrary, gained new force by the argument over the most effective way for the United States to extricate itself from Viet Nam: by stepping up or by scaling down the level of violence there.

This diversification of external goals has its counterpart in the diversity of roles and functions to be performed within the military. Here, too, technology has had a major impact. The content and authorship of articles in American service journals over the past few decades reflect changes in professional identity and self-image. Feld notes (175) how authors writing for these journals have changed their approach. In the prenuclear era military officers addressed their thoughts and ideas about subjects of historical and narrowly technical interest to a body of general practitioners. Now broad conceptual-type articles dealing with applied strategy and civil-military issues are written by specialists for a broader community. Contributions by junior officers are fewer, while those by civilians have increased in number. Perhaps the technical specialist is the officer of the future, but meanwhile science tends to break down the core of common experience on which professional esprit de corps has traditionally been founded (92, 183, and 191). As the focus of interest widens, the polymorphic character of military activity becomes more evident. A professional military identity in which the old ethos is reconciled with a pragmatic and technocratic orientation becomes something to be consciously achieved.

All these developments have contributed to the potential for internal conflict—over strategic doctrines, over the capability of some weapon system, or over the relative priority to be given to some theatre, mission, or function. The advocates of divergent viewpoints are under strong temptation to seek civilian allies in the cabinet or legislature and among the gamut of scientific, academic or journalistic experts. This dependence on civilians is likely, on the one hand, to make the military more critical of the society and more conscious of its own place within it and, on the other, to produce within the armed forces the cleavages that will duplicate some of the political cleavages of the society at large. The professional military has in its political leanings usually sided with the Right. In some countries retired officers have often stood for election to parliament where as a rule they represented the monarchist and conservative parties, as they did, for example, in France (173). Nevertheless, George A. Kelly writing about the political views prevalent among French officers of the late 1950's characterizes them as "modified leftism" (787). Others have written of St. Simonism in the French army (170).

We have only a few surveys of social and political attitudes held by professional officers. Janowitz's data on American officers obtained in the 1950's—a period of relative stability—reveals their clearly "conservative" identification (88). The German officer corps is judged by Waldman (349) on the basis of survey responses in the early 1960's as "basically democratic" in attitude. Certainly those in the higher rankings pay lip service to the constitutionality and rule of law that are tenets of official ideology, but steps toward far-reaching restructuring of internal relations have met with less than enthusiastic acceptance. The most recent and by far the most detailed survey of attitudes among the military is Ochoa de Equileor and Beltran's study of the Argentine armed forces (190). Attitudes on a wide range of subjects were covered and the findings separately reported for various ranks. A rather detailed picture of the diversity of views was thus obtained.

Although military tradition generally frowns on involvement in party politics, the tradition seems to be breaking down—and this not only in countries where the processes of governmental succession function poorly so that the military habitually intervenes to effect change. Electoral participation among high-ranking American officers as indexed by voting was found to be inversely related to the length of time spent in military service, to having a military family background, and to being committed to a full career as a regular officer (194). Voting, to be sure, is hardly an indicator of high political participation, nor the only or even the most important such activity. Yet the organizationally more mobile officers were by this indicator the ones more involved in politics. This suggests that the political goals officers pursue within the conventional party system arise from nonmilitary influences, such as perhaps their family or origin.

The significance of being an officer has obviously changed for many who wear the uniform. Insofar as the entire military establishment ceases to represent a single universe of discourse through which a particular set of professional values is expressed but incorporates into its organization elements of many other professions, traditional motivations will weaken. Already this is happening everywhere. Not only are the occupational choices of sons less likely to follow family tradition, but occupational mobility within a single life span has become far more typical a career than it once was. Experience in many military career fields nowadays has transfer value for a subsequent civilian career. This is not equally true across the board, of course. The opportunities diverge sharply, depending on an individual's age, educational qualifications, and particular military specialty (105 and 109; see 129 for an earlier era). An officer with a successful career usually can, if he should wish to, convert it upon retirement into remunerative employment (133). So obsessed have some become with the occasional entry of such ex-officers into politics or lucrative positions in industry that they fail to see the forest for the few trees. The problem of military retirement is part of a broader set of problems raised by the extension of life expectancy and the technological revolution. The very developments that have brought military and civilian skills more in line with one another have also sped up the obsolescence of these skills. The presence of a large number of unemployed, retired officers without means of support would be a major social problem, especially since an increasing number retire as soon as they reach the twenty-year mark and become eligible for benefits. Increasing attention is therefore being paid to how military experience can serve and prepare the prospective retiree for a "second career." Officers are in fact encouraged to think about this, and programs to orient them have been implemented. While the individual officer stands only to gain from these efforts, the effect on professional self-images remains dubious and in need of further investigation.

## N O T E S

1. See W. Thielens, "Some Comparisons of Entrants to Medical and Law Schools." J. Legal Educ., 1958, 2: 156 and S. Warkov, *Lawyers in the Making.* Chicago: Aldine, 1965.

2. See R. W. Hodge, P. Siegel, and P. Rossi, "Occupational Prestige in the United States, 1925-1963." Amer. J. Sociol., 1964, 70: 286-302.

Chapter 3:

# MILITARY ORGANIZATIONS

Armed forces are complex organizations. Given their size and internal diversity, they obviously share many features with civilian organizations of comparable complexity. There is nevertheless one fundamental difference that, however elementary, cannot be ignored: military forces are organized threat systems designed to produce counterforce (998). An organizational structure adapted to this task somehow differs from other organizational structures into whose calculus violence enters only, if at all, as an incidental or illegitimate disturbance, not as a point of focal orientation. Broad theoretical discussions of military organizations like Janowitz and Little (18), van Doorn (213 and 214), Lang (206), and Lehouck (207) certainly pay tribute to the existence of both basic commonalities and irreducible differences.

*Military-Civil Comparisons.* Comparative studies based on identical data about the military and some other type of organization are still few in number. The bibliography contains a total of twelve such items. By topics they break down as follows: five deal in one way or another with managerial and/or leadership roles (235, 239, 241, 245, and 328); two focus on satisfaction in the particular work setting (228 and 404); another treats the effects of organizational succession (120); and still another communication patterns (237) in comparable organizational settings. Only three address themselves to structural characteristics clearly applicable to the entire organization. Of these one is a comparison of military and civilian occupational structure (594), hence not really an organization study. On the other hand, Evan's analysis of appeals systems (267) and Segal and Willick's of changes in recruitment pattern in agencies under stress (136) clearly concern patterns of relevance for the entire organization.

Most of these studies emphasize the similarities. On the other hand, the discontinuities between the military and the civilian environment stand out sharply when the military is viewed through the eyes of new recruits, particularly of conscripts for whom the conditions of military service entail severe status deprivations. The change in life style is rather abrupt. According to findings summarized in Chapter 2 of the first volume of *The American Soldier* (309), both volunteers and draftees in the U.S. army during World War II resented especially the system of differential privilege associated with military rank. But they were equally critical of the army's undue emphasis on the traditional way of doing things as laid down in army regulations and of the arbitrary orders with which they had to comply or risk disciplinary sanctions. According to McDonagh (273), all controls in the military, formal as well as informal, were in some way or other shaped by the Articles of War. One encounters such themes in nearly every other account based on participant observation (e.g., 173, 201, 202, 204, 209, 220, 280, and 387). Whatever the main objects of complaint and negative feelings used to adumbrate the military social structure, civilian-military differences stand out sharply. One must, however, place these perceptions of the military milieu in a perspective that takes account not only of the disruptions in personal life but of organizational structure as related to the task environment.

In his critique of *The American Soldier,* Speier (229) exposed some of the inadequacies of inferring what military social structure is primarily from the complaints of individual soldiers. Traditionalism, hierarchical stratification, and authoritarianism—the three elements most often singled out for criticism by the men—are certainly not, he contends, unique to the army environment, while the all-male character of a society of soldiers separated from normal female companionship and the degree of consensus among the ranks on many matters not related to differential privileges were largely ignored. Moreover as the authors of *The American Soldier* point out themselves, the rapid pace of mobilization accentuated many problems. The army was unable in this short a span of time to develop new cadres and to adapt long-standing practices to a type of recruit entirely different from the one who had provided the bulk of military manpower in the interwar period. Some of the most annoying practices dissolved rapidly and most completely at the front where concern with procedural detail and forced compliance with seemingly arbitrary standards were at a minimum. To depict military social structure without reference to combat conditions will at best result in a one-sided view.

Etzioni's typology of organizations (203) offers a more systematic approach in terms of compliance structures. Although one may quarrel with some of the details of his formulation, including the way he applies it to the military, some findings from *The American Soldier* can readily be assimilated into his scheme. According to Etzioni organizational compliance structures are the joint effect of member commitments and the predominant methods of control. In his scheme alienative commitments are associated with high reliance on coercive sanctions. The wartime army was made up mostly of draftees and of volunteers who stepped forth only under the pressure of the draft; their membership was involuntary. It was therefore natural for the military compliance structure to be essentially coercive—at least for the lower participants. Organizational controls over member behavior are also pervasive in that they extend beyond work activity; the military seeks to regulate many phases of personal life. This in itself will strengthen the alienative dispositions of even those initially inclined to accept military life and of others generally satisfied with their job assignment (309 and 387).

The concept of total institution as a "place of residence and work where a large number of like-situated individuals, cut off from the wider society for an appreciable period of time, together lead an enclosed and formally administered life" seems an apt description, particularly with regard to the situation of recruits undergoing their initial training or to soldiers at isolated posts and sailors on tours of duty at sea.[1] The cleavage between permanent cadres who act as overseers and draftees undergoing forced socialization has been described by Zurcher (398) with reference to this concept. The same idea is explicit in the discussions of the preinduction treatment in the army examination station by Bramson (357) and of the basic training process by Marlowe (366) and by Bourne (444) and at least implicit in what Vidich and Stein (369) call the "dissolution of personal identity" in military life. Yet these aspects of the military environment do not impinge everywhere to the same degree. They are certainly not the major source of deprivation in combat, and there are many situations in which the conditions of garrison life begin to approximate those of a regular job, particularly in the cold-war army (397). In addition Gross and Miller (295) found that the opportunities on four U.S. Air Force bases for contact with urban civilians had a discernible impact on both satisfaction and morale. Although airmen stationed at isolated sites were about as satisfied as others with their job and equally committed to organizational goals, their complaints focused on different objects. Specifically the men at the isolated sites dissatisfied over the lack of outside contact were also generally dissatisfied with the Air Force; at less isolated sites the discontent of the generally dissatisfied men was often focused on the lack of promotions, pay, and working conditions. Life in the military is varied. It approximates the total institution in some places more than in others. An across the board application of the concept—and conclusions derived therefrom—imposes a perspective likely to be self-limiting.

One must furthermore recognize that the nature of military duties which traditionally have fostered a quasicommunal existence have changed radically as the nature of military tasks has changed. Given the present state of weapons development, the preoccupation of the military has shifted from counterviolence to the deterrence of violence, a development that, as Janowitz and Little (18) have indicated, tends generally to weaken the distinction between military and civilian functions and activities. Thus the majority of "military" jobs today are only indirectly related to combat (473, 580, 589, and 595) and only for a relatively few men in uniform does the degree of danger they experience, even in wartime, exceed what civilians may have to face (173 and 208). Although the effect of these changes has been truly profound, there is some sketchy evidence that some constraints imposed by an orientation toward combat are pervasive throughout the organization, even where the duties of military personnel approximate those normally associated with a civilian job.

From among the yardsticks with which to make comparisons, one can select the satisfaction with certain "work factors." Bowers (404) obtained identical information on the importance of four work factors to persons working in two research organizations engaged in essentially similar work—one a military research and development unit, the other a civilian laboratory under contract to the Air Force—and then asked the employees about the extent to which their present job came up to expectation on each. The four work factors were: the "chance to use [one's] ability and knowledge;" the "opportunity to contribute to the nation's welfare and protection"; "freedom and authority to carry out [one's] ideas;" and the "opportunity to contribute to scientific or technical knowledge." For whatever reason, the mean discrepancy—between what each individual considered important and his perception of how well the work situation provided for it—was greater, particularly on the first two of these factors, for personnel in the military laboratory, with officers even more negative in these evaluations than the civilians alongside whom they worked. A more recent study (228), also using a questionnaire, found that military officers serving at an overseas U.S. Air Force command were much more dissatisfied than civilian managers with comparable managerial responsibility. Among the military, satisfaction was clearly related to rank.

There is also the matter of specific demands of organizational roles within different authority systems. Fleishman (235) compared officers in four naval organizations with managers in four industrial enterprises with regard to the time they spent on various activities and the level of responsibility, authority, and delegation (RAD scores) they perceived themselves as having. The results of this particular study "suggest that differences between patterns of performance in industrial and naval organization, on the whole, are generally no greater than difference among either naval organizations or industrial organizations." Still the same discrepancy between actual and "ideal" conditions stands out more clearly within the military: naval officers were less likely than civilian managers to think that the amount of responsibility they had was adequate to the responsibilities they felt they actually carried. Similarly indicative of the way they view the demands of their role are the judgments of a sample of U.S. Air Force officers asked to rate the importance for success of a list of ten adjectives (249). Like the civilian managers given the same list, they considered inner-directed traits far more important than other-directedness for successful performance in their role. But where the managers consistently placed "imaginative" at the top of their list, officers favored "decisive" and—especially at the junior level—"self-confidence" over imagination.

Two studies that compare military and educational establishments also point to the emphasis on hierarchical authority in the military organization. Communication contacts among top level supervisors in an air defense command were predominantly between superior and subordinates with a preference for the written form. Lateral communications were far more frequent in the academic community. Educators also made greater use of conferences which in contrast to the military were far less likely to be called upon the initiative of the man in charge (237). How leadership ideology among aircraft commanders differs from that of administrators in a school system is shown in another comparison: commanders emphasized the need for initiative defining tasks but showed themselves less considerate than educational administrators of the personal needs of subordinates (239, 241).

*Authority and Discretion.* Military authority structure is geared to one overriding requirement: the uniform direction of troops in battle. The ability to reach quick decisions under external pressure is critical. Hierarchy rather than equality provides the basis for unity on a battlefield where to martial superior force—to get there "the fastest with the mostest"—is the guiding principle behind specific operational decisions. Orders always come from above because only the higher echelons have the "big picture," and the level from which an order emanates is to be taken as sufficient proof that it incorporates superior wisdom and knowledge. Such orders are to be obeyed to the letter but with the details of their execution left to the discretion of lower commanders. Thus armed forces constitute models of rational organization at least insofar as the model accords with organizational and military realities.

These priorities shift with the growth of the technological element in military operations. As a consequence strictness in adherence to the principle of hierarchy in decision-making can be dysfunctional, if it stifles initiative at the lower levels and results in rigidities when innovative solutions are called for. Any such investment of organizational means—procedures, structural arrangements, weapons systems, etc.—with a special sanctity has long been recognized as a form of "bureau-pathology."[2] So has the lack of leadership and initiative among those charged with the responsibility for implementing a general directive. It stands to reason, therefore, that administrative malfunctioning within the military, including the patterned evasions of orders and regulations by subordinates, have often been analyzed with reference to its bureaucratic features. Salient as this perspective may be, inasmuch as armed forces are a species of bureaucratic organization, there are also special reasons for the apparent rigidities and conservatism one so frequently encounters within the military.

Some of the archaisms that strike outsiders as especially out of place have been perpetuated by the relative insulation of the military from outside social influences (173 and 209). The autonomy with which the military pursues its own traditions represents, so to speak, the price exacted for its dedication to the pursuit of the martial arts in peacetime when the need for such skills is not generally apparent. Yet this price has often been high as there is another side to the coin: armies have often set out to do battle with strategic concepts and weapons that were improvements over those previously used only in the elimination of obvious deficiencies. In particular, the affinity the officer corps felt for the horse cavalry prevented its replacement with motorized units, even after its military disutility had been fully demonstrated in World War I (246). This is not an atypical example of how tenaciously military organizations have resisted change. England abandoned sails and spars only in 1901, and military managers in all countries were just about equally reluctant to recognize the military value of the airplane. They were suspicious of submarines and fought hard not to abandon battleships for carriers and airplanes for missiles. This "cultural lag" phenomenon of resistance to the diffusion of innovation (1238) is not, of course, uniquely military. What has been unique is the frequent failure of those explicitly charged with anticipating future needs to include in their calculations the effects of technological advance or to anticipate the conditions under which they may have to fight. They tend instead to rely on old plans and tested weapons. In other words, the remote and uncertain advantages promised by change in peacetime must always be balanced against the disruption entailed in any sort of changeover. All too often it has taken a military disaster to drive home the point.

If the officer's romantic attachment to certain weapons appears strangely out of tune with the times, both the military's insistence that certain forms of etiquette and other procedures be followed to the letter and its concern with constant drill and spit and polish have similarly archaic overtones. Their function derives from the seasonal character of military activity. Since war is the exceptional rather than the routine state of affairs, many operating procedures appear strangely inappropriate to existing circumstances. They are not so much rooted in everyday experience as designed to protect against every possible contingency. For all the drill and simulation, there is no direct test—save war itself—of the adequacy of the various practices, at least not under realistic conditions. Battle alone is the pay-off. Although it has been demonstrated that a good showing in training or a high performance rating in peacetime activity has only a loose relationship to combat effectiveness, faith in established procedures and weapons functions to reduce anxieties about an unpredictable future. An insistence on form and ceremony also promotes confidence that, put to direct test, officers and men at all levels of the organization will conduct themselves as they have been trained. To this extent then the postulate Davis (172; see also 201 on this point) applies to the U.S. Naval Officer Corps—that it "builds its routines on the abnormal, its expectations on the unexpected"—can be taken as the calculus underlying all military organizations.

If this depicts armed forces as conservative by their nature, the image must be tempered. In many instances the military have clearly acted as sponsors of change, sometimes setting the pace that the rest of society follows. This is particularly true of some technological areas where the long lead time required to develop a weapon from the drawing board to a point where it becomes operational places a high premium on research and development in anticipation of future contingencies. In the present qualitative arms race so far essentially limited to the Soviet Union and the United States, the effect of failure on the part of either to match a breakthrough by the other seems obvious to all. But being on the forefront of their society is not limited to pushing weapons development. The U.S. military pushed racial integration, when ordered to do so, beyond a point most communities would have been ready to accept then and are not yet ready to accept (372, 378, 381a, and other listings under III. 5(4) on this point). For perhaps somewhat similar reasons, the breakdown of caste barriers has gone farther in the Indian army than in other institutional sectors (373). Some other examples will come to mind.

As noteworthy as the pressures toward change in many parts of the military establishment is the way change itself has become programmed and routinized through established procedures. The ready adoption by the military of new methods of innovation is itself a major innovation, but the old dilemma persists. There is no adequate yardstick against which the returns from implementing an as yet untested proposal can be estimated. Therefore, decisions of every sort, but particularly in weapons, are inevitably based on uncertainties, suspicions, and remote possibilities. In this way the two superpowers have already gone through several generations of missiles which have had to be scrapped and replaced with new ones without any realistic test except under simulated conditions. Computerized simulation on which many decisions are based does not by itself offer any guarantee that the changes and innovation so produced, whether in hardware or in organization practices, will not become as divorced from reality as ceremonial archaisms left over from the prescientific era. Without a continuous monitoring against experience, change programmed in this manner has severe limitations and raises the possibility of new rigidities.

In discussing the military profession, Janowitz (88) refers to "trend-thinking" and a tendency for innovation to occur at the "margins." "Trend-thinking" involves a proclivity for seeking to perfect and elaborate a concept or system already in existence, such as the replacement of a less powerful weapon with a more powerful one of the same type, or the refusal to exploit the capacity of a new weapon, like the airplane, to its fullest extent by failing to acknowledge its independent capabilities and instead assigning it a supporting role within some existing system. Official channels for sponsoring change are generally inhospitable to radically new ideas. Organizational requirements demand that those who seek development support for a system spell out in advance its goal and performance characteristics with progress periodically reviewed against these a priori specifications. Acceptance of findings of operations research on tactical deployment was also delayed at first by this kind of resistance (1148).

Schon (255), surveying the process through which some two dozen major technological inventions with important military uses ultimately gained acceptance, substantially supports the above propositions. In nearly all instances the early development work on the idea was done by an independent inventor using his own resources and without any official sponsorship. If he received military support, it came largely from unallocated funds outside regular research and development programs. Most met with rejection in their initial attempt to approach through official channels and interest those military men whose function it is to screen ideas. The case histories of the process of adoption "look more like crusades or military campaigns, with overtones of fifth-column activity and guerilla warfare" (p. 84). Success generally came after the inventor linked up with a sponsor who then sold the idea through personal channels and contacts. These sponsors were often military mavericks, Billy Mitchell and Hyman G. Rickover being perhaps the most famous, but usually outsiders had to take up the cause before organizational resistance could be overcome. Basic structural innovation has encountered similar resistance. Civilian championing of a separate air force equal to the other two services was crucial in assuring development of the full military potential of the airplane (718). Had the air arm not gained its independence then, the other services could have relegated air power to a supporting role for forces operating on the ground or at sea. In general civilians play a crucial role not only as inventors but also in mediating between the vested interests and service viewpoints. Davis (686) and Armacost (678) have provided us with additional studies of the complex negotiations by which differences are compromised.

The grounds for opposing an innovation are not always "doctrinaire." Yet even legitimate resistance tends to be driven underground by the way the services try to disseminate their technological self-image to a general public. As a consequence real issues are often masked in bureaucratic red tape. The emphasis on modernism in internal managerial practices thus serves a double function. In their search for efficiency, military organizations have readily borrowed from the civilian world the latest and most advanced methods of cost accounting, scientific management, personnel research, and orientation programs and to an extent even pioneered in their application. One suspects that this unrelenting search for internal order through centrally managed control devices has an ideological component as well. Some innovating trends in this area, as Lang (581) suggests, are really the functional equivalents of the more archaic ceremonial practices for coping with uncertainty in the external environment. In this respect, Zuckerman's conclusion (197)—the more technology put into a weapon system, the more likely that its design and development have been the fruits of civilian thinking and the fewer the options about its use—applies equally to internal management. Formula solutions based on systems analysis still require local initiative if they are to be effective means for solving organizational problems. In fact the intent of any general directive can be neutralized by the discretion left to unit commanders and others charged with the responsibility for implementation, either because they do not understand the assumptions behind it or do not support its goal.

As an illustration, commanding officers under considerable pressure to achieve high ratings on morale and to improve the effectiveness of their units can resolve their own difficulties by "passing their problem over to the organization." The British army, faced in the early months of World War II with a severe shortage of officers, issued a call for educationally qualified men with service experience to volunteer for officer training. The response to this call turned out to be most disappointing. It was subsequently discovered by researchers from the Tavistock Institute that officers were generally reluctant to give up their best men and hence gave the directive only token support. Uyeki (278) offers an essentially similar, if converse, account. One company commander faced serious morale problems according to the record based on the usual indicators, because he was complying with a directive to discipline those guilty of infractions and to separate misfits from the service, while less compliant commanders, content merely to have these soldiers transferred, were able to produce higher unit ratings on efficiency and morale.

Orientation programs, the restructuring of officer-enlisted man relationships, and newly instituted legal guarantees have been undermined in similar fashion. In the German Bundeswehr, for example, many of these changes were formally supported but less than enthusiastically endorsed by the permanent cadres (349, 706, 719, 721). Especially instructive in this respect is Evan's study (267) of the appeals system in military versus industrial organizations. In formally granting all personnel the right to communicate directly with officers of the Inspector General without going through regular channels, the U.S. Army, like the Bundeswehr, went farther than industry in its institutionalization of an appeals system. Still this system sometimes failed as a safety valve against abuses because of the way the I.G.'s office was staffed and because of the many men reluctant to avail themselves of its protection. On the one hand, line officers assigned to only brief tours of duty with the IG often shied away from issues that could reflect adversely on officers of superior rank. Their own position within the status hierarchy inclined them to protect a system through which they themselves would ultimately have to advance. On the other hand, men of low educational attainment and high in authoritarianism were often intimidated by the rank of the I.G. officer whom they tended to view as a representative of the hierarchy. Therefore, when they had a problem, they preferred to take it up with representatives of the Chaplain's Corps or with medical officers who could resolve it on a personal basis.

The military authority structure and its corresponding ideology are nevertheless undergoing change from a system based primarily on domination toward a system based on more indirect and flexible controls (244; see also 242 and for the French army, 265). The old system, as we have said, presupposed a single, clear-cut, hierarchical channel for passing down the orders that lower level commanders were duty bound to obey, confining their judgment only to how best to carry them out. As an adjunct to the command channel, higher level commanders also have access to a staff of technical experts who formally, at any rate, wield no authority except in the name of their commander. The latter remains solely responsible, but the officer who would be successful in supervising and coordinating all the diverse components that nowadays come under the direction of even a tactical commander must, like other managers, share with those on whose knowledge and cooperation he depends the authority invested in him by virtue of his rank and formal command responsibility.

The line-staff distinction which provided the central problem for classical organizational analysis is also basic to the military organizational chart. A commanding officer is assisted by a staff of experts upon whom he can rely whenever his own time or knowledge are inadequate. Where the problem is major and exceeds the capacity of his own officers, he can turn for aid and advice to technical specialists at the higher echelons. However, the increasing dependence on technical knowledge at the lower echelons seems to give staff officers considerably more autonomy than is officially allocated to them. At least informally they enjoy a very considerable amount of de facto authority with regard to problems that fall clearly within their competence. In the U.S. Air Force directors of operations and material on the staff of wing commanders have been found to excercise unauthorized power over squadron leaders and over the latter's directors of personnel (260). Other staff officers have been propelled into an informal "trouble shooting" role, intervening to resolve problems at a lower echelon of command without the consent and sometimes even without the knowledge of the officer who is formally charged with command responsibility. Apparently such deviations from "correct" procedures are not only fairly widespread but, as a survey of the attitudes of U.S. Air Force officers indicates, also widely condoned (243).

The existence of such attitudes and practices confronts the commanding officer with a structural dilemma. He can, as one alternative, resist unauthorized intervention from specialists attached to the higher staff by teaching his officers to ignore all such suggestions not first approved by him. In resisting he risks an involvement in the details of operations that exceeds his technical knowledge. But if, as another alternative, he tolerates direct staff intervention outside the hierarchical command structure, he must face the prospect that his own officers, though trained to respect the chain of command, will accept direction, whenever it suits them, from staff officers with evident superior competence. The particular resolution of the dilemma is no doubt a matter of personalities. Yet the deviations of "power structure" from "authority structure"—to quote Thompson (260)—apparently come about because technical requirements have "led wing commanders to approve the exercise of power over squadron commanders by staff directors."

The extension of work relations to include individuals whose spheres of responsibility are normally defined as separate results in some confusion and ambiguity over the relative status and authority of those involved. If Scott's study of naval organization (256) is any guide, individuals and work units readily manage to coordinate their activities despite some ambiguity over formal authority, so long as both parties clearly acknowledge the existence of a work relationship. Too rigid an adherence to hierarchical channels inhibits such acknowledgment and may discourage lateral communication; individuals may share responsibility for a mission, yet not be compelled to keep in touch, each communicating directly with his superiors. During tactical operations the consequences of such breakdowns in lateral communications can be disastrous, as Marshall (431) graphically demonstrates in his diagnosis of panic among ground troops. In all instances he investigated, the precipitous retreat was occasioned by a loss of contact at the flanks. To cope with this problem at the higher levels of command, the German army developed a dual system of communication. The general staff network through which operational decisions were made assured extraordinary rapport in crisis decisions. Not only was each staff officer entitled to full information, but he was not allowed to withhold any information from either the central staff or from his opposite in other units (248). In a most instructive discussion of the general problem, Feld (234) attributes certain deficiencies in hierarchical control to the unresponsiveness of vertical channels to information needs as they arise at different points within the military organization.

The joint participation of several nations subjects the command structure to additional strain. In the Allied operations of World War II, the principle of unity of command which gave undivided authority to a single commander was accepted alongside a system recognizing spheres of national responsibility. This was clearly an attempt to rationalize a fundamental anomaly of coalition warfare, namely the existence of two channels of responsibility, one upward to the theater commander, the other between each commander and his own political head (247). Other anomalies arise when officers of different nations interact within a single staff. Relatively junior officers from the most powerful nation will arouse resentment if they assume authority to which neither their rank nor position entitles them but which, even if they chose not to use it, adheres to them by virtue of their national affiliation (253). In the multinational forces used for peacekeeping, integration may reach down to the tactical level. Cultural disparities may become superimposed on the racial animosity of the host population. In regions where white units find it difficult to operate, the preeminent role assigned to the nationals of nonwhite countries may contradict their logistic contribution and thereby contribute to internal frictions (see 1321; also 648).

*Group Norms and Leadership.* Organizational control structure is one thing; the impingement of military controls on individual soldiers is something quite different. Organizations are human systems that must "satisfice"[3] the needs of individual members.

To begin with, the civilian soldier transition is for most inductees a period of drastic readjustment, likened by Janis (299) to one of the major life crises that all individuals must face. The pressures and deprivations of military life described by novelists as well as sociologists (see Section III.5 of the bibliography) are certainly real, but they are particularly acute when military service necessitates a partial abandonment or, at least, a temporary deferment of occupational goals. Though service may have its compensatory rewards, these are not quite so obvious, nor men so ready to acknowledge them as they are to cite their trials and tribulations. For one thing military service offers opportunities for escape from any number of civilian problems (302), including the domination of females. A French study (548) points out that the emancipation of youths from family control usually coincided with the time of induction, especially for youths from the lower as compared to middle classes. Only in metropolitan Paris, the most urbanized of the departments, was this class difference not found; the role of military service in effecting the emancipation of even lower class youth was less important there. Still another advantage is the anonymity the military environment affords. Where the criminal past of men paroled into the army remains unknown, they usually find it easier to form new and noncriminal associations.

In the United States the enlisted milieu represents one of the last refuges for a genuinely lower class culture. Certain patterns of behavior disapproved almost everywhere else find here a recognized place, and the point has been made by Moskos (208), for example, that with the changeover to an all volunteer army without any reliance on the draft the contrast of the two milieus—the enlisted military and the civilian—is likely to become even greater. There is in the all male culture of the army an informal toleration of many kinds of aggression and intemperance which is compatible with strict supervision and the invocation of stern disciplinary measures when the limits are exceeded. That the more authoritarian, in terms of the conventional F-scale, among a group of airmen recruits should be more positive in their orientation to military service (361) is probably as much a function of the cultural background of these men as it is of their individual personality traits.

To point out that military life has its rewards is not to minimize the shock a recruit inevitably experiences upon induction. The treatment received naturally arouses considerable anxiety, but the anxiety is greatest among those who have never encountered similar disruptions or who have been habituated to an environment that accords them the degree of recognition and respect their personal qualities and previous achievements warrant. These pressures are already experienced during the prospective recruit's first encounter with the military at the induction station (357). From here on the nearly complete absence of privacy, the limited opportunities for self-expression, and the strict regimen to which the inductee is subjected in basic training result in the adoption of new forms of behavior, of new language (391), and of new standards of "morality" (280, 385) as appropriate means for coping with his new situation. These changes extend even to nonduty behavior. Here one of the effects of basic training is to reduce the quiet and peaceful forms of recreation to a fraction of their civilian importance. "Blowing one's top" which is the most unambiguous expression of dissatisfaction was the only nonduty activity quantified by Selvin (346) that became more common during the first few months of army life. Neither patriotic sentiment nor acceptance of military discipline increased significantly in the course of basic training (362).

Whereas the formal group structure around which the basic training cycle is organized is essentially task oriented, the peer groups and interpersonal ties that begin to form almost immediately serve primarily the inductees' social and emotional needs (230, 340, and 366). These ties which are partly a function of common background and tend to be confined to members of the same squad or work group in basic training as well as in "permanent" assignments (333, 343, 344) help attenuate and counteract the pervasive regimentation of life from above. Data collected by Roghmann and Sodeur (342) on recruits in the Bundeswehr show that peer cohesion is especially significant for the more highly authoritarian recruits, as measured by response to F-scale items; in units where cohesion is weak, these soldiers will turn to supervisors for help with personal problems but are clearly disinclined to do so in units where peer groups are strong. In other words, group supports are most important in the adjustment of persons whose prior attitudes dispose them to lean on supervisory authority and to adhere to whatever it demands.

For all their importance the interpersonal ties formed in basic training and, for that matter, a large proportion of ties formed among men on permanent assignments are of a highly tenuous character. They form as demanded by situations in which getting along without a "buddy" is extremely difficult. Insofar as relationships are based on interdependence rather than consensus, Gross (323) calls them "symbiotic." On the Air Force base he studied, the more highly integrated groups were often built around symbiotic relationships. There were also individual differences. Because they did not depend on group support to the same degree, the highly satisfied airmen tended to be less integrated into the structure of even those groups in which they participated, whereas those having difficulties adjusting were more in need of other individuals (322). The point is that many of these relationships, including, as we shall see later on, those formed in combat, fall far short of friendship as that term is understood in civilian life. Furthermore, even soldiers who appear to be isolates frequently have a high rate of interaction; their ineptness and deviance make them objects of general attention. Others who are satisfied with their assignment but not otherwise committed can afford to be selective about whom they associate with.

A leadership style that includes consideration for and sensitivity to the well-being of subordinates does much to reduce unnecessary tension and therefore should have a positive effect on personal adjustment and general satisfaction within a unit. Evidence from several sources supports this hypothesis. The level of satisfaction of airmen on a base was found to be higher where officers practiced a "human relations" approach instead of merely issuing orders (418, 419, 420). Similarly a leadership climate that has been variously described as "persuasive" or "equalitarian" also, because it eliminates unnecessary tensions, tends to hold down the number of hostile and aggressive reactions (346), unauthorized leaves, and other disciplinary infractions and at the same time encourages a larger number of men to reenlist (294, 317, 348, 363), but according to the study of

Härnqvist (363), the effect of the treatment Swedish naval officers meted to conscripts was nil in relation to the latter's satisfaction with military regulations.

The last finding points to limits in the ability of officers and noncoms to look after the welfare of their men. Both exercise authority within a system that obligates them to comply with orders and to enforce regulations, even when they result in hardships or restrict the freedom of those whom they supervise. Yet Holloman (328) in comparing the civilian and military supervisory role as perceived by both superiors and subordinates of supervisors in an Air Force installation points to the generally high demands made on military supervisors from both above and below. On the one side, both his superiors and subordinates expect from a military supervisor more direction and structuring of tasks than they expect from his civilian counterpart. On the other, they also seem to expect more from him in the way of consideration. There are some small but interesting differences between the perceptions of soldiers and civilians in this regard. Soldiers expect more consideration from their military supervisors than civilian subordinates expect from theirs, but the amount of consideration these soldiers expect is still less than what the military superiors of these supervisors judge to be appropriate for a military leader.

Whatever these perceptions of the leadership role, it is what the leader does that counts. His actions must demonstrate concern with the needs his followers have, while his ability to get results must measure up to standards set by superiors. According to a study of bomber crews (411, 412), the aircraft commander who showed consideration for the needs and desires of his men increased crew satisfaction but lowered the performance rating he received from his superiors. It seems that superiors expect a unit leader to be concerned about the welfare of his men but at the same time make other demands that, if met, make it difficult for him to look after the men in the way he might like to. Here is where the attitude and behavior of commanding officers and not just their philosophy become important. Those who delegate authority and rely on the initiative of subordinates seem to produce a chain reaction right down the line. Findings from the Ohio State University leadership studies as summarized by Shartle (257) indicate that the assistants of commanding officers who themselves delegate more than the normal amount of authority are likely to do the same with regard to their own subordinates. A similar effect is evident for officers in charge of training. The previously cited study of Swedish conscripts (363) showed that a convincing demonstration by officers of their genuine concern over the welfare of trainees caused the latter to look more favorably on their own NCO platoon and squad leaders.

Officers in command but otherwise remote from their men may have an easier time than their noncoms. American studies give evidence that the enlisted leader is often caught in the middle. In one survey enlisted men and officers who were asked about what qualities they valued in their NCO's (218) agreed least on the importance of sociability. Officers generally ranked it low, not only relative to other qualities, but also in comparison with the high value placed on it by enlisted men. Specifically first sergeants often felt themselves by-passed by company officers who would issue orders directly to the men but then hold the NCO in charge responsible for seeing that these were carried out expeditiously (415). Research in the Navy suggests that the chief petty officer frequently gets into a similar squeeze.

The concern of NCO's over the amount of authority they are actually free to exercise inclines them, according to one U.S. Air Force study (215), to be strict disciplinarians, carrying out regulations to the letter and favoring harsh sanctions for any infractions. Moreover the higher the rank of such NCO's, the more likely were they to favor reliance on disciplinary and punitive sanctions. This was quite the reverse of the pattern found among officers. The authority of high ranking officers tends to be clear and unquestioned. They have no need to worry about being "undercut" and thus could better afford some leniency in their dealing with troops. Factors, other than rank, like education and personality, also influence leadership behavior and account, no doubt, for individual variations within the general pattern. Using authoritarian F-scale items, Korpi (334) was able to show that squad leaders with equalitarian ideology, though perhaps less sensitive to requests from above, clearly had more accurate estimates of the attitudes and opinions of the men they led.

Noncommissioned officers are not the only ones caught between competing demands. Requests for special consideration to be granted either in the name of friendship or as a prerogative of rank often exceed the authority of the person to whom the request is directed. Such role conflicts have been described with regard to the naval disbursing officer (261) and the army clerk (396). Others with marginal positions in the military find themselves pressured to accept the premises of military authority though this contravenes other professional and moral commitments, as in the case of the military chaplain (263) and the civilian education advisor (972) working with the military.

It is difficult to overrate the importance of interpersonal ties and of informal groups for organizational effectiveness. Insofar as the members of cohesive groups are moved toward greater consensus on norms (365), they are better able to cooperate spontaneously. The informal group is indispensable as the potential mediating mechanism between the prescriptions of formal organizational authority and their implementation at the work group level. On first impressions one is apt to be overwhelmed by the prevalence of behavior patterns in clear contravention of regulations and the impunity with which such behavior is pursued; yet closer scrutiny makes it apparent that many such practices by cutting through red tape and side-stepping certain cumbersome procedures actually promote rather than hinder group goals. Soldiers learn quickly how to avoid unnecessary work details without attracting the kind of adverse notice that would deprive them of cherished privileges, e.g., their weekend pass, and without transgressing the claims of fellow soldiers for cooperation on tasks that cannot be shirked. The informal group is nevertheless prepared to impose sanctions where deviations clearly threaten the general safety and well-being of its members.

An anonymous article in the American Journal of Sociology (354) describes the assimiliation of recruits into the infantry. The acquisition of skills together with a feeling that "we" have withstood a joint ordeal quickly results in deprecatory attitudes against new arrivals who are less versed in army ways and have not yet proven that they can take it. Such attitudes are even more prevalent among paratroopers and other "elite" units (440) where the deprecation is less openly tinged with envy. There are some intermediate linkages, however. Thus it takes the right kind of tactical leadership to develop esprit and weld men together into cohesive groups. This problem has been most systematically explored, not with regard to the infantry, paratroopers, or special forces, but with regard to bomber crews.

Officer candidates undergoing aviation training obviously thought that the model leader as they saw it set forth in official regulations incorporated certain "authoritarian" traits; they nevertheless expressed a clear preference for the less "authoritarian" of their peers as "the kind of leader they would like to serve under" (327). Once these men are formed into crews, the informal group structure that develops within the more formal structure of roles showed a convergence of attitudes toward a common standard of leader behavior with the leader himself progressively conforming to the standard set by the group. Evidence collected by Hall (325) confirms such a convergence only on the matter of how "intimate" a leader should be with his men; no general consensus on the amount of "nurturance" or "militariness" expected of the leader had emerged during the formative period within the groups he studied. Perceptions of member motivations are also important, particularly where crew cohesion is low. In the less cohesive crews, effectiveness was directly related to the discrepancy between perceived member motivations and what these motivations actually were. Large discrepancies were associated with low effectiveness regardless of the actual motivations of individual crew members. However, when individuals assigned to crews had been transformed into cohesive groups, the motivations of the individual members were directly reflected in the performance of the crew (403). Be this as it may, the informal structure must clearly support and complement the formal structure if a crew is to function effectively. On the basis of their observation of crews in survival training, Levi et al. (219) concluded that in the more effective crews the official leader was also the person the men would have chosen as their preferred leader had they been given the choice.

The development of cohesion and of other desirable attitudes among the members of a newly formed crew is, according to Christner and Hemphill (318), itself affected by the character of the crew leader. Where the leader proves himself "considerate," crew members more easily gain confidence in one another and are more willing to go into combat. The importance of consideration demonstrated in the study of small groups is confirmed by the testimony of combat infantry and artillery officers. Only 5 percent of officers interviewed (309) said that they had ever known a company grade officer who showed little concern for his men before combat and who then turned out to be a successful combat leader.

Still sympathetic understanding and other equalitarian qualities of a leader, however important they are in developing rapport, are not enough. Even the most considerate aircraft commander, for example, must also be competent. His competence as a leader, assessed by his men and based on performance during crisis, depends in part on his ability to define tasks for subordinates and to see that they are carried out. Christner and Hemphill (318) in a study of air crews previously mentioned demonstrated how the rapid development of friendship and mutual confidence was affected not only by whether or not the leader was considerate but also by the positive judgments of his crew about his ability to initiate. Indeed, there is some evidence that overzealous pursuit by a crew commander of equalitarian ways can have adverse effects on crew performance (400). The performance of a relatively small number of crew leaders whose consideration for the men was extreme could thus explain the generally inverse correlation between "consideration" as judged by the men and efficiency rating a commander received from a superior commander (412). Otherwise these findings appear contradictory, as crew cohesion, which is related to high performance, seems itself fostered by a more equalitarian leadership.

One must be cautious in generalizing about the relationship of the various dimensions of leader behavior to group performance, because it is influenced by both organizational practices and national character. British soldiers, at least during World War II, seemed to care much less than Americans about the sociability of their noncoms. Such differences may also reflect the official ideology. The post-Hitler Bundeswehr in particular placed great stress on the necessity of good relations between the NCO leader and the men he led. Also, Belgian officers (53), unlike American officers surveyed by Stouffer (309), considered the social qualities of their noncoms the cornerstone in their success. All these factors come into sharper focus when one examines units in combat.

*Cohesion Under Stress.* We state this as a cardinal rule: the closer a unit is to the line of actual combat and the more directly the men in it are engaged in action against the enemy, the more the formal organizational control becomes diluted. Under the makeshift character of front line living arrangements with officers and men alike exposed to very considerable risks and suffering extreme deprivations, the military social structure, as officially defined, undergoes a partial disintegration and is replaced by an emergency social system. Although the men are still subject to formal disciplinary sanctions— something they never completely forget—they orient their activities toward coping with the problem of joint survival. As a rule conflicts between immediate needs and formal regulations are unhesitatingly resolved in favor of the former. Those in echelons of lesser risk who are also the source of the regulations come in for nearly universal deprecation. Adjacent companies and support units also receive their share of derogatory attention, but the sentiment in this case is colored by sympathy and a sense of solidarity and kinship that extends at least vicariously to all combat soldiers.

The general tolerance for deviations from prescribed procedures is expressed in many ways. One manifestation is the casualness with which property is treated and equipment expended. The seasoned veteran feels he has earned this right, a right he is not as ready to concede to others (230, 429). Another is the near total disappearance of all etiquette surrounding rank, a tendency that has been noted by every observer of front line behavior. Although the deprivational functions of officers are minimal under these circumstances (437), the men nevertheless maintain some social distance from officers (433). The two still interact within a framework of military command with responsibility falling almost exclusively on the latter. The officer's access to information also can be used by him to maintain and solidify his position (443), but the respect which he also needs can be earned only by proving his capacity in combat.

Thus the structure of the military group becomes meaningful in the light of operations and any changes that occur as troops move in and out of combat or between shore duties and going to sea are essentially adaptive (329, 386, 398, 429, and others). For one thing the association between the two leadership dimensions of "initiating structure" and "consideration" and the indicators of effectiveness, such as superior ratings of bomber crew performance and of crew satisfaction, shift as a group goes into combat (412). The shift merely demonstrates that leadership in extreme situations becomes more task oriented and that men are judged by clearer performance standards. This happens even under the simulated conditions of a seven day survival exercise. Post-"survival" leadership "choices" deviated considerably from those made beforehand by crew members (219, 476, and 477). The so-called "dropout" crews, that is to say, the ones who did not "survive," rearranged their choices most dramatically, largely because of evident failure in leadership.

The effectiveness of any tactical unit is strongly contingent on the initiative displayed by its individual members and their capacity for spontaneous cooperation. In the typical infantry squad, leadership functions are widely shared (406). The initiative tends to pass to those best able to exercise it at any given moment. One encounters the same spontaneous cooperation in air crews (409, 421). Not only are the more effective crews characterized by greater participation, greater initial divergence of expressed opinions, and greater acceptance of subsequent decisions, but all crews in combat, whether effective or not, tend to exhibit more of these characteristics than those who have never seen combat (477). The tactical group in combat is clearly integrated on a functional basis, but the patterns of performance differ from group to group. In an elite unit, like the Special Forces troops described by Bourne and his associates (445), competition among the men for acceptance and power impels them to prove themselves in combat. By earning respect for their courageous feats, they can advance in the hierarchy based on combat skill. The men in the ordinary infantry unit are far more inclined to play it "safe," to risk their lives only when necessary for their mutual safety (208, 434). Where the effectiveness of a unit is largely determined by the performance of individuals carrying out disparate and complementary functions, as in bombers or submarines, there is little room for the "heroic" gesture. The basis for cohesion is the proficiency with which each performs his assigned task.

Research on combat effectiveness continues to be geared to searching out character traits predictive of combat performance, so as to use them as guides in the selection of personnel. Within a cluster of traits which includes physical stamina, vitality, and intelligence, the quality of social adaptability assumes a special importance because it points to the significance of interpersonal relationships. In studies of ground combat soldiers in Korea identified by their peers as especially aggressive fighters (472) and of intercepter pilots who qualified as aces, this relatively small group of highly effective soldiers scored well above average on social adaptability as measured on several psychological scales. Previous observations in World War II had also pointed to the significance of social factors in the early breakdown of infantrymen. It was found to have been most frequent among men who had joined established units as replacements without any opportunity, prior to combat, to form attachments to others in the unit. The man who joined an established unit while it was in reserve was in a far better position to withstand the initial baptism of fire than the man who first caught up with his unit in the field (473). Individual replacements of the latter type rarely made effective soldiers, and if they ultimately did, this was only after they had become integrated into the informal group. A field experiment in Korea attempted a systematic test of conclusions drawn from this earlier study by comparing the performance of soldiers brought to the front as members of a four man replacement team and those assigned on an individual basis (424). Though the experiment was never completed, the data collected underline the role of group cohesion in the formation of attitudes related to combat readiness. The team replacements scored higher than the individual replacements on a number of morale measures of proven value in predicting performance.

Sociological analysis has sustained the intuitions of such military commentators as Ardant du Picq (423), Kurt Hesse (326), and S.L.A. Marshall (431) from their own observations of combat behavior. "Four brave men who do not know each other will not care to attack the lion," wrote the first in his *Battle Studies.* "Four less brave men, but knowing each other well, sure of their reliability and consequently of mutual aid, will attack resolutely. There is the science of organization in a nutshell." However convincing and dramatic this elementary truth may be, as formulated here without the necessary qualifications, it constitutes a rather considerable exaggeration. The primary group is indeed the major source of motivational support for troops in combat, and as long as it remains intact, soldiers are better able to endure the anxiety and deprivations of the battlefield. They are willing to court danger up to a point and face injury in the performance of their duties. It does not follow, however, that these groups are uniquely determining in the sense that the context of formal and coercive authority within which the smaller groups function have no effect on the performance norms they transmit. For a summary and interpretations of the various findings by sociologists, the reader is encouraged to turn to such sources as Stouffer (473, Chapter 5), Shils (437), Mandelbaum (430), Bigler (199), Lang (206), and Janowitz and Little (18).

In studying the effects of anxiety on individuals, psychiatrists and social psychologists have also been forced to recognize the significance of interpersonal and organizational factors. Controlled observations by a team of medical specialists of the somatic and psychological reactions of airborne troops in parachute training indicate that harm anxiety focused on the fear of personal injury had far more disruptive effects than anxiety about personal failure, i.e., about the individual's ability to measure up to some group standard (440). In fact the latter provides a motive for overcoming the former. Consequently any event or experience that directs attention to the very real possibility of injury is likely to have adverse effects on performance. Thus, neuropsychiatric breakdowns and other non-battle casualties seem to increase whenever a unit suffers heavy losses from enemy action. The parallel movement of these rates, i.e., battle and nonbattle casualties, has been documented for different units in a variety of situations (450, 473, and 1147). The number of flying personnel grounded for psychiatric reasons varies with the type of duty. It is inversely correlated to the average number of hours in the air before one can be expected to be shot down or suffer a serious accident (469, 475). An additional factor is whether or not a man has been touched by the loss of a close friend. In ground combat units with equally high casualty rates, men who had seen such a friend killed suffered the greater number of fear symptoms (473). In general the immediate group with whom a soldier has shared the ordeal of "joint survival" is almost universally regarded by combat psychiatrists as the last and probably the most critical defense against anxiety (470; see also 427).

Further support for the importance of groups comes from the relationship between what the infantry man says he invokes as his main psychic aid when things get really rough and the number of anxiety symptoms he experiences (473), as well as the likelihood that he would become a neuropsychiatric case (459). The man driven by the feeling that he could not let his buddies down was more likely to remain effective than the man who tried to cope with anxiety through prayer and to this extent found himself alone. The point is further borne out by numerous observations reported by Marshall (431). He notes, for example, that individual stragglers separated from the units during a fluid situation were of little use when temporarily attached to a company other than their own, but in this same situation groups of stragglers usually retained their effectiveness.

Time spent in combat is also a factor in performance which seems to rise and fall in a curve. It usually builds up after the initial adaptation period during which individuals and groups mobilize their emergency resources. But since none can function indefinitely at its peak of efficiency, some break inevitably occurs. Suffering privations, like going without food or without sleep for an extended period, weakens the efficacy of certain group norms (435, 436). In this respect combat units are almost always in a state of partial disintegration. Not only do few men fight until the last bullet is expended, but even fewer units resist to the last man. The intentness with which ground combat troops engage the enemy has often fallen far below what the army command considers an acceptable minimum, as measured by the number of men who direct fire at an available target and as expected on the basis of their physical well-being (431). Part of the explanation lies, no doubt, in the utter psychological isolation men under fire experience. In addition the informal tolerance of combat men for many such lapses—including their sympathetic understanding of why men in some situations are apt to go "over the hill"—demonstrates that the support official prescriptions receive from the norms of the informal group does not apply equally to all matters (437). This last point has been lent special force by the observations of Moskos (208) on U.S. ground combat troops in Viet Nam.

These generalizations must be refined to take account of organizational practices that reflect both national character and the nature of the war being fought. First, an official policy that treats anxiety primarily as a medical problem is an acknowledgment that some forms of "deviance" in combat are natural and to this extent unavoidable. By emphasizing treatment and relying on disciplinary sanctions only when psychiatric measures fail, the U.S. armed forces seek to limit the number of cases leading to long term psychological damage and the permanent impairment of health. Glass (449), an army psychiatrist, believes that the true extent of psychiatric disability is always obscured by other forms of ineffective behavior, among them desertion, self-inflicted wounds, and physical illness. Sometimes the latter do not come to the attention of psychiatrists. Rose's data (463) on desertion in combat indicate, for example, that many who left their station under fire had previously sought and been refused evacuation through medical channels. Conversely, the neuropsychiatric casualty was less likely than the so-called normal soldier to have entertained thoughts of going AWOL before he turned up at the medical evacuation station (459). To this extent then, desertion and psychiatric breakdown are alternative modes of escape from what appears to the individual as an untenable situation.

The whole role of the healing professions, especially of psychiatric (264, 266, 270, 278, and 390) and religious (263, 268, and 281) counseling, merits far more attention than it has so far received from a relatively few sociologists. Most writing on the role of military psychiatry is by psychiatrists themselves. The members of all these professions are subject to conflicting pressures in performing their military duties. As members of an organiation, they are expected like others to contribute toward the achievement of an objective, for example, victory, but as members of the healing professions their primary obligation is to each individual client. So far the dilemmas themselves as well as the way individuals may resolve them have not been fully matched by sociological analysis of what the prevailing practices imply for the organization at large. At times the practice of combat psychiatry is itself contaminated by considerations only tangentially related to strictly medical evaluations of how "sick" a soldier actually is. Medical officers in making their determination are likely to consider its effect on the morale of other men (270, 427). A comparison of the anxiety symptoms of soldiers evacuated as neuropsychiatric cases with others who requested such evacuation but were sent back to the front (276) suggests that some administrative criteria were as important as the symptoms themselves. A man was more likely to be granted a rest cure if he held noncommissioned rank and carried responsibility; any break of efficiency on his part was apt to be serious. Similarly the longer a person had been in combat, the more likely were medical officers to accede to his request for evacuation.

World War II psychiatric casualty rates among American troops may also have been inflated by the widely held conviction that there was, indeed, an objective "breaking point" beyond which a man could not go on (262). Moreover as a man approached the point of eligibility for rotation, various symptoms of stress began to manifest themselves, regardless of the absolute number of days in combat or flying missions he actually had to his credit (473). In Korea medical officers and troops identified a short termer's syndrome. Nervousness increased as the contractual period of service neared its end, as it did also among U.S. troops in Vietnam (208 and 457). British troops in World War II unlike their American counterparts could not look forward to rotation. Consequently they fought for longer periods but were given frequent periods of rest.

Comparative data that help to explain the cohesion of troops in battle are as yet scarce. A paper by Spindler (211) attempts a specific comparison of the U.S. and German armies of World War II. Both armies are seen to reflect certain national character traits. Americans, for example, do not accept to the same degree as Germans the masculine soldier ideal. Hardness and virility are far less valued. But even if these and other differences can be substantiated, as they probably can, such a listing of traits explains little about the effectiveness of troops in combat.[4] Studies that combine observations on the battle behavior of troops with prisoner of war interrogation still point to the overriding importance of the informal group and of the sources from which it draws its strength. Shils and Janowitz (438) attribute the continued resistance in Hitler's Wehrmacht at a time when most men deemed defeat inevitable to the success with which experienced noncommissioned officers sustained interpersonal loyalties. Only after heavy losses had physically decimated these groups did the will to resist begin to founder seriously. On the other hand, the disastrous defeat of Arab armies in two short wars by the Israelis has been attributed to a basic cultural characteristic: a congenital distrust of others and a tendency to be devious that makes the kind of primary group formed in other armies most tenuous (428). The fabric disintegrates at the first sign of real pressure.

The basic process by which motives erode when primary groups disintegrate may be the same everywhere, but the strength which they attain is at least partly a function of organizational practices. Group solidarity in the Wehrmacht of World War II was fostered by the geographical lines along which units, including replacement companies, were mostly organized, at least until the closing phases of the war. Americans, by contrast, have tended to assign soldiers on a highly individual basis. Nowhere has this been more true, previous lessons notwithstanding, than in Viet Nam. Each soldier there knows the exact date his tour ends. Moskos (208) sees in this the cause of the tenuous nature of primary relations among combat GI's; yet, he also believes that, given the general lack of support for the war, assured rotation after one year helped what dissatisfactions there inevitably were from rising even higher.

The goals for which a war is fought also have an effect on combat motivation. The high esprit so far displayed by Israeli troops in every battle encounter is an indication that these recent ventures have enjoyed a popular backing (432, 813). Israeli soldiers and civilians both know that a defeat jeopardizes their chances of national survival. No clear pattern of motives exists for guerillas engaged in unconventional warfare. Some join under duress and then continue to fight because such activities hold out the clear prospect of gain or because once committed they see no way out of an untenable situation without attracting severe sanctions from both sides (1192). Although in a revolutionary situation the cadres are often enthusiasts, their ranks when swelled by an influx representing a broad cross section of the population are also likely to attract a share of antisocial elements, men who are looking for a formalized excuse to use violence (1208). One can nevertheless infer from the responses of Americans who volunteered to fight with the Republicans in Spain (448) that a belief in the broad goals for which a war is being fought is an important element in motivation. Asked about the things that helped them to hold down their fears, the volunteers mentioned ideological convictions far more often than faith in their leaders, comrades, or weapons.

When an army faces defeat, ideological convictions about the legitimacy of the government and of the war it is waging probably gain in importance over other sources of motivational support. In the Czarist army, for example, those regiments with the largest number of socialists among their officers and troops were the first to join the revolt (691). This would be true even though the flag waving type of expression of patriotic sentiment has always been totally unacceptable to the typical American GI in World War II as well as after. The overwhelming majority among them never seriously questioned the war aims announced by national leaders, so that official orders whose basic legitimacy was at least tacitly recognized rarely encountered open opposition but only a great deal of grumbling. This very suspiciousness of all explicitly ideological formulations apparently helped Americans taken captive in Korea to withstand the coercive indoctrination attempts of their Chinese captors (442, 464).

The ideological control system of other armies has often been far more stringent. The German Wehrmacht coupled its efforts to maintain the integrity of its informal group structure with a coercive repression of all ideologically deviant tendencies. Although it is difficult to gauge the success of this practice for the army as a whole, its effects on the individual unit can be attested: the higher the proportion of confirmed Nazis in a unit, the higher the probability of last ditch resistance, particularly if the unit also enjoyed elite status (438). The basis for interpersonal cohesion in Communist armies seems even more explicitly ideological.[5] Most striking in this regard are the accounts of the means by which the Chinese People's Liberation Army using a basic three man cell was able to bring its political control right down to the level of the individual soldier. In addition to providing mutual tactical support, the members of these cells were also expected to survey one another's political views and to bring any evidence of less than full loyalty to the attention of authorities. Repressive as it may appear, the system worked well enough under combat conditions (426). But the distrust and suspiciousness it generated seems to have inhibited the formation of close ties on a personal basis. Consequently once the system was disrupted by military defeat, the complete disintegration of units became all the more difficult to stem. The number of defections among Chinese soldiers taken captive was far greater than among troops on the Allied side (455). It appears unlikely, in any event, that without some faith in their cause and some sense of group worth derived from service to this cause soldiers can for long maintain their effectiveness under fire. Where these conditions are absent, the cohesive military group can easily become a center from which subversive influence spreads.

#### NOTES

1. E. Goffman, *Asylums.* Garden City, N.Y.: Doubleday-Anchor, 1961, p. xiii.

2. Robert K. Merton, *Social Theory and Social Structure.* New York: Free Press, 1957. Also Robert Presthus, *The Organizational Society.* New York: Knopf, 1962.

3. The term is from James G. March and Herbert Simon, *Organizations.* New York: John Wiley, 1958; see also Chester I. Barnard, *The Functions of the Executive.* Cambridge, Mass.: Harvard University Press, 1938.

4. On this point an unpublished paper by H. V. Dicks is instructive. See *The Psychological Foundation of the Wehrmacht.* Directory of Army Psychiatry, Research Memorandum, War Office, London, 1944 (mimeo).

5. See the unpublished Rand Report by H. V. Dicks and E. A. Shils, August 25, 1951 (R-213).

*Chapter 4:*

*THE MILITARY SYSTEM*

Military effectiveness defined in terms of organizational roles is no sure clue to the military might of a society, because armed forces cannot maintain themselves for very long if deprived of their base of support. The military is mainly a consumer rather than producer of resources. How much a society can invest in organized violence for legitimate social purposes depends on the level of technological development. Technology not only puts more powerful means of destruction into the hands of man but resultant increases in productivity mean that fewer men can produce more wealth. It then becomes more possible to divert manpower and resources to military purposes, while the cost of standing forces and arsenals is the more easily borne. It does not follow, however, that there are no reverse effects. On the one hand, military requirements draw on the same limited pool of resources, manpower, and talent from which other social needs have to be met; on the other, they may result in spurts of industrial growth or scientific activity. Although some potential productivity always remains unused, the consequences of reallocating activities and resources are usually felt throughout society.

From such a perspective the military appears as a complex system functionally interdependent with the civilian sector. The interdependence is more than economic; it applies equally to the internal arrangements of the military which must in some manner articulate or be attuned to the civilian social structure. In the simplest model the two are closely interwoven. The civil-military distinction is temporal rather than structural in a system that requires all men to equip themselves at the proper time in response to a call to war. In that case participation in military activity is simply an outgrowth of membership in the community. Military rank and social rank are closely attuned and the military sector does not visibly differentiate itself from the general social system. If a privileged warrior class does develop in the kind of society just described, it does so only by external conquest. Only within a more complex division of labor, particularly when standing armies are large and armaments costly, does privilege come to be associated with differences in the functions performed within the military. The privileges martial men enjoy in most societies demonstrate how much the distribution of status or wealth is determined by their possession or control of the means of violence. Yet regardless of how it arises, privilege always contains the danger of disarticulation between the principles on which stratification in the military is based and the distribution of power and privilege with the society at large. This requires some adjustment. The two must always be somehow brought in line with one another.

*Military Participation.* Andreski (482) has analyzed the influence of military requirements on the relation between social structure and the internal characteristics of military organization, i.e., military system. He singles out the "military participation ratio," i.e., the proportion of population under arms, as one of the critical variables affecting the degree of stratification in both civil society and the military. Other factors such as the state of military technology, the method of recruiting soldiers, and the terms of service exercise their influence mostly in conjunction with changes in the participation ratio, i.e., as either their cause or their consequence. Three attributes of military systems—participation ratio, subordination of the military to a leader, and internal cohesion—are used to construct a typology, which then becomes a basis for generating propositions, in this case, on a fairly general and abstract level, which are then illustrated with case material from every conceivable historical period and region of the world. More quantitative comparisons among contemporary nations reveal considerable variation in the military participation ratio as in the proportion of the gross national product allocated to the military effort (491, 506). Military expenditures take up a larger part of the gross national product, but not of the government budgets, in the industrialized nations of Europe and the United States than they do in other parts of the world. These variations are partly regional and influenced by strategic exigencies, but they also reflect the world-wide commitments of some major old world powers.

The yield from correlations between these type of data and other social indicators has not, so far at any rate, been highly promising either in terms of firm conclusions or new ideas. The approach is too crude. The data are expected to yield results without the researcher's paying attention to such less tangible factors as the dependence of the military system on the bases from which power holders derive their legitimacy. Typologies derived from an examination of particular historical circumstances have been more productive. An article by Hintze (497) first published in 1904 traces the development of the military system in Germany by explicitly linking peasant armies to feudalism; mercenaries and the conscript armies that replaced them were judged to be uniquely suited to the needs of absolute rule. Finally, a militia based on popular participation represented the first signs of an emerging democratic order where, insofar as service was voluntary, the diversity of interests characteristic of a pluralistic society received its first recognition. Such promilitary publicists as Werner Picht (503) and Benoist-Mechin (511) also believed that the thrust of history was toward universal service rendered on a voluntary basis. What potential tension there may be between the freedom of the citizen and the discipline enforced on soldiers resolves itself easily when all are patriotic. The actual thrust of history hardly is that clear. Janowitz (658) identifies several models that can replace the old aristocratic army, i.e., the "democratic," the "totalitarian," and the "garrison state" model, distinguishing each by its elite structure without giving any weight in his typology to other aspects of the military system.

Among the attempts to develop a schema for comparative analysis (e.g. 500, 502, 507), the ideal-typical constructs suggested by Feld (492) strike me as especially promising. Feld identifies the substantive content of five types of military systems and depicts the connection of each with a corresponding policy base. Thus, systems differ in terms of both the principle from which legitimacy is derived and the criteria by which military leaders must qualify for command. Accordingly a military system is based on dominance if any other basis for unity between the military and nonmilitary sector is lacking; in equality systems, on the other hand, military leaders occupy a recognizable, though distinct, position within a common social order. There are two types of dominant systems and three types of equality systems.

Dominant systems are either externally imposed or internally replenished. An imperium imposed on a conquered society represents external dominance, whereas military elites distributed throughout the society but, nevertheless, in sole possession of the instruments of violence arise from a policy base that is feudal and result in an internally dominant system. Systems of equality differentiate themselves from one another by their varying degrees of "openness." In closed equality systems the armed forces are still aristocratic but military command has become subordinated to the problem of administering the general social order. Officership remains a privilege, but instead of being inherited as a birth right, it is bestowed on those who, because they personify national values, are judged as best qualified to command the mass of conscripts that civil society continuously provides. A system of open equality emerges together with an industrial order; the management of the new technological instruments requires special skill. At this time elements of other professions are progressively assimilated into the armed forces. Emulation and competition among the branches and arms based on different technologies and the multiplication of specialized career lines begin to reflect a basically entrepreneurial model of organization. One alternative to this system of pluralistic division and indirect control is the subjection of the military to a political elite that personifies the goals presumed to be common to the entire community which are then formulated into an ideology that may be said to express the national "destiny." This destiny is shared. Everyone must show enthusiasm and involve himself in the effort to spread the true word by force of arms. Within the system the right of command falls on those who display the proper doctrinal commitment. The system is one of ideological equality. All those who do not subscribe to the dominant ideology become unworthy to serve. They are declared subversive and must be treated as enemies. Hence, the structure of power within this kind of military organization, writes Feld, comes to approximate the structure of power within the nation at arms. It is clear that such a system has its own built-in instabilities. When there are too many undesirables to be liquidated, a system based on the ideological equality model may revert to one of the dominant types. They take on a civilizing mission whence political representation will again bring modification.

Constructs of this kind, however useful to the theorist concerned with broad synthesis, cannot take fully into account the diversity of existing arrangements. Most military systems do not embody a single concept but rather are mixed systems in which the elements of service traditions have fused with specific measures adopted in response to contingencies that arose. For example, armed forces today continue to draw a fairly sharp line of division between officers who qualify as gentlemen and other ranks who, assumedly, do not. This two-class system once mirrored social and military realities in a fairly authentic fashion. The two categories were indeed differentially recruited with commissions going to men from the ranks in only the rarest instances. Class background offered the best assurance that a man was qualified for command and socially acceptable to his fellow officers. The unskilled foot soldier required little except sufficient physical stamina to perform his duties.

This two-class system was able to survive in many European countries long after it had outlived its usefulness, because newly emerging middle classes and traditional aristocracies formed political alliances. Members of the nobility continued to provide a disproportionate share of professional officers in return for which they exacted from a parliament, anxious to assure itself of their loyalty, high grain tariffs and a market for the mounts raised on their estates (102). At the same time, the middle classes could either purchase total exemption from obligatory service for their sons or have them, if educated, commissioned in the reserve (524). The vast rural population made "surplus" by industrialization contained more than a sufficient reservoir to perform the menial tasks; careers as noncommissioned officers were open to those among them who showed an inclination and aptitude for service beyond the obligatory term. These men provided the permanent cadres for processing and training of troops.

This pattern of differential military service participation persists even today, though due less to open class discrimination than to personnel policies that assign individuals on the basis of certain criteria of aptitude and competence. For example in the United States, universal liability for service is accepted in principle, but the system of selective call ups, as it has operated since World War II, has in fact favored the college educated groups, a disproportionate number of whom were able to continue repeated deferments granted on educational or occupational grounds until they were past the age of eligibility. H. Wool (595) present a summary of the several survey findings on the military service experience of different categories of persons within the same cohort. This bias in favor of the already favored has been partly offset by higher rates of rejection among the disadvantaged, many failing to meet the minimal physical and mental standards for induction (578; see also 573, 591, 592). Such inaptitude is a stigma on the labor market, and the limited use in the military for unskilled personnel only compounds whatever difficulties these persons face in finding employment. Their "escape" from military service thus represents the very obverse of privilege.

Moreover, many of the men who did serve were still able, if they had aptitude, education, or special occupational qualifications, to avail themselves of special options, like special officer training programs or joining the reserve, and consequently escape the full impact of the draft, insofar as they obtained the "better" assignments or reduced the period of service to a minimum (560, 574, and 1257). The point is that such options, wherever they exist, work to the advantage of the middle classes. The criteria governing the utilization of military manpower also result in inequities. Even in wartime a system of universal services does not ensure that risk and sacrifice are borne equally by all as a democratic political ethic commands. To be sure, officers in positions where combat casualties are disproportionately high undergo the greatest risks. In spite of this the overall association between risk and social status is probably negative. One study using ecological data (582) demonstrated that the poorer the neighborhood, the greater the number of combat deaths. Though the finding was far from definitive, it is in line with what is known about assignment practices. Since most men seek assignments of lesser risk, branches with more favorable technological images usually succeed in attracting and retaining a disproportionate share of the more highly qualified men, even for jobs that do not involve much skill. Those who lack special qualifications are thus steered to the less glamorous ground combat assignments where risks are correspondingly higher (565). Hence the artillery and infantry have unusually large numbers of men who in terms of ability as judged by test scores are marginal. The proportion of such men in these two basic combat specialties is exceeded only in certain service and unskilled assignments (595).

In this connection the role played by minorities is of considerable interest. In the past some armies have recruited mainly from ethnic minorities with a martial tradition. Without these troops, officered as a rule by members of the dominant nationality, the major colonial powers—Britain, France, and to a lesser degree, The Netherlands and Spain—could never have controlled their overseas possessions as long as they did. Yet for these troops, who were paid to carry the brunt of any fighting and to perform the many menial duties involved in policing an area, the segregation into ethnically distinct units under the command of Europeans was a constant reminder that the minorities from which they were recruited lacked full social equality.

In the long run the national allegiances of these troops proved to be of dubious reliability. Where the European powers in World War II suffered a temporary defeat, these units often collaborated with the enemy so as to advance the claims of their own people. With the liberation of most of the Third World, this type of army has largely disappeared, as in India (520), but there remain in some old and many new nations obvious discrepancies between the ethnic composition of the armed forces and the population as a whole that can produce or exacerbate tensions (499).

The casualties among American Negroes in Viet Nam, disproportionately high relative to their number in the general population, became an issue linked with general criticism of the draft system (552). Until all official restrictions on the assignment of Negroes in the U.S. armed forces were removed by order of President Truman in 1948, opportunities open to them had been severely curtailed. They served in segregated units and were mostly relegated to certain support and service activities (378, 569, and 588). Some minor breaks in this pattern of segregation occurred in World War II when the army suddenly faced by a severe shortage of combat replacements issued a call for Negro volunteers. The all-Negro rifle platoons thereby formed were then integrated into white companies. Reactions of both Negroes and whites to this experiment, however limited in scope, were strongly positive (309, 380), and further steps in the same direction taken under the impetus of the Korean War met with equally positive reactions among most troops (372). Yet even though the armed forces had gone farther than any other sector of society in banning all forms of racial discrimination, equal treatment has not yet been fully ensured. Socioeconomic characteristics of the Negro population attributable to the effects of past discrimination, as well as the persistence of attitudes and practices not amenable to administrative control, continue to influence the assignment and utilization of Negroes in military service.

Despite the disproportionately high rates of rejection within any disadvantaged population, the number of Negroes in enlisted ranks is rapidly approaching and will, if this trend continues, soon surpass their proportion in the general population (545). These figures provide graphic evidence that military service is attractive to many members of this group. Not only do many Negroes volunteer for service, but they also reenlist in larger numbers than the rest. Their lack of educational qualifications is no barrier to their advancement into the more senior ranks, particularly in view of their concentration in certain ground combat assignments where the chances for rapid promotion are somewhat better. Yet they are still under-represented at the officer level. Moreover they continue to suffer some discrimination that even an official order cannot fully eradicate. This affects especially their off-duty activities, as many military bases are located in the South where the civilian population is most reluctant to abandon its traditional racial attitudes, and informal groups continue to form along largely racial lines (208). Also despite full integration of combat troops in Korea, the effect of race still influenced some of their sociometric choices (371 and 375). The degree of social equality Negroes enjoy is far more complete while in overseas assignments, combat related or not, where they share equally with their white comrades any privileges accorded them as Americans, representatives of a preeminent power.

*Manpower Requirements and Occupational Structure.* The procurement and allocation of military manpower is always subject to constraints, the case of the Negro in the U.S. armed forces being only a special illustration of factors that everywhere help determine manpower policy and its effects. It seems unnecessary to detail here the variety of alternative arrangements for meeting manpower requirements, such as a volunteer army based on career incentives, a conscript force supplemented by a relatively small contingent of career personnel, an organized militia system in which all men have some military obligation to meet simply as an outgrowth of their other statuses, and so forth (537). Modern nations usually recruit their military manpower by some combination of methods depending on the specific circumstances. For the variety of existing arrangements, the reader is referred to the survey under the auspices of the Institute of Strategic Studies (544).

Each military system must be responsive to both societal and military imperatives. That is to say, it must, on the one hand, conform in its operations to prevailing ideological viewpoints and, on the other, provide the armed services with qualified personnel in adequate numbers. Some permanent cadre consisting of career personnel is an obvious necessity, both as a framework for expansion in case of war and to assure that an adequate number of military jobs are manned by persons already trained. In this respect a system of universal military training, though designed to be fair and to prevent too deep a gulf or too sharp a separation between army and nation, has evident weaknesses. The men released into civilian life after completing their brief training may not be highly effective soldiers when called back to the colors during an emergency mobilization. It was such a system which, according to Challener (535), assured French inferiority to the Germans in two separate wars.

The armed forces have traditionally met their manpower needs from among the rural population who were made surplus by the advance of industrialization and who by sheer force of number provided the necessary muscle power to man the military establishment with a permanent cadre of noncommissioned officers usually selected from the ablest among them. They were well suited for military service insofar as there was nothing in the background of these men often fresh from the countryside to dispose them toward rebellion against barracks discipline or against compliance with the norms governing the relations between officers and men. Recent investigations still show those from a rural background to be more favorably motivated than others toward military service as a career and more ready to accommodate to the pattern of military life (363). In many countries this source of manpower, both relatively and absolutely, has shrunk to a fraction of its former size (581). However, industrialization when it advances beyond a point produces its own population surplus among the undereducated youths in the cities who because of their lack of technical skill and education are chronically unemployed.

Whether these two sources will continue to provide the military with a sufficient number of new recruits depends on such circumstances as the size of the male cohorts, the magnitude of military requirements, and job opportunities in the civilian labor market. In any event the main manpower problem does not lie primarily in the shortages that occasionally arise, as these can usually be made up by some form of compulsory service, especially in those periods when a nation believes itself acutely threatened and its armed forces undermanned and unable to respond. Problems in this area involve above all the need to strike a proper balance between various alternatives—between men who are motivated to serve and men who have the qualifications for a specific job, between stability and turnover, between the requirements as defined by the services and such other highly valued objectives as giving young men the chance to pursue an orderly career without undue disruption. (See such symposia as 550 and 560.) Today more than at any previous time, the military in the industrially advanced nations is competing with industry for the same limited pool of skilled manpower.

Everyone is aware of the upgrading of the civilian work force. A large number of jobs based on muscular energy have been eliminated over the past century to be replaced by occupational activities requiring a higher order of professional or technical competence. Less well known is the parallel shift within military occupational structure during this same period, exemplified most strikingly by the replacement of foot soldiers by a variety of military occupational specialties. Basically unskilled ground combat assignments which a hundred years ago accounted for the large majority of the enlisted force has diminished to less than twenty percent of the enlisted assignments in the American military today. The first attempt to specify the exact dimensions of this shift appeared in Appendix IV to the report of the U.S. President's Commission on Veterans' Pensions (589). Figures presented by Janowitz and Little (18) are from this source. (For later information, see 581, 590, 594, and 595). For example, tables of organization and equipment of an infantry division reflect the introduction and proliferation since World War II of such previously nonexistent activities as fire control and air support. But the mechanization of ground combat is only one and not necessarily the most important factor in the transformation. The emergence of air power as the predominant strategic weapon and reliance on intercontinental missiles as the basic deterrent indicate the extent to which military power has come to rest on a technological' base. A larger proportion of the total effort goes into maintaining and repairing the new military hardware. Beyond this the many and varied activities through which the United States attempts to meet its world-wide commitments need to be carefully coordinated. Hence, more soldiers than ever before are involved in transport, communication, and support activities that cannot be shifted to the local population. Any expansion in the number of men under arms, including the policy of frequent rotation for soldiers stationed in distant theatres, also increases the number of military personnel needed for processing troops performing the traditional military duties.

The skill structure of the truly modern army differs markedly from that of its predecessors. That the majority of enlisted men in the U.S. armed forces today are employed in occupations broadly analogous either to those in the skilled tradesmen category or to those of white-collar workers performing administrative or professional services of the type for which a degree is not usually a requirement creates problems. For one thing, the image of military service has not kept step with these facts. American teenagers, like adults, continue to rank the enlisted career in terms of both its desirability and prestige below that of other skilled occupations.[1] In other industrially advanced nations, the situation is broadly similar to that in the United States. The persistence within the military of a clearly delineated two-class system is one cause for this discrepancy (see especially 226). A system in which only a few skilled artisans were given specialist ratings and extra pay no longer accords with the military occupational structure; neither does the ceiling on the mobility potential of enlisted men repeat the stress on self-improvement and mobility everywhere else in society. To be sure, the ceiling has been lifted for some categories, so that men with rare specialties and long service now have the chance to advance into the officer ranks where previously they would have remained noncoms. In some respects, too, the hard work discipline to which enlisted men in all assignments had traditionally been subjected has been eased, and they also enjoy greater freedom to arrange their nonworking lives in whatever manner they please. Significant differences nevertheless remain, and most of these favor the civilian work environment.

Although voluntary enlistments are also affected by conditions on the labor market, the capacity of industrial unemployment, periodic as well as chronic, to generate an adequately staffed career force is limited. Men induced to volunteer because they have lost out in the competition for civilian jobs may still suffice to fill the declining number of unskilled and service jobs in the military, but their usefulness to the services is often limited by their lack of education and other kinds of inaptitude. These problems are compounded by a tendency of reenlistments at the expiration of the first tour of duty to be inversely related with both educational attainments and performance ratings (581 and 587). Moreover the losses in certain enlisted job categories requiring the most extensive training have been disproportionately high despite the practice of making attendance at some service schools conditional on the prior extension of the period of contractual commitment.

In the postindustrial society where education is both widely available and the major prerequisite for occupational mobility, failure to complete minimal schooling often implies more than just a lack of the skills to meet the demands of a technological civilization. It can also be symptomatic of a more basic inaptitude, one that accounts for the difficulties such persons have experienced in adjusting to school. The findings from the extensive studies by Ginzberg and his associates (573) on the ineffective soldier in World War II showed conclusively that breakdown from all causes, including ineffectiveness in ground combat, occurred much more frequently among the undereducated. This observation, replicated many times since, has come to be taken so much for granted that it is rarely reported nowadays in academic journals. (See 564 for a more recent study.) It should nevertheless be obvious from the preceding discussion that to raise minimal educational requirements for eligibility in order to separate potential misfits, as the services have done, merely shifts without solving the basic problem of meeting military manpower requirements. Such a policy would disqualify the very groups for whom a career in military service still holds considerable attraction, namely the poor and often undereducated youths from rural and urban areas who are more strongly motivated and also stand to benefit more from training offered in many service schools.

There are two conventional solutions to this basic dilemma. Both have been variously tried and each has its costs (544). One is to improve screening to identify from the pool of available volunteers those who regardless of formal credentials give evidence that with training they can still become useful soldiers (572, 573, vol. 1; and 577). Yet there are limits to the effectiveness of screening procedures. Because at some point the risks of subsequent failure exceed the possible returns from the larger training investment (575), the armed services are often unwilling to assume a large share of the burden for rehabilitating the nation's manpower resources. They have nevertheless reluctantly taken on this mission because of their concern that the pool of qualified manpower might dry up, especially if they had to do without conscription. An example of such a response is the so-called 100,000 man project of the United States under McNamara. There have been reports that these men did not have significantly higher rates of inaptitude than others, supporting earlier World War II studies and others since that a large proportion among them can be "salvaged" and trained. Nevertheless, this system continues to discriminate against the poor in terms of assignments. Those with the better qualifications, as judged by their education and performance on tests, are in a better position to avail themselves, if they should wish, of opportunities for specialist training and in the course of this to reduce their risks. The tendency to channel the more marginally qualified manpower into combat assignments goes against the principle of equality of sacrifice. Although that principle can never be fully enforced, the high casualty rates of Negroes in Viet Nam have resulted in charges of deliberate discrimination, and it is likely that such charges will be aired wherever similar circumstances prevail.

Compulsory service represents the second alternative for meeting the manpower needs of the military. Such a system appears more equitable in that it requires the same minimum period of service from all who meet the standards of eligibility. A majority of the American soldiers in combat in Viet Nam toward the end of the buildup there have been draftees, while the excess of Negroes among them has been reduced and the Negro casualty rate nearly brought in line with that of whites (208). Compulsory service is also likely to improve the average caliber of the men in the armed forces, directly because many of those called would never otherwise serve and indirectly because the impending draft calls cause an undetermined number to volunteer in order to obtain a preferred assignment while still others enter programs that will lead to their being commissioned when still in civilian life. Accordingly the draft has also come in for a good deal of criticism. When military manpower needs can be met by only a minority of the age eligible cohorts, the system begins to appear arbitrary and capricious. The decision of who shall be called when not all serve has generally been entrusted to local boards. The intention has been to assure flexibility in an impersonal system. Yet the unrepresentativeness of the membership of these boards meant that local needs were often interpreted so as to perpetuate and magnify existing social differences. Only recently has this aspect of selective service come under scrutiny from investigators employing social science perspectives (538 and 562).

Comparing the draft with forced labor (542) and involuntary servitude is hardly an apt basis for criticism, since in other times this method has found general acceptance. What is important is that, except under conditions of national emergency when a country is united, most men involuntarily called will be poorly motivated. Whatever deprecatory views they hold of military service are then communicated to others, including some whose propensity to delinquency is held in check only as long as it receives no reinforcement from the disaffection that this kind of draftee is far more likely to express openly than the ordinary career soldier. The short period most draftees serve also means constant turnover. The cost of training will be high relative to the period a man can be utilized. Yet long terms of service for conscripts, especially when they are negatively motivated to begin with, are obviously impractical, whereas for volunteers the effect is different. Experience shows that the longer a person has served, the greater the likelihood that he will extend his commitment. Hence, long first term engagements for volunteers tend to result in a larger number of renewals; too long an extension of this period will, on the other hand, deter some of the very men who might otherwise be induced to volunteer.

A balance always has to be struck among several considerations. One is between military requirements and other pressing social needs. Another is between military needs and the equalization of risks. In connection with the latter, one should recognize that whether a man serves or not is most important for some, but what he does while in the service is more important for others. Although all military personnel simply because they wear the uniform can on occasion be called to risk their lives in combat or while performing their duties under enemy fire, it is also true that the armed forces are increasingly manned by specialists with many opportunities for training. Men continue to enter and leave military service with varying effects of the time spent there on their subsequent careers. There is likewise a continuous flow of resources from the civilian into the military sector. The use to which they are put has obvious consequences for the total society and the distribution of values within it.

*Functions.* One issue concerns the side effects of military service. There is little doubt that such service has been one of the main avenues for geographical and social mobility. To leave home always offers opportunities for new experience, and countless young men have found an escape from narrow provincialism and a restrictive milieu after being called to the colors (302). Particularly in the new nations, military service often provides the first sustained contact with modern ways and a stepping stone to altogether new types of occupational activities. This is illustrated by a recent study of exservicemen in Ghana (624). Still, the data from various countries on the long term impact of military service on the subsequent career of exsoldiers and on the occupational structure are sketchy and difficult to interpret in any systematic fashion.

What has attracted considerable attention is the problem of reassimiliating large numbers of men discharged from service into civilian life. (See also Section VI.3 of bibliography.) The problem is hardly acute where a short period of service rendered at a time specifiable in advance causes a minimum of disruption. It is not unusual to ease the transition of career soldiers by giving them preference in certain positions as a recognition of their service and to supplement their pension. Unlike many other countries, the United States has only recently had to cope with the impact of large scale retirement from the military of men still in the prime of life (597). But the problem of mass demobilization it faced at the end of World War II was similar to that of other belligerent nations. Hence, some findings concerning this experience have general relevance.

Gross comparisons made sometime after World War II between who had and who had not seen wartime service showed veterans to be generally better off. This was not necessarily a consequence of either their service experience or of veterans benefits received. The status of the exservicemen also reflected their aptitude and social background. As we have seen already, the very characteristics that disqualify men from military service may also handicap them in competing for the better civilian jobs. The real issue in terms of career advancement is whether the experience in the military assignment helps to build a career or whether in terms of personal gain the time so spent could have been put to better use. So far data collected on this issue are far from definitive because of small samples (611) and because the many factors that affect careers have to be controlled in any objective analysis (606).

The majority of veterans, when asked, said that their service experience had been a help rather than a hindrance in postservice jobs they had held (589). But the question put in this manner is loaded; perhaps other experiences would have been of more help still. Many have inferred from the overall convergence of the military and civilian occupational structures so evident in the period since World War II that the reassimilation of veterans and retirees would be greatly eased by the skills acquired in a military job that carried a designation identical to one in the civilian work force. It appears nevertheless as if the actual transfer value of most military experience has been greatly exaggerated (109, 598, 605, 617, and 625). There is, to be sure, a special demand for men trained and utilized in certain military specialties where there are serious civilian shortages. Yet most men discharged as well as those retired from the armed forces settle in jobs that have little to do with what they did during most of their military career. Retirees often feel that their skills are seriously underutilized in the jobs they ultimately land.

That this should be is not surprising considering the intrinsically "parochial" nature of a military career. The value of the esoteric knowledge a person acquires through long service in any organization diminishes sharply when he transfers out. For example, even though a military specialty may be by designation identical with a civilian job, the specific knowledge required is often geared to particular equipment and, hence, much narrower than that required to fill an identically designated job in civilian life (594 and 595). Many military retirees, even specialists, encounter difficulties in finding civilian employment with status and level of pay they expected on the basis of their attainments in the military (566). Their separation from the service represents downward mobility. (See also 129.) The degree of success in finding a commensurate position depends on education, age, length of prior service, and rank achieved. Certainly the young, those with a good academic background, and those whose achieved position in the military has made them highly visible, given them cosmopolitan perspectives, and afforded opportunity to establish contacts find interorganizational mobility much easier. This has been the normal road to success in the advanced countries.

For most military personnel a "second career" is not just a way to improve one's mobility potential; it has become a necessity even for those prepared to make a long term commitment to military service. In this line of activity the emphasis has always been on youth, except that in times of stability and retrenchment the age of the men under arms, as that of military leaders, has shown an inexorable tendency to rise (122 and 137). The new technology and the need for continuous innovation require institutional devices to assure the most talented enough chance to advance within the military establishment. This requirement tends to conflict with the hierarchical rank structure. There is a sharp curtailment of opportunity as one approaches the apex of the rank pyramid. Despite an expansion in the number of ranks at the middle level largely in recognition of the new skill structure, there comes a point in the careers of many officers and enlisted men when they find themselves frozen in rank with little chance of further promotion. They have, in fact, become supernumerary. It is to their best interest and that of the organization that these men should now become eligible for retirement after twenty years of service, and an increasing number choose to leave despite the fact that they are still in the prime of life and their financial needs usually near the maximum. This situation also creates an obligation to ease their transition to civilian life for which the retirement benefits alone do not suffice.

Although the training of men has always been one of the major preoccupations of the military (629), the content of the various programs has not been geared primarily to easing this transition. To be sure, both technical training and academic education are sometimes offered in return for past service. It has also been used as a deliberate retention device when the men who receive such schooling most obligate themselves for a specified period following its completion. Some basic literacy and vocational courses may, in fact, be the last chance of salvage for school dropouts (615; see also 631). Yet it is not unusual for schooling beyond the basic courses to be deliberately narrowed to correspond to the requirements of a specific job or piece of equipment in order to reduce its costs and to diminish the chances for a man so trained to transfer easily to a more remunerative civilian position, thereby nullifying one of the main advantages this training has for the individual receiving it.

Another factor that impedes the transition resides in the unusual concentration within the military job structure of some occupational specialties—electronics again being one of them—that, in spite of their critical importance in the economy, nevertheless account for a much smaller proportion of the civilian work forces. The availability of these men on the job market may be a gain for infant industries that develop around the technology in which the military has pioneered (629). For example, the growth of civil aviation in the United States after World War II was no doubt speeded by the pool of men trained to meet the needs of the Air Force. Yet the gains for the economy are not automatically gains for the individual. An oversupply of men narrowly specialized means that they will encounter difficulties in finding suitable employment in the particular field for which their military training has prepared them.

In their general emphasis on the modernizing role performed by the military in many countries of the third world, writers like Shils (674) and Pye (622) seem in this respect to be echoing the view of Sombart (626). Yet the relationship between the armed forces and society in the newly developing nations is different from what it was in Europe during the 16th and 17th centuries. The apparent "modernism" of military institutions in the new states is basically an outgrowth of the interstate system. Military aid and assistance training programs given by the industrially developed nations serve as a channel for important innovations both technological and organizational which the industrial and scientific base of the receiving society could not possibly sustain on its own (604, 609, 621, 627, 635, and

639). As a result the armed forces are equipped with modern weapons; they also are organized along explicitly modern lines (480). Despite the sharp contrast between the "modernism" of military institutions and the "backwardness" of many other sectors, the armed forces themselves are not necessarily the prime movers of change.

Entrepreneurial activity is obviously critical for autonomous development. Usually this role is recognized only in connection with the commercial and industrial—not the military—enterprise, but many industrially underdeveloped societies are deficient in both. Redlich (529) has recently given us a well-documented account of the men for the most part aristocrats who provided for profit the services necessary to wage large-scale wars in Europe between 1350 and 1800. By contrast the entrepreneurial activities of the military in the newly emerging nations are more likely to be directed toward the consolidation of political power. In this regard it falls to the state and its organs of administration to create the conditions for economic development. However, when a disproportionate share of the resources flows through the military apparatus, a disproportionate number of ambitious young men will likewise be drawn into the armed forces which provide one of the best means of social mobility. A military that commands the skill and resources generally in short supply but essential to development is likely to expand its role into many activities only indirectly related to the primary military function. In some countries like Burma, the military have assumed major responsibility for industrial activities (525). They are also deeply involved in a variety of "civic" missions.

The accounting scheme devised by Bobrow (599) represents an effort to identify and ultimately to measure the various types of input from the military to national development. The measures may lack precision as there is no way to balance benefits against costs or to weigh the relative advantages of alternative patterns. Yet one point has been widely acknowledged: wherever tribal divisions, linguistic diversity, and poor communications have inhibited the emergence of a national identity, the military has helped discipline the population into loyal subjects of the state. In Europe where the military once served and saw itself as a "school for nationhood" (521), this function has been progressively relegated to civil institutions. Once developed, they appear to fill this function much better. The military still represents the most visible symbol of nationhood in much of the third world where the organs of civil administration have not yet fully penetrated the countryside and the outlying districts. In these circumstances unity depends very much on military force, not necessarily on subjugation by conquest, but nevertheless on the means and the nation-wide network that only the armed forces command.

The military is also one of the original forms of public enterprise; in many countries the army predates even the postal service. The incentive to expand its role depends in large part on how well other institutions are developed (525). There may be few alternatives, and the military, because opportunities in the private economic sector are limited, attracts a disproportionate share of the technical and entrepreneurial talent as well as the resources from the government. The factors that determine the allocation functions to the military call for a good deal more study. One interesting first step in this direction is an article by Anderson (481) which reports on the disaster role played by the armed forces of several countries.

The diversion of resources and talent from the civil to the military sector, particularly when the institutions within the first are weak, can produce serious distortions in priorities. Though clearly a stimulus for many activities, it is highly probable that the resources allocated to armaments and armies and the manpower trained to perform military tasks could have been put to better use. The potential for distortion exists equally in countries that have the prerequisites for self-sustained economic growth. In the latter the lion's share of defense contracts has often gone to those groups and regions most highly developed and, therefore, in the best position to meet the requirements, the very ones which because they are already developed are least in need of this infusion. Yet economy and efficiency demand that existing industrial and laboratory facilities be kept working at capacity.

The problem is economic insofar as it is allocational, but the allocations among the different institutional sectors involve not only commodities but other social values. One of these concerns the impact of military requirements on intellectual productions. Thus Merton (618) has shown how the direction of scientific inquiry in 17th century England, a period of unusually high scientific productivity, was influenced by military factors. Development in the field of military ballistics made the discovery of the laws governing trajectories or the expansion of gases especially relevant. The intellectual effort itself had other roots in religion and in the humanism of the era. In no sense can it be considered merely, or even primarily, a by-product of the military effort (1248). When a good deal of the support for scientific research is governed by its potential military utility and significant fractions of the professionals in some disciplines like physics and psychology are either directly employed by or under contract to the military (969), the pattern of growth is inevitably affected. Whether scientific progress is more helped than hindered by support given in this form remains an issue of considerable sociological interest.

Military influence is exerted by means of patronage. Regardless of the explicit intent, vested interests that inevitably evolve around whatever pattern has emerged then raise obstacles to change of any sort. This in essence is the problem popularly articulated by reference to the military-industrial complex. Yet functional integration denotes more than just the dependence of some industries on military contracts and vice versa. It refers equally to the tendency of scientific, educational, social welfare, and other establishments to look to the military, so that activities initially undertaken to meet military needs or simply channeled through the military as a matter of convenience gain a momentum of their own (602). Despite the significance of these relationships, very few sociologists of the military have attempted any kind of systematic analysis (502, 947). The subject is usually left to the journalist, and when economists take it up, as some have, they tend to see it more narrowly, focusing by and large on how important these activities are to prosperity and on whether disarmament or reconversion can be achieved without dislocations likely to lead to a recession.

No a priori distinction can be made between what is appropriately military and what represents an inappropriate institutional intrusion into a separate civil sector. Military sponsored projects in such diverse fields as public health, education, earth and space exploration are often justified as national defense. This rationale, whatever the legal lines of authority, reflects the position of the military within an overall system of social stratification. The definition of the military as a distinctive type of expertise alongside other types and strictly limited in its applications is, of course, a heritage of liberalism, but the separation of the institutional spheres as well as the clear assertion of civil supremacy can equally be grounded in a caste system as, for example, in ancient India (685). The military sector need not be dominant. Whether or not it is depends to a large extent on how significant warfare looms as an activity. It depends also on the nature and degree of integration between the military and civilian elites. Even the interpenetration of the two spheres does not preclude control by the basic civilian values to which both soldiers and civilians aspire. That, however, is a problem not of functional integration but of norms and of the distribution of political power.

### NOTE

1. See Chapter 2.

*Chapter 5:*

*CIVIL-MILITARY RELATIONS*

The concept of civil-military relations has meaning only if the institutional sector identified as military has begun to differentiate itself from a more encompassing social order. Along with functional specialization goes another development; military scales of values lose their universal validity and the ideals personified by the military are assigned a place within a general scale of values. Civil-military relationships are inevitably fraught with conflict insofar as the claims by the military and its leaders for power and privilege exceed what civilians are ready to grant. The resolution of these conflicts over the legitimate limits of the influence of the military gives rise to a normative order.

Where the military is dominant within the state and society, one customarily speaks of this situation as "militarism." (1040).[1] As an analytic construct this term has little use unless it discriminates clearly among the various conditions on which this dominance is founded. Thus, there are societies where the dominance of a warrior class represents, so to speak, a natural condition; the social and political order incorporates this principle. Most of the time, however, militarism denotes a more specific state of affairs in which the military has somehow usurped power in contravention to the principle of civil rule and/or has extended its influence beyond the technical requirements of a specifiable mission. As Vagts (102) reminds us, militarism in the modern world has little to do with military efficiency. Ritter (818, Vol. II, p. 32) likewise speaks of militarism only where the primacy of the political leadership and civilian perspectives have been challenged by the military. (For other definitional essays, see 677, 681, 710, 717, and 729.)

This challenge can manifest itself in different ways. Militarism in its classic European form rests on the social and normative power military men have enjoyed by virtue of their close association with civilian elites. The harsh discipline prevailing in the armed forces became exalted as a virtue and also set the tone for authority relations in other spheres of social life. These norms, obvious survivals from the postfeudal era, were deliberately exploited by some political leaders to maintain civil peace and acquiescence by the people to a government in which rising industrial interests had allied themselves with members of the old aristocracy. The posture of many statesmen and some of their decisions reflected these same ideological premises. Hence, the term militarism is also applied with reference to the content of the foreign policies pursued by states, such as extreme aggressiveness or expansionist tendencies as well as the one-sided preponderance of military considerations in policy decisions. Yet ideological militarism of the first type is hardly the sole or even the main cause of a militarist foreign policy. Similarly the tendency of civilian leaders to defer to military advice can be enhanced by insufficient knowledge or lack of the unity necessary to reject the collective presentation of a viewpoint expressed by the military. This is often the case with decisions made under the shadow of impending war. Finally there is the phenomenon of coercive intervention by the military into the process of government with or without an actual military takeover, but in clear violation of legally institutionalized procedures. This, too, has been called militarism, mostly by reference to Latin America (see 770 and 802), regardless of whether the coercive power in the hands of the military is used to advance their own narrow interests or to promote a variety of social objectives. Militarism in this third form is in some respects antithetical to the other two. It often flourishes when the armed forces have no viable foreign policy mission and their links to the governing civilian elites are tenuous.

This threefold categorization of the variety of referents given to the term militarism seems to overlap to some extent with a typology developed by Janowitz (88, 660). "Designed" militarism flows from a fairly well developed ideology of military preeminence. By contrast "unanticipated" militarism is the result of a lack of traditions and of institutional mechanisms for asserting civilian control, with "reactive" militarism a response to persistent failures on the part of civil government. The second and third are essentially ad hoc formulations intended to highlight the clear differences between the classic forms of militarism as they existed in Europe and the potential threat to civil supremacy in modern nations with a highly professionalized military establishment, on the one hand, and in the new nations, on the other. However useful this classification of the dynamics and "motives," one must recognize that all three may be present though in different mixtures, and that what began as an unanticipated move into an institutional vacuum or as a reactive takeover can become institutionalized military rule and perpetuate itself as designed militarism.

*Normative Influences.* The ideological and social dominance of officers within society and the state appears to be most closely associated with the dynastic state during its decline when many rulers came to rely on the military in order to shore up their own power. Though primarily a European phenomenon, it has also been experienced in other parts of the world. In both Japan and Turkey, for example, officers also exercised considerable influence, at times overtly, but usually because their close ties to the head of the state provided them with a shield. A somewhat pallid version of this form of militarism once existed in some Latin American countries where its antecedents had been imported from Europe long ago and where political instability had opened the way to the usurpation of political power by those who had the requisite means of force. Yet the traditional symbols of aristocracy from which officers derived their social respectability and ideological preeminence have everywhere lost much of their legitimacy. What prestige the military enjoys resides increasingly in the opportunities it offers; that is to say, the officer career has come to be valued less for its intrinsic content and more as a means to gain access to other values. Therefore, what ideological support the military is able to mobilize flows largely from its success in identifying itself with the aspirations of the people. Even in those new nations where officers have seized political power, the requirements of technology and the gradual penetration of the countryside by modern means of communication make it unlikely that the pattern of civil-military relations there will ever duplicate those once so prevalent in Europe.

What conditions favor the social dominance of the military? One of them appears to be the military participation ratio (482). Although having a large number of men under arms implies the diffusion of military values into other phases of social and political life, this tendency can be offset by other normative influences. We have already in another context referred to the caste system in ancient India. Because the preeminence of the Brahmin caste in all ideological matters was assured, this restricted the influence of the military even under conditions of high military participation (685). The contrast with Europe is clear. There dynastic wars tended to overlap with religious conflicts, and the influence of the church often depended on the secular sovereign. As the church lost its unchallenged power as a unifying force, the military became the primary instrument in the hands of principals for ensuring the loyalty of their subjects and socializing them politically (672). The principle that those unworthy of citizenship were also unworthy to wear their country's uniform is compatible with both universal conscription and a militia system. Both incorporate the idea of the unity of the armed forces and the nation, an idea that receives its penultimate expression in the slogan of the nation in arms. (See 497 and 504 on the relation between recruitment and political system.)

The scope within which military values are assumed to be valid is always enhanced by a close relationship between military leaders and the head of the state, particularly when the latter sees in the armed forces one of his mainstays of political support. These values, in other words, express a political bias and because of this are often challenged by political opponents (690). Yet such a contest always finds some civilian ready to rally to the defense of the corporate interests of the military, if not to the defense of the regime itself. The case of Germany's iron chancellor, von Bismarck, who simply overrode the Reichstag with the support of the Emperor and the Emperor's personal military cabinet when his requests for military appropriations were voted down is only too well known. The example is, of course, an extreme one, and wherever parliamentary traditions are firmly entrenched, no prime minister willing to match this audacity can expect to be sustained. Because public acquiescence is questionable, organized pressure groups explicitly formed to support the demands of the armed services for larger appropriations, for internal autonomy, or for the adoption of some specific military policy come to represent a major political asset. Sometimes these groups are dominated by ex-officers; sometimes by demobilized soldiers. Even the latter are apt to press not only for increased veterans' benefits, but also for what they perceive to be the interests of the services and therefore concern themselves with a variety of policy issues. The case study by Martha Derthick of the National Guard in the United States (760) and our knowledge of the important role associations of ex-soldiers are known to have played

in Germany during the nineteen twenties, in France during decolonization, and in England after World War II (953) whet the appetite for
more material.

The political roles assumed by ex-officers represent another
channel of potential influence. Although nothing remotely approaching a full documentation of the military backgrounds of legislators
and of "civilian" officials exists, their representation in the parliamentary bodies of many countries is by no means negligible even
today (195). Retired professional officers sat in significant numbers,
second only to lawyers, in the British House of Commons between
the two world wars (88, p. 339) and their number is still large. They
were likewise significant among the deputies of the Third French
Republic where they were far from equally distributed among the
parties. The overwhelming majority among them represented the
right-wing and conservative parties and could be counted upon not
only to side with the military, but also to give their support on most
of the major issues to the monarchist, clerical, and antilabor position
(173). In Germany the disdain the members of the old imperial
officer corps felt for democratic institutions expressed itself in an
official attitude of political neutrality, but when as officers they
stood for election, it was usually, like their counterparts in other
countries, under the banner of the nationalists. Among the Nazis
elected to the Reichstag in 1930, former officers made up a
significant fraction (102).

Political involvement goes against the professional military ethic as
it is depicted by Huntington (657). What he has called "objective
forms" of civilian control rests on a set of norms that confine the
activities of officers to the sphere of their expert competence; yet
the meaning of political neutrality as practiced is not without its
ambiguities. In the first place, the recognition as experts enjoyed by
a corporate body like the officer corps actually gives them
considerable political leverage, particularly when it comes to decisions where the national interest is believed at stake. This is not only
a function of their technical advice, but there appears to be a trend
to rely on ex-officers in many kinds of quasipolitical assignments,
including but not confined to their use in diplomatic missions (88,
946, 949, and 958). In the second place, being politically neutral has
usually been interpreted as standing aloof from the partisan political
struggle, an aloofness that has often served as a cover for the exercise
of influence behind the scenes and outside of normal political
channels. This nearly every case study of the policy process

documents. Often overlooked, however, is the way the many formal and informal ties members of the military elite inevitably form with key civilians tend to tie them to the status quo. Not only are officers often slow to accommodate to a change of political regime, but there has been evidence of connections, often of a clandestine nature, between professional officers and representatives of the extreme right wing (169, 188, 761, and 793). This represents still a third type of political activity, one that grows out of a search for a viable political ideology. It is impossible to say how widely these views are diffused, but military men are professionally concerned over the denigration of patriotism among men in the service and among the general population.

Given the traditionally conservative orientation of the military, its "political neutrality" in the above sense is strongly contingent on two conditions: close integration of the officer corps with the governing stratum (736) and the relative absence of popular unrest (751). When they are met, the assimilation of military values can pass for character training. (See Chapter 4.) Moreover, the weaker the roots of enlisted men in civilian society—that is to say, when they enter without firm political convictions and serve in relative isolation—the greater the domination of their thinking by the officer corps. Whether or not such a force includes a broad cross section of the population does little to undermine this control until political dissent is carried into the army from outside or disaffected soldiers have formed their revolutionary cells. Lacking contingents of proven reliability and no longer certain of at least the tacit acquiescence of significant segments of the people, the military become dependent on the governing authority. Hence, the typical response of the armed forces to a change in political structure through an uprising from below has been one of reluctant and reserved accommodation, so Katherine Chorley (751) concludes from her study of the role of the European armies in some 150 cases of internal disorder. Threats to public order arising from working class protests were successfully quelled by armed force except in those instances where the military control structure had already disintegrated because of military defeat.

The ability of the military to stem the tide of political change depends on its having some measure of structural autonomy. Through screening of personnel, through its indoctrination, through the special regulations and disciplinary procedures that apply only to military personnel, and so forth, the armed forces could to some extent preserve a separate enclave, existing as foreign bodies in their societies and insulating themselves from new ideological currents defined as subversive. There were, of course, limits to their success in this regard. New political leaders, particularly those brought to the fore in a major political change, invariably turned their attention to the armed forces. They sought structural reforms designed to assure themselves of the military's political loyalty.

One of the foci of conflict and accommodation concerns the control over personnel selection. Criteria of professional expertise often clash with political considerations. It stands to reason that senior commanders have to be men of proven political reliability, but they must also be qualified to assume major responsibility for the direction of troops and enjoy the confidence of their subordinates. The problem is somewhat simplified at the highest echelon. The top positions are always filled by political appointments, and the decisions taken at the highest level of government are the result of extensive consultation among all those involved. Hence, it may not occasion surprise that in the newly formed Soviet Red Army and the Chinese People's Liberation Army the distinction between military and political leaders customarily made in the West had little validity (691, 716). Yet many of the intermediary positions must still be filled with professionally qualified officers whose adherence to the regime may be open to question.

Effective political control over an army of revolutionary origin therefore requires that it be penetrated by men ideologically committed to the new regime at every level. There are two alternative means to achieve this whenever the fusion of army and party is incomplete: by the institution of a parallel hierarchy whereby a commissar who represents the dominant political ideology is directly attached to every major unit and by the formation of party cells among soldiers as countervailing influence to the command authority of officers (679; see 683 on Nazi Germany). Both place commanding officers under "outside" scrutiny and enforce conformity of the leadership practices and indoctrination effort to the principles set forth by the dominant political party. In comparison with this pervasive form of control, the various efforts of the liberal and left-wing critics of the military in the parliaments of pluralistic democracies have always been limited by the fact that they lacked such means to enforce compliance. Nevertheless, the commissar system and the reliance on control from below do not resolve all conflict; they merely succeed in transferring it from the parliamentary to the unit level, where the advocates of reform pit their strength against traditionalist officers who see their prerogatives threatened by alien political forces. Experience shows, however, that commissars also tend to interfere with normal command functions even when these concern matters only professionals are qualified to decide. Hence, resistance is not just an expression of political conservatism. According to such Sovietologists as Kolkowicz (182, 183) and Wolfe (196), the requirement that military officers participate in political activity and provide in the army a "school for communism" contradicts professional orientations that have emerged most strongly in the technical branches. In other words, where the traditional officer role included all kinds of "character training," such training, whatever its content, is becoming incompatible with this role as a new breed of technologists and administrators are coming to define it.

It is easy to exaggerate the impact of service experience on the social and political attitudes of those who serve. On the one hand, the effectiveness such an indoctrination effort has depends on how men view their military obligation, that is to say, on the way anticipatory socialization affects the nature of their commitment. We have already referred to survey findings, scanty as they may be, that indicate fairly general dissatisfaction with military regulations and no visible increment in patriotism. (See Chapter 3, above, and discussion of officer socialization in Chapter 2.) On the other hand, the criticisms and complaints expressed by soldiers can build up momentum for structural reform. In the United States negative attitudes toward the military among men demobilized at the end of World War II stimulated critical self-examination. The substance of many criticisms was affirmed in the report of a specially appointed board headed by General Doolittle, a war hero, and whose membership included also some former enlisted men (724). That report helped legitimate some reforms. Popular distrust of the military was especially widespread and had a political basis in Germany, where officers of the old army had discredited themselves. The support many of them had lent willingly to Hitler's political ventures—all in the name of military duty—and the way conventional military discipline was alleged to have conditioned soldiers to unquestioning obedience had left a strong residue of public hostility. In the reconstituted Bundeswehr all traces of what the Germans call Kadavergehorsam were to be eradicated at every level, once and for all. As a result the Germans have moved farther than many others in their legislation to guarantee full civil rights for all soldiers, in the code requiring that criminal offenses by soldiers be tried before civil courts, in the appeals system with review by a parliamentary commissioner, in theory, a kind of ombudsman, and in the election of "shop stewards" to ensure comradely relations (349, 706, 719, 721). Yet form and substance do not always coincide.

These and other efforts at reform express the desire to lend substance to a new concept of military service as a special form of service to the community in partial fulfillment of the political responsibility that falls on every citizen, whether "in uniform" or not. This is the explicit principle that the legislation and regulations governing the German army have sought to incorporate. The French officer corps had likewise attempted for some time to restructure itself along new lines. Through its emphasis on what was called "le rôle social de l'officier," the military acknowledged that the concept of a "people's army" would govern both the relations of officers and their troops and those of the officer corps in its entirety to the Republican regime (684). Yet the continuing debate over these matters testifies to the degree to which these reforms have fallen short of the more extravagant expectations its sponsors harbored, partly for lack of support in many military and in some civilian places. The nonlogical elements in the military ethos are not readily amenable to change from outside. Until new traditions more congruent with representative and participatory democracy are established, some vestiges of the old will inevitably persist to plague the reformer.

Problems of civil-military relations also arise in working relationships, all the more as civilians take over a large number of tasks related to military management, including the development of strategy and tactics. This trend seems irreversible. The blending of civilian and military skills at the central staffs where professional officers must deal with the officials of the ministry set up to oversee the armed forces has led to something approaching psychological parity between the two types of administrators—at least in the United States (967). No longer are the inner workings of the military a complete mystery to civilians. In not being subject to rotation as officers are, the latter have in fact an advantage, and some have made a career of some aspect of military management. Although both officers and civilians equally subscribe to civilian control as a principle, they do not necessarily agree on its meaning. As Hammond (933) describes the pattern of operation in the U.S. Army and Navy departments, officers because they tended to consider Congress the appropriate agency for maintaining civil supremacy were prone to resent the direct intervention by civilian administrators into the internal affairs of the services. Some strain in these relationships, regardless of how they were structured, is therefore unavoidable. The resolution of these strains in the two departments occurred in an essentially similar manner despite some differences in the allocation of responsibility as described in organizational charts.

The experience in agencies where civilians and military collaborate is similarly instructive insofar as the division of responsibility does not always reflect the actual inputs by the different groups. Scientists (197 and 1148) who in World War II lent their services to the military Scientific Advisory Board, applying the techniques of operations research to all kinds of problems including the deployment of tactical weapons, gave evidence of an occasional reluctance to use their findings as sufficient ground for changing procedures. This particular problem has been resolved to some extent with operations research now a routine adjunct to all kinds of military planning. Recently the status of reserve officer training in American colleges, where officers had enjoyed long-standing and usually harmonious relations with campus officials (155), has emerged as a prominent civil-military issue whose political dimensions, as those of other issues, tend to contaminate the day-to-day work relations. Some of these things belong essentially to the microsociology of organizations. For example, civilian officials involved in the administration of occupied territories have sometimes found the long term objectives they sought to be neutralized by actions of military commanders formally in charge. The latters' overriding concern with security, for which they alone shouldered responsibility, went together with a disinclination to consider fully some of the unintended effects of their measures (976). More careful documentation is needed of the conditions conducive to effective collaboration at all levels of managerial policy and administration, whether in research, in education and training, or in the government of occupied territories.

Military installations always involve commanders and troops in relations with the host community. Whether they are inside their own country or on foreign soil, the contacts between men in uniform and civilians are a source of potential friction between the two (982, 983, 987, and 988). These matters have attracted considerable attention especially when the number of incidents gives reason for concern, but official investigations are usually directed toward determining the specific causes rather than at sociological generalizations. Barth's study (977) of several American communities located near a military base points to the economic dependence of the former on the latter as a major variable that affects both the number of incidents and the ability of the base commander to cooperate with the local power structure in order to eliminate major sources of difficulty. Some interesting comments on the impact of military occupation are available in the books by Rodnick (985) and Gimbel (981), but neither of them uses civil-military relations as a framework of analysis. In general, reaction within the host society to foreign troops and military bases is only partly determined by the occurrence of incidents, but also reflects attitudes toward political leaders whose domestic and foreign policies support their continued presence. The monograph by the Kyres (984) which deals comprehensively with several American occupations approaches this subject largely in terms of policy objectives and only secondarily in terms of the civil-military relationships involved.

*The Policy Process.* The process by which military policy is formulated has been a central interest of political scientists who are naturally concerned both about the substance of decisions and about the means by which effective civilian control can be maintained. Substantive issues related to strategic decisions are not particularly relevant to military sociology, but insofar as they are relevant properly fall into the sociology of war. Issues related to the subordination of the military to civil authority are, of course, an important aspect of civil-military relations.

A highly professionalized military is often acknowledged to be more willing to confine its activities to technical tasks, military management and to leave political decisions to civilians (see especially Huntington, 657; also 99). Control is then "objective"; it is based on the common acceptance by the military and the civilian leadership of an impersonal legal framework that spells out the division of responsibility. However, definitions of what is policy and, therefore, the responsibility of political leaders, what is strategy and, therefore, the specialized competency of the military are more likely to converge when the requirements of the armed forces are small and their missions clearly specifiable in advance. Where national security begins to hinge upon an adequate scientific and industrial base and on the psychological mobilization of the entire people, the line between policy and strategy becomes blurred. Civilians may still make the final decisions, but this does not preclude deferring to military judgments in decisions affecting the national interest. Whether it does or not depends in part on the range of alternatives with which political leaders are provided. If the number of alternatives is too sharply limited, civilians instead of initiating policy would merely be ratifying a viewpoint that enjoys strong backing from the military. The real issue is the point at which the political leadership enters to balance the military advice because it determines, according to Fox (928), the way civil supremacy is implemented. Imbalances arise even where this principle is sanctioned by tradition to which not only civilians but also military officers profess to adhere. In other words, the faith in military professionalism as the best assurance against their exercise of undue influence is perhaps misplaced. Only comparisons between countries with similar polities but different levels of professionalization and case studies focusing on the behavior of individual officers with different orientations can clarify the issue.

The famous dictum first formulated by Clausewitz that war unless clearly subordinated to policy tends to become absolute to a point where strictly military considerations override all other considerations has been echoed by many other writers since. Strategy is intimately related to policy, and whenever people take seriously the possibility that war will break out, the military component in foreign policy gains in importance and along with it the weight given to the soldier expert in the counsels of government. This opens the door to the "garrison state" (663, 664). Because the demand for their skill is great, military men begin to wield dominant power in civil-military coalitions. They come to exercise a larger number of functions and demands for efficiency will further assure their ascendancy (see 929). In these circumstances professionalization, far from being a restraint, provides the major impetus for expansion of military influence in the policy process.

Civil-military relations in Germany, Italy, and Japan at one point did apparently conform to the garrison state model, but the fit, even in Japan where the development went farthest, was far from perfect during this particular period. The point is that soldiers nearly everywhere have moved into diplomacy (958), especially since demonstrations of military force are one of its indispensable instruments. Also, there has always been some amalgamation between the military establishment and those sectors of industry heavily dependent on military contracts. In the United States one is, of course, forced to acknowledge the possibility that civil-military relations may be moving toward the garrison state, especially in view of the important role the Department of Defense has played in many foreign policy decisions. In the opinion of Mills (946), Cook (603), Swomley (956), and some others, this possibility has already become a fait accompli. Yet such anecdotal evidence as is marshaled by the above, particularly Mills, tends to exaggerate the degree of unity among the various segments out of which the American power elite recruits itself. To be sure, military-industrial interests have at times lobbied successfully for the development of new weapon systems of dubious military value or against the abandonment of those about to become obsolescent (602). Some retired generals have also taken major jobs in industrial corporations. However, such observations by themselves are not an adequate test for the fit of the garrison state model. They do not, moreover, substitute for a systematic analysis of how military policy comes to be formulated.

Case studies covering a variety of specific decision-making episodes in the United States (920, 931, 955, 1279) point to the diverse groups and factional interests involved. Consensus is in no sense automatic but comes only through negotiation and compromise. This is true of civil-military relations in other countries as well (640, 654). Insofar as students of this subject across the world have focused on the unique and particular, as most of these case studies have, their contribution to the kind of theory on which cross-national comparison must ultimately be founded is rather limited. In a critical review of some of these studies, Edinger (925) has proposed a simple two-dimensional paradigm for ordering the many ad hoc observations. Thus, he distinguishes, on the one hand, between the use of formal and informal channels to gain access to the heads of government and, on the other, between direct and indirect approaches to the decision-makers. He then goes on to identify a number of relevant sociological variables but does little to gauge the effect of each on the capacity of the military to determine the outcome.

There is a fair amount of agreement today that the process by which consensus on military policy is reached in the United States is primarily a matter of negotiation among the various agencies in the executive branch (937). The progressive adjustment of the divergent viewpoints held by agencies that must pass on different aspects of policy involves genuine political bargaining in which military leaders participate. They nevertheless define their role as "nonpolitical" as long as they do not associate themselves with a particular party or otherwise take sides in electoral contests. When testifying before Congress, they likewise do so only in their capacity as experts and as representatives of service viewpoints, whether the military policy issue to which they address themselves has become embroiled in partisan politics or not (757). Yet on only rare occasions do the fundamental assumptions on which military policy and budgets are based receive a full review and critical examination from the legislative bodies whose responsibilities in this area are constitutionally mandated. This is true despite the fact that the statutory power Congress has over key appointments and over appropriations places in its hands important means of control. In the past the power of the purse had enabled Congress to hold down the size of the army (938), but its role has greatly declined since World War II and the budgetary review no longer represents a very effective brake on the demands of the armed forces (923, 942, 943, and 952). There are several reasons for this lack of effective Congressional power (937). In the first place, just about every public scrutiny of military policy in Congress has been confined to a single issue—a jurisdictional dispute among the services, the effectiveness of a particular weapon system, some particular instance of alleged bungling by the military, or some military reverse that required explanation. The review of military budget requests tends to be cursory and sporadic with a good deal of the concern directed at setting overall levels of force but with the actual revisions usually confined to fairly narrow limits. In the second place, Congress itself is fragmented; the constituencies represented in it regional. To develop any degree of strategic consensus is difficult. Even a strong legislative leadership must acknowledge the political forces whose backing individual Congressmen seek for reelection. Finally, executive agencies have sources of specialized information that only a few legislators can hope to match.

The likelihood of head-on collisions between representatives of the armed forces and either the executive or legislative branch of civil government is reduced by interservice rivalry. The more intense this rivalry, the more does it divert conflicts that could result in direct civil-military confrontation into competition among the various groups to have their special claims honored, since each service is itself a conglomeration of interests. To marshal support for a service viewpoint or for a specific program, officers are forced to involve themselves in the mesh of civilian administrative and congressional relations. They also erect a political and institutional bulwark to assure themselves of outside support. Observations such as these have led Huntington (699) to reason that the internal pluralism of the military has the same moderating effect as have intersecting interests for society as a whole. The presentation of a unified viewpoint requires prior adjustment and balancing. Hence, service spokesmen must maintain flexibility and become less committed to a preconceived point of view. At the same time their solicitation of outside support strengthens the hands of civilians who in this situation are thrust into the role of arbiters rather than that of opponents. Thus, these multiple conflicts arising from this internal pluralism help in their totality to sustain the supremacy of the civilian executive.

This reassuring conclusion overlooks the fact that the balance of power may still rest with the military in those issues on which politicians disagree, a possibility made all the more likely by the small size of the military policy public. If data from a decade ago can be taken as guide, sustained interest in military affairs and strategic questions is concentrated within a relatively small group—a group that is disproportionately young, male, and well-educated and that also has a slight Democratic bias (917, 921). It is easy to ignore pressure from this rather small and apparently rather liberal public who have no choice politically except that between the major parties, while the officials on whom effective civil supremacy ultimately rests may themselves have assimilated excessive acquiescence to certain military viewpoints. Similar information on public opinion relevant to control of the military is beginning to become available from other countries (e.g. 732).

A pluralistic system of such complexity also has its built-in stabilizers. In their article on the military-industrial complex, Pilisuk and Hayden (947) also take a far less favorable view than Huntington of the countervailing power each group exercises on the others in preventing the dominance of any single interest or viewpoint. The result is a system which in its entirety is highly resistant to change because built into it are certain assumptions concerning the national interest, the inviolability of property rights, and the intrinsic superiority of the American version of constitutional government. However harmonious civil-military relationships may be, they do not necessarily lead to substantive rationality in foreign politics. Hammond (934), too, concludes, but from a set of altogether different observations, that the process by which military budgets are generated and approved within the Department of Defense may kill any tendency toward innovation in policy. Making the budget conform to rational standards is not just a matter of applying substantively informed judgments; it involves above all adherence to proper procedures and making the necessary political accommodations. In addition to this "rationalizing" function of the budgetary process, the steps by which it takes shape must "distribute responsibility" and minimize political risks as well as make the whole process appear "legitimate."

Perhaps totalitarian polities are in a stronger position to exploit the factionalism and career ambitions that exist within the military (723, 755, 880). The proposition is difficult to prove, for even here they wield considerable power as long as there is need for their professional expertise. Thus during the disunity and maneuvering among political leaders that followed the death of Stalin, the support of the military became a major political resource. Yet most of the time they have been relegated to providing expert advice while retaining considerable autonomy in the technical and strategic area. Some believe that their quiet bid for influence made in the name of the military-technological revolution has been made ineffective by the continuing struggle between traditionalists and modernists within the officer corps (182, 183, 196, 768, and 769). The analysis by Kolkowicz (708) of the role of the Soviet army against a background of internal politics is of special interest. In China, by contrast, where the majority of high ranking military came from among the old revolutionaries who also held political office and in that role issued orders that they themselves had to carry out (716), the lines of conflict are only beginning to emerge. Some Sinologists (140, 696, 700, and 701) conclude from information available to them that the cleavages within the military and conflicts between the army and other interest groups there are beginning to conform in some ways to patterns familiar in other countries with a technologically sophisticated military establishment.

*Coercive Intervention.* Any reliance on military force, actual or threatened, to bring about a change of government or to contest the claims of other groups in society constitutes coercive intervention into the political process. There are all kinds of nuances which may range from a mere threat to withhold support from a government about to be formed to a full seizure of power. To create some order within this diversity, we shall distinguish among three types: limited intervention, occult intervention, and military takeover. (See 676 for a somewhat similar typology.)

Sometimes the military may step in without appearing to pursue any political goals of its own but merely in order to cope with extraordinary circumstances such as may have arisen from the overthrow of a dictatorship by popular revolt, as in Santo Domingo following the fall of Trujillo, or when intense factionalism among the parties is accompanied by a breakdown of public order beyond the capacity of civil government to cope, as happened to some extent in the Congo and in Pakistan. The move by the military to fill a temporary political vacuum is usually accompanied by declarations that its rule is merely provisional. The intervention serves a strictly limited purpose with a full restoration of constitutional government at the first sign that conditions have returned to a point where normal political processes can again function. This does not, of course, prevent a military once in power from finding new reasons to justify its continued rule.

In other situations the military no longer acts as an avowedly neutral power. Rather it intervenes for the express purpose of either altering or preventing change in the balance of political forces. Although the officers involved may still lack a program of their own and merely intercede between groups of civilians in a contest for power, they decide either by themselves or in consultation with their civilian allies when and how they should act. The amount of overt force used varies greatly. Thus, the military may do nothing beyond making its obedience conditional, exercising an occult veto over the government whose fall it threatens to cause merely by its withdrawal of support; or, alternately, it can act as a shield for a civilian group without the political base to stay in power. This form of intervention when institutionalized culminates in the kind of gendarmist state found in some countries of Europe and Latin America, but is not confined to those parts of the world. An open takeover is rarely necessary. The behind-the-scenes influence the military enjoys, usually but not invariably by virtue of its alliance with conservative forces, assures that its own interests will be protected.

Both the above differ from a third situation where the military, or some segment of it is clearly the prime mover in a coup d'etat. Officers seize power in order to proclaim their own version of what the nation needs. Military rule becomes institutionalized in a junta: the pretorian regime. The characteristics of this type of civil-military polity have been outlined in Rapoport (504), Huntington (783), and Perlmutter (669). Initially many positions in government are filled by officers, but the new ruling group once established undergoes a process of civilianization. On the one hand, its coercive functions begin to wither away; on the other, the discords of public life start making their entrance into the governing circles. Without a solid base of popular support, the military regime will soon face the danger of being itself displaced by a new coup headed by officers still excluded from the sources of power. In this respect military regimes often encounter the same difficulties in achieving stability as the civilian regimes they displaced; the recent rash of military coups amply demonstrates this tendency.

The prevalence of intervention by the military has sparked a rapidly growing literature on the subject. Much of it is in the form of case studies, descriptive as well as analytic, and confined to a single country or even to a single crisis in civil-military relations. The literature is far too vast to review in any detail, and the reader is advised to turn to any one of the summaries for an introduction to the field. What interests us here are the broader cross-national generalizations about the conditions with which the so-called propensity to intervene is associated and which affect the forms it is likely to take. On the one hand, there are the highly general and formal paradigms about the role of the military in political development; on the other, one finds an increasing number of investigations making full use of quantitative techniques in order to search out and test some propositions about the relationships between military intervention—as measured by the number of military coups within some time period, differences in the persistence of military rule, or the extent of military domination of the government—and a variety of economic and social indicators. In all this the contrast between the new nations and those of the old world seems a natural point of departure and so it has been but mostly implicitly. Only Aron (638), Ronneberger (672), and Janowitz in some introductory passages of his comparative essay (660) make any serious attempt to depict and explain these differences in any systematic fashion. Again, some like Finer (765), draw their illustrations from all parts of the world, but a study by Feit (896) contrasting military rule in Spain and Ghana extends comparative analysis to a former colonial power and a former colony only recently carried past the threshold of nationhood.

On one point the evidence is certainly unambiguous: the propensity for intervention by the military of a country is related to its level of economic and political development. A tabulation of coups during the years 1958 to 1965 by Finer (839) shows their incidence to be highest in the new nations that gained independence since World War II. Many of these had already fallen under military rule, but irrespective of this the lower the per capita wealth and the smaller the percentage of the nation's population living in cities the greater the likelihood of one or more attempts at a coup by the country's military. The pattern of coups in Latin America over a sixty year period (840) is essentially similar. In this region with its long history of continuous military intervention, the larger and poorer the country the greater the instability during these years, as indexed by the number of coups staged, with poverty more important than size. Further evidence of the importance of economic conditions comes from the timing of coups in these countries. They have tended to occur in years of economic deterioration while periods of prosperity have been relatively free of them (858: also 864). The effect of size is ambiguous by comparison. To be sure, the size of a country adds to the difficulties any government, military or civilian, faces in its efforts to create or maintain a viable political order in the face of intractable economic difficulties. Accordingly Wyckoff (881) found continued military rule of one sort or another to be most typical of the small and relatively isolated countries of Latin America where the lower classes were politically least acculturated and, therefore, most inclined to tolerate whatever regime was in power.

The civil government of no nation is entirely immune against coercive intervention by the military. Yet the frequency with which such threats arise and the form they take, varies. This phenomenon, which Finer in his book *The Man on Horseback* (764) calls the propensity to intervene, can be viewed as the joint product of motives and capabilities. Motives are of course situational and capabilities must always be judged relative to those of other groups. Of course, very little hardware capability is required to control a population that is politically quiescent. Very modest defense expenditures suffice to ensure the physical superiority of even a relatively small military force over the unarmed citizenry. In his little, though hardly unbiased, classic on the coup d'etat, Malaparte (854a) showed how easily the vital centers could be seized by a determined body of men. Yet the overemphasis on tactics led him to overlook the political factors. Officers who challenge civil authority expect to be obeyed by soldiers and sustained by public opinion. Both are questionable wherever countervailing political forces exist to balance the physical means of force. Hence, in Finer's book the level of political culture emerges as the main contextual variable that mediates the effect of the other two, but the distribution of skills between the military and civil groups as well as the latter's proximity to the dominant centers of power are equally important (853).

More specifically, in weak and nonconstitutional states where peaceful forms of pressure lie outside the range of practical affairs, the army is more easily induced to pave the way for political change. At the same time extreme fragmentation among the political parties under a parliamentary regime which prevents them from forming an effective governing coalition has also been a motive for intervention as it has been, for example, in Argentina which ranks fairly high on both urbanization and literacy but has been under almost continuous military rule for several decades (737, 765, 814, 841). In a modernizing nation a multiparty system is usually associated with instability, a condition that invites military intervention. As part of his more extensive discussion of political order in changing societies, Huntington (783) shows with statistics that the larger the number of parties contending for power, the more susceptible to a military coup is the government of a country; the proposition has its limits in that a political system without any effective parties represents the extreme of vulnerability. Where the political parties are little more than political cliques, the army becomes one of the few and often the only organization with the capacity for disciplined action on a national scale. Still, as the examples of Indonesia, Ghana, and Algeria demonstrate, the military has displaced the civil government in even some one party states. So far only the regimes under communist domination with their close fusion of army and party have altogether escaped a military coup but not all forms of pressure from their armed forces.

Both the causes and character of military intervention change as a nation approaches "modernity." Some rather elaborate paradigms, far more complex than the mere combination of motives and capabilities implies, have been devised by various authors (643 and 853). However, the patterns themselves are too diverse for more than a crude fit, or the variables which the paradigm incorporates are compounded from too many factors to permit an empirical test.

Putnam's attempt (867) to explain differences among the nations of Latin America, a region with a generally high level of military intervention, is based on a correlational analysis of several indicators of both economic growth and social mobilization over a fifty year period. From the pattern of correlations between each and the dominance of the military, Putnam infers that the direct and short run effect of economic growth is to encourage a military takeover. Yet this direct effect is mitigated over the long run by the evident linkage between economic development and social mobilization, so that we can look forward to a progressive reduction of the coercive role of the military in politics even in this part of the world where intervention has been chronic for over a century. Putnam also notes that the correlation between his indicators of social and economic development, on the one hand, and intervention, on the other, was weaker for the 1960's than for the year 1910. The military in some of these countries apparently had become habituated to a political role and military rule was the institutionalized form of government.

Such indications of the increasing autonomy of the political sphere seem confirmed by tabulations Janowitz (660) made of the political regimes in Asian and African nations excluding those under communism. At least within the range represented by these countries, the level of economic development and the character of the regime in power was a poor predictor of the character of the political regime. The structural conditions in all of them are conducive to takeover attempts, and the frequency with which these have met with success testifies to the impotency of other institutions to resist intervention from politically motivated officers. These same conditions which influence the likelihood that a given country will fall under military rule also determine the dynamics of the civil-military conflicts that lead to a coup d'etat.

Even in the nations with a highly developed political culture, officers have occasionally been moved to revolt against their government. But because of their relative rarity and because of the unique circumstances attending each, these cases have had far more interest for historians than for sociologists intent on studying the general pattern underlying such events. Case studies point to the frequency with which civil-military relations in these countries have approached the boiling point, particularly over issues related to the conduct of military operations in wartime. One thing that keeps them from boiling over is that officers generally accept and have internalized the norm of civil supremacy. Given the availability of political channels, they will as a rule prefer other forms of influence to an open challenge unless the stakes are extremely high and their grievances cumulative. Only when issues of sufficient gravity arise directly involving the national interest will officers ultimately put justice above law and perhaps force the kind of peace settlement that makes the cause for which soldiers have bled "worthwhile" (638).

Yet no matter how great their disaffection, they are still inhibited by the fact that they cannot expect to succeed without political leaders to rally the people and to make their withdrawal of obedience stick. Lacking such leaders within their own ranks limits the goals they can expect to achieve by their forcible intervention. In the two most recent attempts at coups d'etat in fully modernized nations— Germany in 1944 and France in 1961—the military were therefore forced to act under the cover of a simulated internal uprising by others. This "crisis" of public order they then hoped to exploit to gain support from the majority. Important field commanders expected the public to acquiesce once the fall of the government had become a fait accompli (852; see also the case studies of civil-military relations in Germany and France during this period).

Both attempts were failures militarily as well as politically, as in each case the head of the state was able to appeal directly through the media of mass communication to the people and to the troops while officers were divided among themselves over what course to follow. Some agreed with the policy of the government, and many more remained politically uncommitted. Most preferred to play it safe by first awaiting the outcome. Lack of broad popular support made it impossible for such a coup to succeed.

Military coups follow a different logic in states whose unity rests primarily on bureaucratic centralization. In what Handman (845) calls the "bureaucratic culture pattern," found in many parts of the world although some Latin American countries are no doubt the archtypical examples, a large share of the economic and other values are dispensed through the government (791b). Public office and positions of political influence become objects of intense competition, much of which would in other circumstances be directed toward the private sector, while the absence of mass parties makes possession of the means of physical force one of the major resources in political struggle, all the more so since elections, even when they are held, may not be exactly honest. The instability of the political system is dramatized by the succession of coups, very few of which represent any change in the pattern of civil-military relations as they only replace the rule of one group of military officers with that of another. Although the military coup is in this respect the functional equivalent of an electoral system with viable parties, Horowitz (847) who speaks of a "norm of illegitimacy" may be pushing this idea beyond the point of validity, especially since many coups are timed either to forestall an election or to overturn the results of an election just held. At the same time, the political bargaining among officers seeking to form a coalition capable of staging a successful coup does not assure the stability of the new government. The critical swing man whose support makes the difference often gains a major voice and may even emerge as the official leader. This moderates the extremism of the original instigators of the coup, but these divisions within the junta then become the basis for a subsequent coup (858).

In many new nations just past the threshold of independence and still torn by tribal and ethnic divisions which the former colonial presence helped to contain, the problem of creating a viable political order is closely linked with the problem of maintaining civil peace. Nowhere has this been more true than in some parts of Africa. The surveys of armed forces there by Gutteridge (648) and even more so by Lee (499) address themselves to this very problem and some of the case studies in the volume edited by Bienen (830) analyze the role of military intervention in connection with widespread public disorder. As a general rule the armies that function as internal security forces become by this fact alone an important factor in politics even when the struggle is not waged by violent means. By the same token, armies forged in the struggle for colonial liberation, like revolutionary armies everywhere, ordinarily will not relinquish on their own all political influence. Thus, India, unlike Burma, did not move into independence with a highly politicized army and has so far been spared a coup (819). Similarly the civil governments of Tunisia and Morocco where independent status was attained peacefully have not fallen prey to an army claiming sole credit for the victory as happened in neighboring Algeria. In his study *The Military and Society in Latin America,* Johnson (785) even goes so far as to suggest that the relatively orderly and peaceful manner in which Brazil gained its independence may have had something to do with the lower dominance of the military, but in recent years the armed forces there have intervened several times, and the present military regime came to power by a coup that overthrew the duly elected civil government. (See 687.)

Although intervention has been triggered by military defeat, it is the lack of foreign threat that most often characterizes the countries under chronic military rule. The armed forces in these countries continue to symbolize their sovereign status, even when they are far too weak to serve as instruments of diplomacy. This is certainly the case in many of the new African states (493 and 647) and to a lesser extent in Latin America (784). The resources and manpower under military control facilitate intervention, but do not always have this consequence. It is in the great powers that military outlays have been highest, both absolutely and as a proportion of the national product. These mammoth military establishments have been principally geared toward meeting these nations' world-wide commitments and deterring potential attacks. In countries outside the European state system, the level of military effort has as a rule been lower and the borders relatively secure. This leaves the leaders of the armed forces more freedom to satisfy what political ambitions they may harbor and/or to assure themselves of a government that looks with favor on high levels of support, even when this cuts into funds available for other programs. A strong correlation between military intervention and the military's share of the gross national product was observed by Putnam (867) for Latin America, while the correlation with absolute size was in the opposite direction. Such correlations do not always enable one to distinguish between causes and consequences. Yet the typical pattern of expenditures for countries under the most continuous military domination was to invest heavily in infantry armaments with a few tanks and airplanes, rather than to acquire the high cost items that contribute most to improving a country's strategic position (621).

Their mission alone tends to make the ground forces more interventionist; naval forces removed from the population centers and on long tours away from their home base are less likely for that reason to become the prime movers in a takeover. Too much should not be made of this difference, however. It takes only a very small concentration of troops to seize the vital centers, and officers whose proximity to the capital involves them in all types of political intrigues are always a potential threat because the troops they command—be they ground, naval, or air force units—usually have sufficient capability. Sometimes an uprising at the capital is quelled by troops from the hinterland or vice versa, as loyal commanders can appeal to regional or religious loyalties. In this way cleavages within the armed forces, and within the officer corps in particular, limit the prospects of any among them staging a successful coup. When these cleavages run deep and moreover mirror the divisions within civil society, intervention raises the specter of civil war. On the other hand, an impasse caused by extreme fragmentation which renders civil power ineffective provides its own motives for intervention. Divisions within the armed forces will then become an additional cause of instability as, for example, in Argentina (868).

It is increasingly evident that most cases of intervention arise from specifically military imperatives including some idea of the national interest, rather than from a civil-military coalition advancing the interest of some group. Thus, most observers today hold the view that career experiences are a stronger determination of officer political behavior than the social origins of these officers (650, for example). This does not mean, however, that background and other social affiliations have nothing to do with the persistent tendency of Latin American armies, for example, to intervene against liberation movements (662). In the first place, an officer corps recruited from a narrow segment of the population is more likely to become encapsulated in its own traditions and, therefore, less responsive to new political currents. Second, a large influx of lower middle class elements, former students, and ex-activists harboring unorthodox and sometimes even revolutionary political ideas may provide new motives for intervention. This will also affect the political coloration of any coup (784). In the third place, whatever the effects of changes in the pattern of recruitment, they are sometimes reinforced by other factors which introduce a spurious element into any relationship between the social origin and background of an officer and his political behavior. According to Lieuwen (798) the lower the rank of the officers who were the prime movers behind several of the coups in Latin American countries, the greater the likelihood that their program encompassed radical reforms, whereas intervention by officers of higher rank, often from an upper class background, tended to have a politically more conservative character. Nevertheless, the apparent radicalism of the former in comparison with the latter is not necessarily a function of differences in social background. It may, on the one hand, grow out of the poor career prospects these officers face and, on the other, reflect the generational consciousness of the younger officer cohort, a consciousness far more important than either the class background or achieved status of the officers involved.

The generational factor is of special significance in the new nations where passage from colonial status to full independence has been abrupt. Thus, nearly all the leading participants in Nasser's coup against Farouk had been members of the same class in the Egyptian military academy. The principles they sought to implement date back from that period (885, 910). East Africa, which did not enjoy the same degree of autonomy as Egypt, had by virtue of its status as a protectorate achieved independence without an indigenous officer cadre of its own, and an uprising against the civil government took the form of a mutiny headed by enlisted men. It was aimed primarily at raising levels of pay with the demand for the Africanization of the officer corps the only genuinely political issue (854b). More generally the large number of vacancies in the new army facilitate rapid advancement. Young officers attain high rank at an early age but, if this blocks opportunities for the next cohort, the new frustrations may ultimately become linked to a new ideology.

Foreign influences also play an important role. For one thing the cadres trained in the colonial forces assimilate at least some of the traditions that characterize the military of the dominant power. Still, the relative importance of the different elements in this tradition are usually reworked as they interact with others indigenous to the country. Hence, the specific effects of the colonial heritage are sometimes subtle as indicated, for example, by the different course of events in India and Pakistan, both of whose officers were schooled in the British tradition (819). In India the nationalists in the forefront of the struggle for liberation insisted on a dominant role for parliament. They ousted the officers who had fought England's wars but did not replace them with any of the Indian Nationalist Army heroes and thereby helped keep the army nonpolitical. In these circumstances the quest of officers to improve their status was redirected into the marriage market. By contrast, the main residue of British tradition in Pakistan was associated not so much with parliament as with elements of the viceroy tradition. Hence, when politics failed, it became natural for the military to ensure continuity by establishing itself as the "caretaker government." Comparisons between neighboring or otherwise similar countries along such lines, like Ghana and neighboring Nigeria, both of them former British colonies (79, 642, and 837), can be highly instructive.

Contact with foreign powers has above all stirred the passion of the military to modernize their country. Insofar as the professional military self-image is everywhere permeated by notions of discipline and efficiency, though not to the exclusion of other notions, their idea of progress has usually been far more closely tied to technological advancement than to the rule of law and parliamentary forms of government. The orientations of the military also contrast sharply in this respect with those of the economic elites in their country. The presence of the colonial power had left the latter little scope for independent entrepreneurial activities. They led a parasitic existence and tended to be exploitive and mercantile in their orientations.

These contrasts are a major theme in a number of essays on the role of the military in the political development of new nations, particularly in those by Shils (674), Janowitz (660), Hopkins (650), and Pye (622), but so far only Hong (697) for Korea has documented the orientations of the military by reference to a civilian comparison group in the same country. (See also 688 on Burma.)

The nationalism of officers can itself be traced in part to foreign influences. Being the major recipients of aid from abroad, including schooling in foreign military academies, gives many officers a unique vantage point from which to observe the failings of their own countries as measured by international standards. In Latin America, an area especially open to neocolonial penetration of all sorts, military assistance seems not only to have strengthened the hands of officers intent on establishing military domination (881) but also, as the findings from a study of one coup show (874), those with the more extensive foreign experience and the closest contacts abroad were the ones most likely to be involved. It does not follow, of course, that the technically most accomplished men in the country are invariably found in the officer ranks, nor that they have the capability to mobilize their people for the tasks of development. In the long run success depends on harnessing the energies of groups at the grass roots level. Military regimes may perpetuate themselves in power where unfavorable conditions make the coup d'etat the primary mechanism of political change. The case for the military as the agent uniquely suited to play a major part in the modernization process remains to be proven (189). If the basic problems remain unsolved, uprisings from below are likely to result, even though so far this has not happened except, perhaps, in China where the special circumstances of the Japanese occupation was a significant factor.

### NOTE

1. See, for example, G. Mosca, *The Ruling Class*. New York: McGraw-Hill, 1939, pp. 53-56.

# Chapter 6:

# WAR AND WARFARE

In his study of war which in its comprehensiveness borders on the encyclopedic, Wright (1049) distinguishes among its four manifestations: the military, the psychological, the legal, and the sociological. Military activities are essential. There can be no war unless violence is actively used or at least seriously threatened by an open display of military force. On occasion the course of history has been greatly affected by the outcome of battles and campaigns. The rise in tension and hostility is another direct manifestation of war, one that occurs on the psychological level. Still, fighting and aggression are "complex cultural responses due not to any direct dictates of impulse, but to collective forms of sentiment and value" (1024). Fighting, private and angry, is usually regarded as a breach of the law and the mores, whereas the hostilities aroused in organized fighting are distinctly group related. Hence, war also creates an abnormal juridical situation. No state of war exists unless the break in peaceful relations is reciprocally recognized with or without a formal declaration of war. Finally, viewed sociologically, war represents a generic form of intergroup conflict characterized by organized violence between two or more juridical equals who accord one another belligerent status.

The phenomenon of war occurs in many variations. Most of the time we tend to think of war only in relation to the nation-state and as an instrument of diplomacy. Primitive war does not have this character. The sportive element prevails in many manhunting expeditions in a search for trophies and glory. War also serves as a juridical mechanism for the adjustment of differences between culturally similar groups. In both cases the violence is likely to be subject to strict rules. Institutionalized warfare in primitive society is a subject studied primarily by anthropologists (996, 1013, and 1042, but also 1007). Although hard and fast divisions have no validity here, the sociological study of war is more directly concerned with the role of organized violence at higher levels of political organization.

Here, too, one encounters little appearance of uniformity, so that one cannot get along without some minimal distinctions. External wars are between two or more politically independent and sovereign nations; civil wars between social groups within a sovereign state. Yet the sovereignty of the two parties often establishes itself only in the course of the war. Some wars have been the impetus for ethnically homogeneous groups to consolidate into the rudimentary nation-state; others for the extension of boundaries through the conquest of peoples among whom state formation had not yet taken place. There are also wars of national liberation which involve a group that looks upon itself as a separate nation but is politically subservient to another. These struggles become regular wars when the former subject group attains some legitimacy in the eyes of the other. This asymmetry is also important in wars of consolidation or colonial conquest.

*Consequences and Functions.* Data on battles, campaigns, and wars and on the losses of life and wealth attributable to fighting can be used to estimate the impact of war in different periods (see, for example, 1049, 1076, 1084, and 1212). From an index based on the number of wars in each century between the 12th and the 20th, with each war weighted by its duration, the size of the participating armies, the number of casualties, the number of belligerents, and the proportion of combatants among the population, Sorokin (1084) infers a generally rising trend in the magnitude of war activity with significant breaks in the 17th century, a period of intense warfare, and in the 19th century, an era of comparative peace. The index points to a long-term increase in the level of violence among the nations within the European state system.

War is a cyclical phenomenon. Periods of active hostilities alternate with periods of peace. According to Wright (1049), Chapter 11 of whose book contains an excellent compendium of most pre-World War II studies, the wars of the modern period have been characterized by an increase in the size of the participating armies, a decrease in the average duration of wars but with more continuous and intense fighting in the period between the declaration of war and the formal cessation of hostilities together with a tendency for the war to spread over a larger area and to embroil more countries. The net effect of these trends was an increase in the human and economic costs of war in both absolute and relative terms.

Advancing technology is the factor most directly responsible for this tendency of wars to become more destructive and disruptive (1143; see also 1149a, 1153). The immense improvement in weapons has led to an increase in battle casualties, but the size of the participating armies and of the states at war has tended to increase even more. Until the present century, moreover, epidemics were a far more important cause of mortality, even among troops, than death in battle. Better medical facilities have contained the spread of disease as well as the ratio of deaths to wounded in action. Yet these risks are hardly distributed evenly. Some elite units suffer the heaviest casualties (473, 1040, 1147), but overall the burdens are greatest for persons of lower socioeconomic status who have fewer resources and are in a worse position to obtain a favored assignment where risks are at a minimum. The advent of airpower and advances in ballistics have made the eugenic implications of differential war fatalities less germane than ever. Civilians far from the zone of combat now come within the potential range of enemy fire. As a result Germany and England in World War II suffered civilian casualties at more than a hundred times the rate in World War I (1143). An all-out nuclear exchange raises the prospect of mutual annihilation, but quite apart from this possibility, the cost of waging even a "conventional" war has become astronomical, so that a nation courts bankruptcy if it becomes embroiled in a major conflict. It is impossible not to pay special tribute to the tome of J. Block (1149a) for the arguments with which he supports his contention that major wars have become impossible and for the way in which it anticipates present arguments based on the capability of mutual annihilation.

All this is true but to a degree irrelevant. The actual losses in a war do not depend solely on the technological capability of the means of destruction insofar as they can cause death. They depend equally on what a nation is willing to endure, on the loss of life it is prepared to suffer, and on the proportion of wealth it is ready to invest in the military effort (1049; also 1292 and 1299). The level of technology may determine the nature of the battlefield but not, therefore, the character of the war. The latter is a matter of social definition. Modern wars have not as a rule been wars of extinction, and the belligerents have almost always imposed some restraint on the level of violence. Hence, the losses and destructiveness incurred on the battlefield are the joint effect of technological factors and of the strategic and social considerations that impose limits (1194). Sometimes the more deadly weapons may cause a nation to surrender at the first threat; they may similarly expedite a settlement before serious loss has been suffered. The present deterrent strategy is based on precisely such an assumption about the potency of the carefully graduated and decisive use of force (1278, 1293, and 1298, for example).

Too exclusive a focus on the battlefield has led the polemologist Bouthoul (999, 1001) to mistake an unavoidable cost of war for its essential function. Because every war involves some killing of men, wars in general are mechanisms for demographic relaxation, a process which, according to him, is activated by population pressure. This view not only finds little acceptance among sociologists but has been severely criticized (e.g., 1008 and 1273) for not taking adequate account of the facts and evidence. The first criticism is that the rhythm of population is hardly geared to subsistence. The optimum population a territory can support is contingent on technology and, therefore, highly variable. Whatever overpopulation there may be relative to resources will no doubt be aggravated by their diversion during war from productive activities and by armies supporting themselves "off the country" and by pillaging. Famine, epidemics, and other "positive checks" far more often follow than precede the outbreak of war. Thus, more people fell victim to the Spanish influenza in the wake of World War I than had been struck down by machine gun fire. These, too, can of course be considered among the losses of war, but if this is so the killing of men in combat would seem a most ineffective way of relieving population pressure, especially if it left unimpaired the potential for demographic recovery. Shećerov's theory of war (1082), statistically worked out more carefully and applied only to violence in the modern world, raises somewhat similar difficulties.

The social functions of war are rooted not so much in nature as in the nature of group life. In most general terms wars occur when functional relationships extend beyond the realm of common attitudes and understandings. Armed conflict everywhere acts as a mechanism of societal selection (1041). The conquests or accommodations that follow wars cause new relationships to be established and so result in higher forms of political organization. Thus, the enlargement of the area in which peace prevails must be judged as another of the cumulative consequences of war (1027). But armed conflict remains one of the major means for settling disputes between politically sovereign societies even after the emergence of the modern nation-state (1005, 1055). This may be, as Steinmetz (1040) and others have argued, because peoples and governments accept the outcome of a war, at least temporarily; they recognize that war, more than any other form of conflict, measures the collective strength and determination of a group to survive and to impose its will on others. The demographic effects of most wars are quite small when compared with their social and political consequences. War expresses not the Malthusean struggle for existence; it rather grows out of what Sumner has called the competition for life between groups at odds over the differences between them.

Not only the external relations, but the groups and societies at war are themselves transformed by the struggle. Some heightening of in-group solidarity is at least a short-run consequence of every war because hostile and potentially divisive sentiments focus on the external enemy. Partisan interests of every sort are subordinated to the higher cause—be it religious, national, or ideological—for which the war is fought. Public opinion, normally apprehensive about war and reluctant to support a foreign policy that seems to bring a violent collision closer (921, 926, 1137, 1142, and 1310), almost invariably rallies to support the war once it has been declared (1095, 1096, 1099, 1119, 1121). When the security of the nation is clearly at stake, people become more ready to bear the difficulties and deprivations associated with war (1122, 1127, and 1136), especially since leaders can always point to the enemy as their ultimate source. Insofar as the outbreak of war is associated with elite instability, it appears that some statesmen may deliberately have pursued foreign policy objectives, even at a high risk of war, as a means of stilling domestic discontent. The external danger becomes a club with which to browbeat critics, and this helps to deflect attention from intractable domestic problems. The opposition is silenced because it, too, is forced to recognize that the nation must stand united for the foreign policy crisis to be weathered and war to be waged effectively. When political conflicts are shelved for the duration, there is strong pressure to form a coalition government or, at least, to conduct the war under the mantle of bipartisanship.

It is nevertheless a fair assumption that popular support is always fraught with some ambivalence. On the one hand, the common threat is an impetus toward mutual aid and spontaneous cooperation; on the other hand, too prolonged a threat causes the balance gradually to tilt the other way. The more directly and visibly a population is touched by enemy action, the greater the tendency to turn latent in-group hostilities into active animosity against the enemy. Accordingly, wars in defense of the homeland usually call forth extraordinary collective energies even among groups not known for their martial dispositions. The marked increase in hatred of the enemy and the short run gains in morale which were the immediate consequences of bombings in World War II on the centers of population in Britain, Germany, and Japan (1201, 1202) bear out this point. Populations everywhere exhibited a remarkable capacity to adapt emotionally to the continuous threat of air raids (1236) as well as to improvise in order to limit its damage (1235), but only as long as the conflict had a meaningful purpose and they retained their faith in collective survival. Cleavages do not disappear; they are merely buried, and once damage to a community passes the point at which resources from the undamaged sector can compensate, personal and interpersonal aggravations begin to accumulate. Dissension over who has responsibility for any defeat, over the general conduct of war, and over perceived inequalities of sacrifice in particular express war weariness. Issues like these arise from the war itself and can be highly disruptive. In a rigidly stratified society, these cleavages tend to form along a vertical axis, and it is more than likely, as both Simmel (1038) and Coser (1006) suggest, that sharp class divisions favor a reliance on despotic forms of control as a means to prop sagging morale in wartime, while this is by no means a necessary consequence in more equalitarian societies.

From his examination of the role warfare has played in primitive society, Fried (607) concludes that armed conflict itself is not a sufficient cause for the emergence of rank differences where none had existed but that it operates to institutionalize whatever rankings are already recognized. This long term consequence probably results from the rise in the military participation ratio (482) and should perhaps be considered an effect of the military system and of the number of men under arms rather than of war itself. Znaniecki (1272) hypothesized on the basis of observations during World Wars I and II that war caused a shift in the lines of stratification away from status and more toward functional lines. Modern war increases social participation (1179) and therefore promotes some leveling. This is due also to a greater willingness to accept government controls in many areas, to the suppression of obvious profiteering, and to the general discouragement of conspicuous consumption in wartime (1247). Yet the war economy also enables some groups to improve their position relative to that of other groups, largely by population shifts into industries and localities of labor scarcity. Only the stringency of regulations and the general reduction in the level of consumption prevent these changes from becoming immediately apparent. On this point Speier (1261) has summarized the evidence from World War I and Sorokin (1260) gives a preliminary picture of what could have been expected as a result of World War II, but the whole matter has not had much attention from sociologists since.

War has serious unsettling effects on all aspects of institutional life (1046). In part these are due to the dislocation of large numbers of people from their locality and from their normal occupations. (See in particular the studies of the Carnegie Commission on the social and economic consequences of World War I, as listed in 34, for which there is no World War II equivalent.) Such movements have many consequences. People separated from their social group become emancipated and freed from any informal sanctions against the violation of mores. While the status of middle-class women improved noticeably in two world wars (1249), family life was disrupted and children grew up under abnormal circumstances. Not only does this cause emotional strain, but it also impedes the transmission of traditional values, so that many indicators of social disorganization show a marked rise during war. Yet the postwar "climate" is not simply a function of the magnitude of the catastrophe as Sorokin (1258) contends. It is equally a function of institutional change. New agencies are created during war in order to cope with new circumstances, while many existing institutions are forced to adapt by finding new functions. Temporary measures to meet the exigencies of war have a way of becoming permanent. For one thing, the involvement of minority groups in the mainstream of society results in gains that are unlikely to be relinquished without a struggle once the emergency has passed (1224); for another, new institutional relationships of an improvised character between government and education or government and science and new services of all sorts set precedents that may become binding for the postwar society.

It is often difficult to demonstrate that any of the long term social changes are directly attributable to the impact of war. Many involve complex causal processes for which the war acts only as a catalyst. Werner (1270) has raised this whole issue in the most general terms and not only with regard to technological progress as does

Kaempffert (1237, 1238). Unfortunately we lack community studies for the World War II period that are comparable in richness of data with those which the Lynds conducted in "Middletown" before and during the depression.[1] The social history of a war boom community by Havighurst (1228) deals with a less than typical situation. Many other studies of wartime changes are confined to some particular institutional sector or concerned with some particular social indicator like crime and therefore, except for the fact that they occur during war, do not bear directly on the sociology of war. Following World War II, interest shifted clearly in other directions.

*The Causes of War.* Whatever contributes to the breakdown of peaceful relations among groups or nations is a cause of war. However, the usefulness of any inventory of such causes is limited if it fails to differentiate between fundamental predisposing conditions and immediate inciting conditions which merely precipitate the eruption of conflicts already endemic. We shall in discussing the causes of war confine ourselves to the general factors and not to the chain of events that contribute to the probability of an outbreak of violence.

Time trends in the incidence and magnitude of war reveal clusters and peaks and periods of relative peace. The element of periodicity in these alternations has attracted the attention of some analysts (1049, 1070, 1071, 1076, 1077, and 1084). Their tabulations of wars with each war weighted by its magnitude point to the existence of both long term cycles and of smaller oscillations within these cycles. The picture that emerges depends to some degree on the length of the intervals compared and whether they span a full century or just a few years. Tabulations by Denton and Phillips (1071) of the amount of war activity in each five-year interval between 1820 and 1949 lend some support to the folk concept of an upswing in the level of violence about once every generation, but tabulations of these same data using intervals of twenty and more years also point to larger cycles with crests after sixty or after eighty to 120 years respectively and with each upswing followed by a sharp decline. The rapid succession within twenty-five years of two highly destructive wars obviously accounts for the peak near the end of the period spanned by these observations. Bouthoul (999) whose views we have already criticized attributes this to the rapid demographic recovery by nearly all the participants of World War I.

Its superficial plausibility notwithstanding, evidence in support of the demographic explanation is shaky insofar as the coincidence between the deadliest wars and periods of rapid population growth is far from complete (1049, 1060, 1267). To be sure, a large population is a potential resource in waging war, while heavy war losses are not only a setback, but also a reminder of how destructive war can be. Still, a country like France did not become more peaceful between 1850 and 1940, when it lost population but remained a major power; nor has Japan's extremely high density, unabated since World War II, prevented it from pursuing a nonaggressive foreign policy since. One finding from a statistical study on the amount of foreign conflict experienced by different countries between 1955 and 1960 should not therefore occasion any surprise: those with the highest population density and those low in urbanization had on the average less foreign conflict (1059). Yet people forced to migrate for various reasons have sometimes served as a pretext and sometimes as the advance guard for invasions of their weaker neighbors.

Recent increases in war damage—battle deaths and property destruction—are largely due to technological advances and two major world wars. Although the violence of war has by these measures increased significantly, the frequency with which wars broke out during this period has not (1079). These two aspects—losses and "quarrels"—are often difficult to separate; a large number of dyadic conflicts can become linked together in a single general war. In his social and cultural dynamics, Sorokin (1084) combines the two measures and then accounts for peaks of violence in the interstate system by reference to culture change; that is to say, he sees them as evidence of the disruption of social relationships caused by transitions from the ideational to the sensate and from the sensate to the ideational phase of culture. Conflicts over values when transferred to the interstate system manifest themselves in bloody wars, as evidenced by the predominantly religious wars of the 17th century during which external violence reached its crest. Similarly the rising curve of war in the 20th century is believed by him to express the accentuation of conflicts over values with those of ideational type once again in the ascendancy and contesting the dominance of values expressing the sensate phase of culture.

The general implication of Sorokin's formulation is more significant than the specific content he gives it. If internal stress of any kind is the main cause of war, then external and internal disturbances

like revolutions should cluster together. The evidence on this point is
rather ambiguous. Even his own data force Sorokin to conclude that
the two curves measuring the magnitude of each had only a mild
tendency to coincide and over long periods of time to fluctuate
"fairly independently" (see also 1076). More recent research still
leaves this question unresolved. According to Denton and Phillips
(1071), the magnitudes of external and civil violence within each
twenty year period during the 19th and 20th centuries were
distinctly correlated. Civil wars became more important during the
20th century when they tended to occur either just before or just
after the larger international conflicts (1070). In cross national
comparisons based on factor analysis of post-World War II data
(1066 and 1080), the factor of foreign conflict was found to separate
itself rather clearly from that of domestic violence, some modest
association between the two notwithstanding.

It is still possible, nevertheless, that the two forms of intergroup
violence, foreign and domestic, stem from the same malintegration of
the social system as long as one assumes, as Sorokin does, that they
are alternative responses that act in a "compensatory fashion."
Accordingly the various mechanisms available for coping with stress
must be credited with having at least a mediating influence. They
determine whether the stress generated by social change is channeled
into external aggression or whether it manifests itself in any one of
several forms of deviance. Industrialization and urbanization, two
major indicators of change, are therefore important not only because
of their unsettling effects which contribute to discontent and
conflict, but also because these structural changes affect the societal
responses to these problems.

Two studies by Haas (1058, 1059) were explicitly designed to
examine the nature of the relationship between internal stress
indicators like unemployment and the prevalence of several forms of
deviance like alcoholism with the international behavior of the
country's government. Some associations do turn up in these studies,
but they are too weak and irregular to yield anything even
approaching a convincing explanation of how what Haas calls the
"societal prerequisites" of war translate themselves into reliance on
military activity as the primary tool of statecraft, even though some
of his findings are clearly consistent with the historical evidence; for
example, the more frequent involvement of the great and wealthy
powers in war, particularly during the period of their expansion
(1049). Industrialization and urbanization which normally cause

some forms of deviance to rise have also coincided with heavy military expenditures (1058), a fact that may also help to account for why the rich countries with the largest gross national product in the world today continue to experience more foreign conflict than the majority of developing nations.

Industrial pursuits may be incompatible with continuous fighting, but contrary to Spencer (507) states do not necessarily become more "peaceful" as industry develops. Certainly the formation of the modern nation-state facilitated the resolution of religious conflict short of war; dynastic rivalries are no longer germane. But, as Raymond Aron (1051) convincingly demonstrates, industrial society developed its own set of symbols to sanction the economic colonial wars which had their peak before World War I (see also 1110). Concern over the protection of vital national interests has not disappeared despite the economic infeasibility of large-scale war and the limited prospects of any long term gains. Meanwhile new ideologies have arisen which call forth allegiances that cut to some extent across national boundaries. Disputes over the relative merit of particular social and political arrangements precipitate war between as well as within nations. Naville (1186) reviews the various "social arguments" to be considered in determining the character of any particular war.

The nature of the society and the content of the supporting symbols are largely ignored in the attempt by Richardson (1079; see also 1078) to derive the probability of war from such measurable characteristics of the interstate system as the number of member states and the number of other countries that bound the territory of each. Richardson focuses on ecological variables. For example, the likelihood of a country's becoming involved in disputes that escalate into war is a function of the number of states with which it shares boundaries. These boundaries are also a rough measure of the area over which a state's interests extend. This, rather than their size or wealth, may again help to account for the propensity of the larger and wealthier nations for war.

Along with this interest in Richardson's approach to war goes the application of systems theory to international relations. This has become increasingly fashionable, as collections such as the one recently edited by Gray (1285) show. Galtung's structural theory of aggression (1056) with its high degree of formalization and explicit use of sociological constructs fits in with the trend to account for the foreign policy and military behavior of states by reference to their position in the interstate system except that, contrary to Richardson, rank disequilibrium rather than common boundaries is used as the primary variable. Rank disequilibrium is a measure of the different positions a country occupies on several dimensions of status. The interstate system is stratified, and a nation whose military capability is far greater than the prestige of its voice in international deliberations or a nation preeminent in science but without the commensurate economic base is apt to behave "aggressively," using as a reference point the criterion it enjoys in parity with other "high status" nations for the parity it seeks on all criteria. Such disequilibrium would also be a potential source of cross pressure in response to which a country might associate itself with "haves" on some issues and with the "have-nots" on some others. Galtung acknowledges that shifting alliances of this sort can be a moderating influence; they also prepare a nation to play a role as mediator. But he believes that the low degree of integration of the interstate system prevents these cross pressures from working this way, thus placing the disequilibriated nation under considerable pressure to rise. Aggression can become a viable response in the absence of effective sanctions against violence when mobility toward a consistent "top dog" configuration is blocked because previously unappropriated resources are scarce.

The freedom of action a nation has to improve its position in the international arena is always limited by the counterforce with which it must reckon. In the absence of superordinate legal and political institutions, nations enter into formal alliances to protect their interests. The implication of Horvath and Foster's study of alliance formation (1289) is that the power of the alliance measured by the number of members rather than by the individual strength of each determines the rate at which nations will join. Membership in an alliance imposes restraints and obligations on the actions of all partners. These would have been much weaker or not existed at all without the formal commitment. As Singer and Small (1083) have shown, alliances do influence the behavior of the signatories. Being linked to another nation in a formal defense pact increases the likelihood that the first will come to the aid of its partner when he is attacked, and knowledge on the part of potential aggressors that such aid deprives him of the superiority necessary for success often has a deterrent effect. Alliance systems function in this regard as balancing mechanisms with major realignments signifying that the balance has broken down. Denton and Phillips (1071) found a distinct tendency for peaks of war activity to coincide with breakups of major alliance systems.

The loss of interaction opportunities as a result of alliance commitments is also significant for the capacity of the international system to absorb conflict without rupture. It is the consequences of this aspect of the different alliance configurations for the onset of war which Singer and Small (1083) set out to test in their longitudinal study. They start from the assumption that "every dyadic relationship [between states] will be a mixture of the cooperative and the conflictual, with political, economic, ideological, and other issues all producing different interest configurations for each possible pair of nations. The net effect . . . is such a welter of cross-cutting ties and such a shifting of friendships and hostilities [on each issue] that no single set of interests can create a self-aggravating and self-reinforcing division or cleavage among the nations" (p. 249). Extreme loss of interaction opportunities occurs when alliances "aggregate" to produce instead a few large coalitions. Consequently the greater the number of alliance commitments and the closer the entire configuration approaches bipolarity, the more war will the system experience. Unfortunately their confirmation of these two propositions, involving conditions whose moderating effect on domestic conflict is almost axiomatic for sociologists (1006, 1056), is less than conclusive because of inadequacies in the measures used (1088).

The theorem concerning the intrinsic instability of the bipolar world has received some elaboration by Haas (1072) and some cogent criticisms from Waltz (1086). The latter points out that the balance that results from the bipolarity of blocs differs fundamentally from the present nuclear stalemate where two, and only two, powers have been clearly preponderant. The first type of bipolarity, he admits, results in a highly fragile balance because it grants any partner of the bloc the power to commit others who have little control over his actions. But in the second type where the intense competition between the superpowers extends over a wide area, the balance cannot be changed by realignment. Each crisis evokes a response, and the determination of each to resist reduces the chance for easy gain at small risks. As a result the foreign policy of the two powers is increasingly dominated by the international system instead of domestic events. However, the restraints this competition imposes on them do not have equal force for many small nations unlikely to become the targets of massive nuclear retaliation but nevertheless eager to turn to their own advantage the great power rivalry (1003a, 1035, and 1298). The gap in the formal and actual status of nations who lack the power to influence world events has been a factor in the recent tightening of internation relationships (1302b), but whatever balance now exists would clearly be upset by the emergence of a third superpower. These considerations also suggest that conflict models based on decision theory may be far more applicable to the present system than the balance of power theories derived from observations of an international system long past.

Another change in the international system of the postwar world whose effect is also amenable to analysis in terms of decision theory is the increased reliance on formal institutional means to settle international conflicts of every sort. The total number of conflicts involving at least the threat of force have not diminished significantly, as Holsti's study (1313) of all such incidents during the inter- and postwar periods—1919 to 1939 and 1945 to 1963—shows. His tabulations also show that some organized violence was used in a clear majority of the conflicts in both periods. Yet formal settlement procedures were far more successful a means of settling disputes during the latter period; the proportion that did not involve the imposition of terms by military conquest, forced submission, and so forth was far larger. To be sure, different procedures met with different degrees of success, but the relatively greater effectiveness of the postwar settlement attempts cannot be explained in this simple a fashion. The international machinery gained results largely by applying pressure that helped freeze the conflict until it could be compromised or the parties would tacitly accept the existing status quo. In fact noninstitutionalized ad hoc measures were among those most frequently used and resulted in settlements about as often as formal juridical and other institutionalized procedures.

International integration is further aided by various transnational bonds. Tensions arising from the intense competition between the superpowers cause the number of such contacts, formal and informal, to fall off but not apparently to a point where they cease to have any effect. By using the escalation of the arms race as a measure of tension and the rate at which international nongovernmental organizations were formed as an indicator of the operation of an "integrative" system, Smoker (1133) attempts to show that these and other agencies caused some slowdown in the arms race. No such institutions had significantly reduced the strain in two prior arms races. There was no visible effect from various transnational bonds on the arms build-up that led up to World War I; in the second they were not strong enough to withstand its disruptive effects.

*The Conduct of War.* Only recently has the interest of sociologists in the causes and consequences of war been matched by an interest in its actual conduct. Bernard's suggestion (993) that a general sociology of conflict be based on the game theory approach to strategic decision-making has had only limited resonance among sociologists, partly because the logical models that differentiate between a strategy of conflict versus one of bargaining (1029) or between a situation of conditional and unconditional viability (997) are too formal and abstract to be of much help in the analysis of reality. Yet the approach taken in particular by Schelling (1035) to the dynamics of conflict, including war, as a mixture of opposing and cooperative moves has helped bring some rapprochement between those primarily interested in formal models and those concerned with the day to day issues of strategy. The interactions between opponents, the considerations on which their choice of strategy and tactics depend, certainly fall within the scope of sociological interest as, for example, those that deal with trust and suspicion (see 1030, 1236).

There is a basic fallacy in viewing war merely as a sign of disturbance and not as the outcome of a decision process which may itself be highly rational. If a political elite or some other group decides to use organized force in ways that transgress the rules normally binding on interstate behavior, it usually acts out of the conviction that goals whose attainment has been blocked can no longer be postponed and more is to be gained than lost by using force. Abel (1090) more than anyone else has stressed the rational character of the deliberations that preceded the outbreak of twenty-five major wars including World War I. Taken up to five years before the start of hostilities, these decisions were in no case, Abel concludes, "precipitated by emotional tensions, sentimentality, crowd behavior, or other irrational motivations" (p. 855).

How useful is this rational-irrational distinction? One can, of course, reasonably assume that a country would be deterred from deliberately starting a war under two conditions: when it own capabilities are inadequate so that instead of attaining any of its goals it would face defeat; or when the image of what the war of the future will bring emphasizes unacceptable losses so that there will be no victors in any meaningful sense. In his *Voices Prophesying War,*

*1763-1984,* Clarke (1101) has given us a vivid account of how the horrors of war have come to overshadow all else in the popular imagination. Concern over its own security can still impel the elite of a country into actions that, though they arouse little enthusiasm, may nevertheless appear necessary in the circumstances and then elicit reactions that escalate and over the long run escape its control.

The progressive competitive increase in armaments between two states or two coalitions of states can serve to illustrate what is likely to happen when there is no understanding about what the proper balance between their respective powers should be. An arms race results only from the sequence of choices by the two antagonists, both of whom are seeking security or power and not from any one decision by either of them. The security of each and, hence, its decision to increase or decrease its preparations for war in peacetime, though partly dependent on the measures it has already taken, is in large measure a reaction to the preparations of the other. Obviously a nation may "overreact" or, alternatively, remain unperturbed by what the other does. How strongly it will react depends according to Richardson (1126) on its general attitude of friendliness or hostility toward the other nation and on a "reaction coefficient" which is a measure of its touchiness. Only prohibitive costs and the inability of either party to gain a decisive advantage ultimately call a halt to these reciprocal increases.

Competition between nations tends to intensify when only a few weapon systems are equally available to all and when any nation that wants to can challenge the existing balance. However, if long-range and relatively invulnerable weapons with the capacity to destroy a country's cities and industries are in the possession of two superpowers, as they are today, little is to be gained by further competitive increases. The "balance" can only be upset by a new weapon system that would provide one side with a nearly foolproof defense and with the unacceptable capability to destroy the other without suffering damage itself. The arms race would receive another spurt with the danger of surprise attack added to the rising costs (1114), creating a situation both parties presumably would be eager to avert but which their reluctance to make any concessions may nevertheless bring about. According to one study (1291) the optimum chance for successful arms control talks, as judged by proposals put forward by the two superpowers incorporating some concessions, seems to come at a point of near parity with the initiating party subject to only mild insecurity, assuming of course that pressure from war related industries with a stake in high armament do not interfere (1053).

An arms race that produces successive shifts in the distribution of power also increases the probability that one or the other of the antagonists may precipitate a conflict to protect a temporary advantage which it sees about to disappear. The bloc character of the arms competition is also a factor insofar as a bipolar situation in which all countries have allied themselves into opposing blocs makes it impossible for anyone to compensate his relative loss of power by diplomatic realignment or to bolster his security by entering into a new defensive alliance. Finally the danger of preventive or preemptive war is greatest in the early phase of an arms race. With the passage of time people learn to live with the insecurity. They adjust their objectives and accept their conditional viability.

These balance theories derive from the postulate that a two-sided sufficiency to render the other nonviable acts as a mutual deterrent. However, it does so only as long as the antagonists keep their heads and do not become overly touchy. Alternatively a nation with a marked superiority of grievances can be held in check by an opponent with equally marked superiority of power. War will be risky in either event. An aggressor who considers the prospect of defeat should refrain from war except when extremely high grievances render him insensitive to the consequences and/or he counts on surprise to offset the superior strength of the other (1111).

Therefore, as Huntington (1113) points out, the impact of an arms race on the likelihood of war depends not only on whether or not a power equilibrium develops, but also on how much each feels aggrieved. The probability of war breaking out is least, as Huntington puts it, when the sum of the grievances and power of one state approximates the sum of the grievances and power of the other. There is good reason to assume that the touchiness to which Richardson refers is not a basic disposition but stems from perceptions of threat and above all injury which if great enough neutralizes an elite's perception of its own inferior capability, all the more so if it feels public opinion is behind it. The point is difficult to prove, but a systematic analysis of communications in the period leading to the outbreak of World War I by a group of political scientists at Stanford University (1089, 1112) tends to substantiate this general proposition. Present injuries have greater salience than future possibilities. A nation of clearly inferior capability may be goaded into war because it expects the ratio of its own power to that of the opponent to undergo further deterioration.

Inadequate information further detracts from the apparent "rationality" of the choices the actors can make. Secrecy may bring short term gains but makes things harder for both opponents; forced to rely on guess work, their sense of insecurity is apt to increase. This can lead in turn to serious miscalculations (1102, 1120). A nation increasing its military preparations or even plunging into preventive war may be trying to redress a balance that it believes to be on the verge of tipping when in fact it has not even begun to change. But regardless of whether an effort to maintain secrecy about capabilities should or should not be made, some uncertainty about what an opponent's actual intention may be and about how third parties will behave in case of war is inevitable. Therefore, a good bit of the maneuvering on the international scene takes the form of probes and threats designed to establish one's own credibility and to test the responses of the other. The purpose of what Schelling (1035) has called "tacit bargaining" is to signal as clearly as possible one's determination to act or not to react in a certain way in the event certain contingencies should arise.

The old-fashioned arms race was viewed long ago by William James as the actual war and not merely as preparation. It has now been replaced by a "game" of limited moves between two parties deterred by the sufficiency that each knows the other to possess. As Kaufmann (1292) was perhaps the first to point out, deterrence to be effective has above all to be credible. Each must demonstrate not only his rational caution, but also what provocations will cause him to throw caution to the wind. Threats of one form or another have always been an instrument of diplomacy. The nuclear stalemate imposes a new limitation, namely the need to achieve one's political goals without crossing the brink to nuclear war. Much effort goes into trying to anticipate all possibilities, and "psychological warfare" instead of being an adjunct of violence emerges as the predominant aspect.

Psychological warfare in peace and war has always received much attention from social scientists who addressed themselves to the conditions on which its success depends as well as to its limitations (1140, 1144, 1174, 1180, and 1199). A casebook on psychological warfare incidents (1151) brings together much useful material, most of it from the prenuclear period. With the present emphasis on deterrence instead of "morale," goals of psychological warfare are progressively shifting away from its exclusive concern with the masses toward influencing the behavior of elites (1198). During World War II, systematic analysis of the enemy propaganda output offered significant clues about his intentions (1163). This is being supplemented by all sorts of political "gaming" (1284) in which role players place themselves in the position they think their opponent is in. The predominant strategy is increasingly geared to this kind of assessment of intentions. The delicate balance to be maintained between psychological, political, and strictly military forms of pressure is well illustrated in Davison's study of the Berlin blockade (1279), one of the major confrontations between the two preeminent nuclear powers, and by George's analysis of the American decision to intervene militarily in Korea (931), a move that was defined juridically as a police action but has since gained recognition as a "real" war.

War may well be the continuation of diplomacy by other means, but the sharp distinction between war and peace has lost much of its operative and some of its juridical validity. In a book aptly entitled *The Politics of Force,* Young (1303) dissects the behavior of the antagonists in a number of the major post-World War II crises for the explicit goal of formulating hypotheses about the prospects for nonviolent resolution. The main danger today resides in a chain of events causing the "peaceful" demonstrations of violence to escalate beyond any nation's power to control simply as the outcome of a series of moves by which each commits himself until he can no longer change course. Both may wish to avoid a collision to which their own actions may nevertheless contribute. Such a war could be viewed as "accidental"; it could also be viewed as a rationally calculated act. The crucial element resides in the time that elapses between the moment at which those controlling foreign policy realize the high probability of their becoming involved in a war (the point of "surprise") and the moment at which they become powerless to prevent it (the point of "no escape"). The shorter the interval, the more clearly is the movement toward war out of the hands of individual statesmen (1128).

Public opinion is also a factor insofar as it leaves these elites free to act as they see fit or ties their hands. Authoritarian regimes may be freer than democracies to engage in all kinds of foreign conflicts (1059), but pressure from domestic opinion if it limits flexibility is as likely to commit the elites to a course that leads to war as to strengthen the resolve to preserve peace even at great risk. World opinion is quite another matter. The nearly universal desire for peace places those involved in conflict under great pressure to settle their differences by means short of war (1137, 1142, 1310, 1318, and others) and, should the peace be disturbed, to limit the scale of violence used. World opinion alone cannot, however, reduce armaments and establish the conditions for peace.

Small and limited wars can either expand or explode. To prevent such escalation the parties in a conflict must make a deliberate effort to limit their military activities. They can do this in several ways: by confining belligerent activity to a particular geographical area, by refusing to acknowledge the involvement of some states who are parties to the conflict, by reciprocally foregoing the use of some weapons, and, finally, by granting immunity to certain targets (1165). The first two prevent local war from expanding into general war; the second two are intended to keep the fighting more humane. Yet should the superpowers confront one another in general war, it is highly unlikely that they will be deterred from making at least some use of their nuclear arsenals, the various attempts to limit violence notwithstanding (1169). As the character of war changes, so do the forms of warfare. Different strategies and different kinds of striking forces become appropriate at different levels of conflict. In this respect the first definite "act of war," to the extent that it involves a decision, is not usually of an all-or-none character by the party commits itself all in one blow to the unrestricted use of force. It consists rather of a series of decisions as a result of which the action progressively shifts to the battlefield until neither feels he can withdraw.

A conventional battlefield encounter may indeed be a conflict of "pure force" with the striking forces of each side seeking the destruction of the other, but the sociological character of the war is a matter of goals, not of means. Only in what Speier (1199) has called "absolute" war—sometimes also called "total"—do the belligerents aim at the annihilation of their enemy, an enemy that is viewed as the personification of all evil and therefore outside the framework of common norms. His other two types can likewise be described in terms of the social definition of the enemy. "Instrumental" war by contrast is oriented toward advantage, toward values under the control of the enemy, and therefore governed by considerations of expediency rather than by blind hatred. Finally, "agonistic fighting" is subject to strict rules; it is oriented toward glory and justice and therefore dissociated from any useful purpose. These types are of course logically "pure" abstractions. In actuality the conduct of war, even that of the absolute variety, is always tempered by some minimal recognition of reciprocity. This may be nothing more than the knowledge that the enemy can retaliate. More specifically, to wage war with maximum ruthlessness may be incompatible with such goals as the economic exploitation of the territory under enemy control or the ideological conversion of the population.

The conception each party has of the enemy (1007) is clearly a major factor in war. Great divergences of culture or social structure are probably inimical to the mutual recognition of common norms in the conduct of war; hence, war between highly dissimilar opponents would tend toward the absolute end of the continuum. This expectation is not confirmed by Rummel's study (1081) of the various dyads involved in war. For the period under consideration (1820-1952), the degree of cultural and racial similarity was unrelated to intensity when time of occurrence was controlled. The measure of intensity was based on the number of dyads, the duration, and the number killed in the war, but even by this measure wars between essentially similar opponents pursuing incompatible goals were among the most intensely fought. The denial of common bonds by the insurrectionists represents treason; the effort to subdue them tends to become a "righteous crusade." Strong commitments on both sides lead to more ruthless fighting than in wars where spoils are the primary issue and where one would want to avoid undue damage to what one hopes to exploit in the future.

"Just war" doctrines inject moral viewpoints which always obscure the concrete interests at stake. They are not therefore to be treated as insignificant, however. The moralizing they contain may sometimes help and sometimes hinder the efforts to make the conduct of war less brutal, but they almost invariably are an obstacle to an early termination of war short of total defeat. Warring nations develop elaborate ideological justifications (1186). Traditionally the emphasis has been on religion; Communist teachings stress divergences of economic position and social structure. Tucker (1135) has described an essentially American version of these "just war" doctrines, one that had never been fully articulated before. It pictures the American people as basically peace loving. Their creed is never to go to war except under extreme provocation from an aggressor who threatens their freedom and liberties. Such a disinclination to enter a conflict to defend concrete national interests, Tucker believes, also implies a disinclination to accept a settlement that does not entail some punishment of the aggressor who because of his actions must accept sole responsibility for the disturbance of the peace.

The character of war as distinct from the forms of fighting reveals itself most clearly in the manner in which it terminates. One might begin with a set of distinctions paralleling those previously made among the three social types of war. The end of agonistic fighting approximates a ritual. It relies on conventions that signify to both parties that further violence has become inappropriate. At the opposite pole of the continuum is the unilateral imposition by superior force of the will of the victor on an opponent rendered totally helpless by utter exhaustion or annihilated physically by the war. As Kecskemeti (1115) has pointed out, every strategic surrender that terminates a war contains at least the rudiments of a bargain. The loser, who is forced to conclude the war, trades his remaining capacity to inflict damage for the best terms he can get under the circumstances. In contrast to a tactical surrender at the end of a battle which may be unconditional, the termination of hostilities constitutes a political act.

When and how does a loser decide to sue for peace and what affects the ability of belligerents to reach an agreement concerning their relative strength? Klingberg (1075) approached this question in terms of the number of battle casualties as a percentage of population. In the wars he examined, the losses suffered by the loser were usually higher than those of the winners. But far more conclusive a sign of impending defeat was the change in the relative size of the armed forces in the months prior to the end of the war when the large number of troops sick or captured caused a rapid erosion in the loser's strength. If, however, the end of the war conforms to some kind of coercive bargain, the victor and loser must still have a common definition of what constitutes defeat, and extremely high polarization with regard to goals and disparate cultural traditions may lead to continued resistance when by all "rules of the game" the loser has clearly lost (1103). The change in fortunes is the easier to gauge when war is conducted by conventional means, when one party is progressively deprived of the means with which to press for better terms. These more conventional definitions are less binding on irregular forces who can dissolve into the population following any defeat. Fighting may gradually subside and finally die out, but its termination by an explicit bargain is a remote possibility except where the irregulars achieve their goals.

Conventional warfare discriminates between soldiers who are legitimate targets and civilian noncombatants who are not. It shades off one side into massive—usually, but not necessarily, nuclear—warfare and on the other into various forms in which irregulars, who do not abide by the conventions that govern the conduct of war and are not accorded belligerent status, carry the brunt of the fighting. In their nonrecognition of the sharp line between soldiers and civilians, the two forms of unconventional warfare are rather alike. There are also similarities between them with regard to the concern each shows for the political effects of violence, actual or potential, other differences in the techniques of coercion notwithstanding. Thus, unchecked nuclear warfare against an enemy who has the power to retaliate on a massive scale would be unreasonable; so would the use of such power against a nation whose lack of retaliatory capability permits it be blackmailed by a credible threat with only a limited demonstration of that power. Irregular warfare which was the natural form of warfare among primitive peoples has become the principal instrument where conventional forms of warfare are ruled out either because of vastly disproportionate capabilities between the opponents or because of the danger of uncontrollable escalation.

Irregular warfare has attracted much attention from those concerned over its danger and from those to whose imagination it speaks. The literature, much of it popular, on the subject of guerilla war has become truly voluminous. The more dispassionate analysts distinguish clearly between its use as an instrument of subversion, of insurrection, and of defense (1191). The use of irregulars (guerillas) for purposes of subversion has the distinct advantage of being compatible with the official nonbelligerency of the country providing them with support. Yet subversive irregular warfare on a significant scale is possible only when such activities coincide with revolutionary or nationalist aspirations already present within a population. Oppressive acts or illegitimate conquest create a reservoir of grievances that an outside power may seek to exploit for its own ends.

Civilian loyalties are critical for the success of irregular forces operating from a domestic base (1172; see also 1192). The effectiveness of this form of warfare depends largely on the psychological impact it has. Janos (1171) in dealing with internal war points to two fundamentally different strategies which are not exclusive so that both of them may be used in a single war. One is insurrection that attempts to transform the attitudes of troops who are defined as potentially friendly. The irregulars lack anything beyond the most minimal military capability but pin their hopes on being able to persuade soldiers to hold their fire and, henceforth, to defect in common cause with the rebels. Guerilla warfare in its narrower sense seeks to achieve its objective by tactics designed to create anxiety, fear, and frustration among the forces of order. By their terror the guerillas mean to deny a superior enemy the fruits of victory. Support of the local population is required primarily for intelligence information and logistic support. The antiguerilla forces' progressive inability to distinguish between friend and foe often sparks indiscriminate counterterror which weakens the government's legitimacy and ultimately hastens its fall.

Military sociologists are just beginning to become sensitive to the issues that relate to the new forms of warfare, including the various methods of keeping the peace. The contribution of the military sociology to policy problems will be increased to the extent that individual investigators manage to free themselves from the perspectives that limit the views of some of the official sponsors of policy research.

We cannot close this chapter without some reference to peace-keeping operations. The nature of such a force (181, 195), the internal problems it is likely to experience (375), the disputes over spheres of authority and responsibility (1315, 1317), and the many other obstacles it faces in its operations (1306, 1320, 1321) are natural subjects for social science analysis. Ultimately one hopes the insights gained from these and other studies can be applied to international organizations of all kinds and help render them more effective.


N O T E

1. Robert S. Lynd and Helen M. Lynd, *Middletown.* New York: Harcourt, Brace & World, 1956 and *Middletown in Transition.* New York: Harcourt, Brace, 1937.

*Part Two.*

**ANNOTATED**

**BIBLIOGRAPHY**

## ANNOTATED BIBLIOGRAPHY

### I. GENERAL

#### I.1 Summaries and critical reviews

1. BARABANSCHIKOV, A. V., PLATONOV, K. K., & FEDENKO, N. F. "On the History of Soviet Military Psychology." Soviet Psychology, 1968, 7(1): 48-57.

2. BINZ, G. "Wehrsoziologie" (Military sociology). Wehrwissenschaftliche Rundschau, 1961, 11: 485-506. A definitional essay.

3. BOLDYREFF, A. W. "A Decade of Military Operations Research in Perspective: a Symposium." Operations Research, 1960, 8: 798-860.

4. BOWERS, R. V. "The Military Establishment." In P. F. Lazarsfeld, W. H. Sewell, & H. L. Wilensky (Eds.) *The Uses of Sociology.* New York: Basic Books, 1967: 234-274.

5. BUSQUEST BRAGULAT, J. "La Sociologia militar" (Military sociology). Revista del Ejército, 1966, No. 320: 25-30.

6. CAMPENEAU, Dr. "Questions de sociologie militaire" (Questions of military sociology). Revista Internacional de Sociologia (Madrid), 1903, 11: 639-650.

7. CHANDESSAIS, C. *La psychologie dans l'armée* (Psychology in the army). Paris: Presses Universitaires de France, 1959. 195 pp. With a bibliography.

8. COATES, C. H., & PELLEGRIN, R. J. *Military Sociology: a Study of American Institutions and Military Life.* University Park, Md.: Social Science Press, 1965. x + 424 pp. A text.

9. CUNIS, R. "Zur Soziologie des Militärs" (On the sociology of the military). Hamburger Jahrbuch für Wirtschafts- und Gesellschafts-Politik, 1967, 12: 325-344.

10. ENGELS, F. *Izbrannye voennye proizvedeniia* (Selected works on military problems). Moscow: Boeh, 1957. 843 pp. With an introduction by A. Strokhov.

11. FEDOSSEEV, P. "Sovremennaja burjoiznaja sociologija o problemakh voïny i mira (What contemporary bourgeois sociology says on problems of war and peace). Bolchévik, 1946, 22: 38-52.

12. GIRARDET, R. "Problèmes militaires contemporains; état de travaux" (Present-day military problems: trend report). Revue Française de Science Politique, 1960, 10: 395-418. A bibliographical essay.

13. GRACZYK, K. "Problematyka zakres badan i spoleczna uzytecsnosc ivspolczesnej socjologii wojny" (Problems, scope, and utility of the contemporary sociology of war). Studia Socjologiczno-Polityczne, 1966, 23: 207-219. Emphasis on causes and prevention of war.

14. HALL, R. L. "Military Sociology." In H. L. Zetterberg (Ed.) *Sociology in the United States of America: a Trend Report.* Paris: UNESCO, 1956. Pp. 59-62.

15. HERTZ, A. "Zagadnienia socjologii wojska i wojny" (Problems of the sociology of the military and war). Prezglad Socjologiczny, 1946, 8: 119-140.

16. HOPPE, G. *Kritik der imperialistischen deutschen Wehrsoziologie; Wehrge-meinschaft wider den Frieden* (Critique of the imperialist German military sociology; common defense against the peace). Berlin (DDR): Deutscher Militärverlag, 1964. 173 pp.

17. HUTCHINSON, C. E. "The Meaning of Military Sociology." Sociology and Social Research, 1957, 41: 427-433.

18. JANOWITZ, M., & LITTLE, R. *Sociology and the Military Establishment.* (Rev. Ed.) New York: Russell Sage Foundation, 1965, 136 pp.

19. KRUPNOW, S. I. *Dialektika i voennaia nauka* (Dialectics and military science). Moscow: Voenzidat, 1964. 201 pp.

20. LANG, K. "Military Sociology: a Trend Report and Bibliography." Current Sociology, 1965. 13(1): 1-55. Whole issue.

21. LENIN, V. I. *O voine, armii i voennoi nauke* (On war, army, and military science). Moscow: Boeh, 1965. 835 pp. Collected articles.

22. RATTENBACH, B. *Sociologia militar; una contribución a su estudio* (Military sociology; a contribution to its study). Buenos Aires: Libraria Perlado, 1958. 158 pp.

23. ROGHMANN, K., & ZIEGLER, R. "Militärsoziologie" (Military sociology). In R. Koenig (Ed.) *Handbuch der empirischen Sozialforschung.* Stuttgart: Ferdinand Enke Verlag, 1969. Pp. 2-30.

24. ROUCEK, J. S. "The Trends in American Military Sociology and its Educational Implications." Duquesne R., 1962, 8(1): 26-49. A review article.

25. ROUCEK, J. S., & LOTTICH, K. V. "American Military Sociology: the American Military Mind." Social Science Information, 3(1): 91-106. A review article.

26. VAN RIPER, P. P. "A Survey of Materials for the Study of Military Management." American Political Science R., 1955, 49: 828-850.

27. VIAL, J. "Introduction à la sociologie militaire" (Introduction to military sociology). Revue de Défense Nationale (Nouvelle Série), 1959, 15: 1225-1235.

28. WALTER, P. "Military Sociology." In J. S. Roucek (Ed.), *Contemporary Sociology.* New York: Philosophical Library, 1958. Pp. 655-672.

29. WIATR, J. J. *Armia i społeczeństwo: wprowadzenie do socjologii wojska* (Army and society: an introduction to military sociology). Warsaw: Wydawnictwo Ministerstwa Obrony Narodowej, 1960, 396 pp. A text.

30. WIATR, J. J. *Socjologia wojska* (Military sociology). Warsaw: Wydawnictwo Ministerstwa Obrony Narodoweij, 1964. 342 pp. A text.

31. WINDLE, C., & VALLANCE, T. R. "The Future of Military Psychology: Paramilitary Psychology." American Psychologist, 1964, 19: 119-129. Growing emphasis on social interaction and cross-cultural communication.

32. ZIEGLER, R. "Einige Ansatzpunkte der Miliärsoziologie und ihr Beitrag zur soziologischen Theorie" (Some tentative propositions of military sociology and its contribution to sociological theory). Kölner Zeitschrift für Soziologie und Sozialpsychologie, 1968, 20 (Special Issue): 38-58.

I.1  See also 531, 536, and 995.

## I.2. Bibliographies

33. BULKLEY, M. E. *Bibliographical Survey of Contemporary Sources for the Economic and Social History of the War.* Oxford: Clarendon Press, 1922, xix + 628 pp. On World War I.

34. CARNEGIE ENDOWMENT FOR INTERNATIONAL PEACE. *Summary of Organization and Work, 1911-1941* (Economic and social history of the World War including comprehensive list of monographs published). Washington, D.C., 1941. xii + 123 pp.

35. EINAUDI, L., & GOLDHAMER, H. "An Annotated Bibliography of Latin American Military Journals." Latin American Research R., 1967, 2 (2): 95-122.

36. GRAHAM, C. C., & BREESE, ELEANOR. *Publications of the Social Science Department of the RAND Corporation, 1948-1967.* (Memorandum RM-3600-4) Santa Monica, Cal.: The Rand Corporation, 1967.

37. HUMAN RESOURCES RESEARCH OFFICE. *Bibliography of Publications; as of 30 June 1966.* Washington, D.C.: The George Washington University Human Resources Research Office, September 1966. 237 pp. Supplementary bibliographies of HumRRO reports are issued periodically.

38. LELAND, W. G., & MERENESS, N. D. (Eds.) *Introduction to the American Official Sources for the Economic and Social History of the World War.* New Haven: Yale University Press, 1926. xlvii + 532 pp. A bibliography on World War I.

39. LISSAK, M. "Selected Literature on Revolutions and Coups d'ètat in the Developing Nations." In M. Janowitz (Ed.) *The New Military: Changing Patterns of Organization.* New York: Russell Sage Foundation, 1964. Pp. 339-362.

40. NEY, V. "Military Sociology—a Select Bibliography." Military Affairs, 1966, 30: 234-237.

41. SELLS, S. B. *Military Small Group Performance under Isolation and Stress—an Annotated Bibliography.* Fort Wainwright, Alaska: Arctic Aeromedical Laboratory, Alaskan Air Command, 1961. Six Volumes. Vol. 1—Basic Psychology of Group Behavior; Vol. 2—Dimensions of Group Structure and Group Behavior; Vol. 3—Environmental Stress and Behavior Ecology; Vol. 4—Organizational Staffing; Vol. 5—Organizational Management and Leadership; Vol. 6—Leadership in Formal Groups.

42. SOCIAL SCIENCE RESEARCH COUNCIL. COMMITTEE ON CIVIL-MILITARY RESEARCH. *Civil-Military Relations; an Annotated Bibliography, 1940-52.* New York: Columbia University Press, 1954. xiv + 140 pp.

43. SPECIAL OPERATIONS RESEARCH OFFICE, AMERICAN UNIVER-

SITY. *A Preliminary Bibliography on Studies of the Roles of Military Establishments in Developing Nations.* Washington, D.C., 1963.

44. U.S. DEPARTMENT OF THE ARMY, OFFICE OF THE ADJUTANT GENERAL. *Military Manpower Policy; a Bibliographic Survey.* Prepared by H. Moskowitz & J. Roberts. Washington, D.C.: U.S. G.P.O., June 1, 1965. x + 142 pp.

45. U.S. DEPARTMENT OF STATE, BUREAU OF INTELLIGENCE AND RESEARCH. *Roles of the Military in Less Developed Countries, Jan. 1954-Feb. 1964; a Selected Bibliography.* Compiled by Nancy Blackenstein and L. Moses. External Research Staff Paper, 1964, No. 147. 11 pp.

46. U.S. SENATE, COMMITTEE ON GOVERNMENT OPERATIONS, Subcommittee on National Policy Machinery, 86th Congress, I Session. *Organizing for National Security: a Bibliography.* Washington, D.C.: U.S. G.P.O., 1959. Bibliography on government, military organization and civil-military relations.

47. U.S. SENATE, COMMITTEE ON GOVERNMENT OPERATIONS, Subcommittee on National Policy Machinery, 86th Congress, II Session. *Organizing for National Security: a Bibliography.* Vol. 2 of 3 volumes of subcommittee hearings. Washington, D.C.: G.P.O., 1961. Pp. 35-111. Bibliography on government, military organization, and civil-military relations.

48. WOJCIK, J. *Bibliografia socjologii wojska i wojny w Polsce po II Woznie Swiatowej* (Bibliography of the sociology of the military and of war in post World War II Poland). Warsaw: Wojskowa Akademia Polityczna, Katedra Socjologii Wojskowej, 1967. 24 pp. From 1945 to 1966.

49. ZIEGLER, R. "Ausgewählte Literatur zur Militärsoziologie" (Selected Bibliography on Military Sociology). Kölner Zeitschrift für Soziologie und Sozialpsychologie, 1968, 20 (Special Issue 12): 327-360.

I.2 See also 673 and 771.

### I.3. Compendia of research not elsewhere classified

50. AMERICAN JOURNAL OF SOCIOLOGY. Human Behavior in Military Society. 1946, 51: 359-508. Special issue consisting of articles based on World War II experience.

51. ARCHIVES EUROPEENES DE SOCIOLOGIE. Armed Forces and Society in Western Europe. 1965, 6: 225-308. Special issue edited by Morris Janowitz with synthetic studies.

52. FAZIK, A. *Sociology and the Armed Forces.* Prague: VPA KG, 1965. Contains articles by M. Purkrábek on political administration and staff of the field army, by O. Miksík on the psychology of work and of command in the armed forces, as well as reviews of military sociological studies in Poland and the United States. In Czech.

53. GELDARD, F. A., & LEE, M. C. (Eds.) *1st International Symposium on Military Psychology Proceedings.* Washington, D.C.: National Academy of Sciences-National Research Council, 1961. 225 pp. Includes papers on the functions of the noncommissioned officers (by L. Delys), on the selection of officers for combat (by L. Carmichael and L. E. Baker), and on the effectiveness of mentally subnormal soldiers (by E. Siro), and others.

54. HUNTINGTON, S. P. (Ed.), *Changing Patterns of Military Politics.* New York: Free Press, 1962. 272 pp. Huntington's "Recent writings in military politics—foci and corpora," 235-266, is a first-rate bibliographic essay; articles by H. D. Lasswell, D. C. Rapoport, L. Radway, R. Girardet, P. Abrams and M. Derthick.

55. JANOWITZ, M. (Ed.) *The New Military; Changing Patterns of Organization.* New York: Russell Sage Foundation, 1964. 369 pp. Introduction-Organizing Multiple Goals: War Making and Arms Control by M. Janowitz; studies dealing with managerial forms and succession, professional socialization, social cohesion under prolonged stress, career commitment and retirement with a bibliographic guide to revolution and coups d'état in developing nations.

56. KOLNER ZEITSCHRIFT FUR SOZIOLOGIE UND SOZIALPSYCHOLO-GIE. *Beiträge zur Militärsoziologie* (Contributions to military sociology). 1968, Special Number 12: 1-360. Contributions on the place of the armed forces in society, internal problems of military organization, research reports, and a bibliography. Edited with an introduction by R. König, assisted by K. Roghmann, W. Sodeur, and R. Ziegler.

57. MERTON, R. K., & LAZARSFELD, P. F. (Eds.) *Continuities in Social Research: Studies in the Scope and Method of "The American Soldier."* New York: Free Press, 1950. 255 pp.

58. PICHT, G. (Ed.) *Studien zur politischen und gesellschaftlichen Situation der Bundeswehr* (Studies of the political and social position of the Bundeswehr). Witten & Berlin: Eckart-Verlag, 1965-1966. 3 vols. 320, 246, and 368 pp. Volume 1 contains articles by G. Picht, H. Herzfeld, K. Frhr. Schenck zu Schweinsberg, and G. Howe; vol. 2, articles by L. von Friedeburg, J. H. von Heiseler, and F. A. Klausenitzer; vol. 3 is a monograph entitled "Rüstung und Gesellschaft" (Armament and society) by G. Brandt.

59. REVUE FRANCAIS DE SOCIOLOGIE. *Guerre, armée, société* (War, army, society). 1961, 2 (2): 1-151. Special issue on a variety of topics in military sociology.

60. SPEIER, H. *Social Order and the Risks of War.* New York: Stewart, 1952. ix + 497 pp. Includes diverse papers on military sociology.

61. VAN DOORN, J. (Ed.) *Armed Forces and Society; Sociological Essays.* The Hague & Paris: Mouton, 1968. 386 pp. Papers selected from those presented at the Sixth World Congress in Sociology on the military profession, on its relation to societal change, and on its role in developing nations.

62. VAN DOORN, J. (Ed.) *Military Profession and Military Regimes: Commitments and Conflicts.* The Hague & Paris: Mouton, 1969. 304 pp. Essays on the military in old, new, and socialist nations by members of the working group on armed forces and society.

63. VAN DOORN, J.A.A. *Organisatie en maatschappij* (Organization and society). Leiden: Stenfert Kroese, 1966. xii + 272 pp. Contains essays on sociology of the military.

64. WILLIAMS, R. H. (Ed.) *Human Factors in Military Operations: Some Applications of the Social Sciences to Operations Research.* Technical memo ORO-T-259. Chevy Chase, Md.: Operations Research Office, 1954. xi + 406 pp. Chapters on manpower problems, training, behavior stress, combat, the military group, and others.

65. WOLFE, J. N., & ERICKSON, J. (Eds.) *The Armed Services and Society: Alienation, Management, and Integration.* Edinburgh: Edinburgh University Press—Chicago: Aldine, 1970.

## II. THE MILITARY PROFESSION: MANAGERS OF VIOLENCE
(also 51, 55, 61, 62, and 65)

### II.1. Social and cultural perspectives on the profession

66. AYCOBERRY, P. "Le corps des officiers allemands: de l'Empire du Nazisme" (The German officer corps from the Empire to National Socialism). Annales, 1957, 22: 370-384.

67. BUSQUEST BRAGULAT, J. "Las cuarto ultimas generaciones militaires" (The last four military generations). Revista Española de la Opinion Pública, 1967, 7: 179-194.

68. BUSQUEST BRAGULAT, J. *El militar de carrera en Espana; estudio de sociologia militar* (The professional soldier in Spain; a study in military sociology). Barcelona: Ediciones Ariel, 1967. 226 pp.

69. BUSQUEST BRAGULAT, J. "Origen del militar de carrera en Espana" (The origin of the military career in Spain). Anales de Sociologia, 1966, 1 (1): 19-39.

70. CHALMIN, P. *L'officier français de 1815 à 1870* (The French officer from 1815 to 1870). Paris: M. Rivière, 1957. 408 pp.

71. COLBY, E. *The Profession of Arms.* New York: D. Appleton. 1924. vii + 183 pp.

72. DEMETER, K. *Das deutsche Offizierskorps in Gesellschaft und Staat, 1650-1945.* Frankfurt/Main: Bernard & Graefe Verlag, 1962. vii + 321 pp. (English translation: *The German Officer-Corps in Society and State, 1650-1945.* New York: Praeger, 1965. xiv + 414 pp.) A sociological study of origins and tradition.

73. DRASCHER, W. "Zur Soziologie des deutschen Seeoffizierskorps" (Sociology of the German naval officer corps). Wehrwissenschaftliche Rundschau, 1962, 12: 555-569.

74. ELIAS, N. "Studies in the Genesis of the Naval Profession." British J. of Sociology, 1950, 1-2: 291-309. Shift from ascription to criteria of competence.

75. GASSLER, C. W. *Offizier und Offizierskorps der Alten Armee in Deutsch-land als Voraussetzung einer Untersuchung über die Transformation der militarischen Hierarchie* (Officer and officer corps in the Imperial German army as the basis for inquiry into the transformation of a military hierarchy). Mannheim: Diss. Heidelberg, 1930. Partial translation by S. Ellison, Columbia University, 1937 (mimeo).

76. GIRARDET, R. (Ed.) *La crise militaire française 1945-1962: aspects sociologiques et idéologiques* (The French military crisis 1945-1962: sociological and ideological aspects). Paris: A. Colin, 1964. 240 pp. Part I—Problèmes de recruitment par R. Girardet et J.-P. H. Thomas; Part II—Problèmes de structure et de mode de vie par P. M. Bouju et J.-P. H. Thomas; Part III—Problèmes idélogiques et moreaux par R. Girardet; Essaie d'interpretation par R. Girardet.

77. GIRARDET, R. *La société militaire dans la France contemporaine* (The military society in contemporary France). Paris: Librairie Plon, 1953. 329 pp. Its emergence over the past century.

78. GORLITZ, W. *Der deutsche Generalstab: Geschichte und Gestalt.* Frankfurt/Main: Verlag der Frankfurter Hefte, 1953. 306 pp. (English translation: *History of the German general staff.* New York: Praeger, 1953. 508 pp.) The military elite nucleus.

79. GUTTERIDGE, W. "Military Elites in Ghana and Nigeria." African Forum, 1966, 2 (1): 31-41.

80. HACKETT, J. W. *The Profession of Arms.* Lees Knowles Lectures, No. 3. London: Times Publ. Co., 1963. 68 pp. Military service as a profession.

81. HILTON, R. "The Soviet Armed Forces." In A. Inkeles & K. Geiger (Eds.) *Soviet society.* Boston: Houghton-Mifflin, 1961. Pp. 241-249. Elite composition.

82. HOROWITZ, I. L. "The Military Elites." In S. M. Lipset & A. Solari (Eds.), *Elites in Latin America.* Oxford University Press, 1967. Pp. 146-189.

83. HUNTINGTON, S. P. "Power, Expertise, and the Military Profession." In K. S. Lynn (Ed.) *The Professions in America.* Boston: Houghton-Mifflin, 1965. Pp. 131-153. Also in Daedalus, 1963, 92: 785-807.

84. IMAZ, J. L. de. *Los que mandan: las fuerzas armadas en Argentina* (Those in command: the armed forces in Argentina). Buenos Aires: Universidad de Buenos Aires, 1964. 250 pp. Social origins, education, and ideology. (See also 85.)

85. IMAZ, J. L. de. "Los que mandan: las fuerzas armadas en Argentina" (Those in command: armed forces in Argentina). América Latina, 1964, 7 (4): 35-69. Social origins, education, and ideology.

86. JANOWITZ, M. "Armed Forces and Society: a World Perspective." In J. van Doorn (Ed.) *Armed Forces and Society.* The Hague & Paris: Mouton, 1968. Pp. 15-38.

87. JANOWITZ, M. "Armed Forces in Western Europe: Uniformity and Diversity." Archives Europèennes de Sociologie, 1965, 6: 225-237.

88. JANOWITZ, M. *The Professional Soldier: a Social and Political Portrait.* New York: Free Press, 1960. xiv + 464 pp. Sociological study of American military professionals.

89. JOHNSON, J. J. "Algunas características sociales de los militares latino-americanos (Some social characteristics of the Latin American military). Revista Paraguaya de Sociologia, 1965, 2 (3): 41-54.

90. KITCHEN, M. *The German Officer Corps 1800-1914.* Oxford: Clarendon Press, 1968. xxix + 242 pp.

91. KJELLBERG, F. "Offiserene som sosial gruppe" (Military officers as a social group). Tidsskrift for Samfunnsforskning, 1962, 3 (2): 113-131.

92. KJELLBERG, F. "Some Cultural Aspects of the Military Profession." Archives Européennes de Sociologie, 1965, 6: 283-293.

93. KREKOLA, A. "Sovilasel itii Suomessa" (The military elite in Finland). Politiikka, 1968, 10: 18-25. Changes concomitant with modernization.

94. LANG, K. "Military." In *International Encyclopedia of the Social Sciences.* Vol. 10. New York: Macmillan & Free Press, 1968. Pp. 305-311.

95. LEWIS, M. A. *England's Sea Officers: the Story of the Naval Profession.* London: Allen & Unwin, 1939. 307 pp.

96. MILITARGESCHICHTLICHES FORSCHUNGSAMT. *Beiträge zur Militar- und Kriegsgeschichte.* Vol. 4. *Untersuchungen zur Geschichte des Offizierskorps; Anciennität und Beförderung nach Leistung* (Studies in the history of the officer corps; seniority and promotion based on performance). Stuttgart: Deutsche Verlagsanstalt, 1962. 342 pp.

97. PAXTON, R. O. *Parades and Politics at Vichy: the French Officer Corps under Marshal Pétain.* Princeton, N.J.: Princeton, 1966. xi + 472 pp.

98. POCH, A. "Diplomacia y fuerzas aramadas en la vida internacional: caracter analogico de ambas professiones" (Diplomatic corps and armed forces in international life: analogy between the two professions). Revista de Politica Internacional (Madrid), 1962, 60: 31-51.

99. RATTENBACH, B. "El profesionalismo militar en el ejército Argentino (Military professionalism in the Argentine army). Temas Militares, 1967, 1 (3): 9-16.

100. RAY, O. A. "The Imperial Russian Army Officer." Political Science Q., 1961, 76: 576-592. Origins and structure as factors in political noninvolvement.

101. TUETEY, L. *Les officiers sous l'ancien régime* (Officers under the prior regime). Paris: Plon, 1908. vi + 407 pp. A social history.

102. VAGTS, A. *A History of Militarism.* (2nd Ed.) New York: Meridian Books, 1959. 542 pp. Romance and reality in the military profession.

103. VAN DOORN, J. "The Officer Corps: a Fusion of Profession and Organization." Archives Européennes de Sociologie, 1965, 6: 262-282.

104. WIATR, J. J. (Ed.) *Z badań nad zawodem oficera: materialy i studia* (Studies in the military profession). Wroclaw: Ossolinskich Wydawnictwo Polskiej Akademii Nauk, 1966. 125 pp. Contributions cover the professional military in Poland, its prestige, military families, and related matters.

II.1 See also 482, 657, 691, and 703.

## II.2. Origins and career patterns

105. ABRAMS, P. "Democracy, Technology, and the Retired British Officer." In S. P. Huntington (Ed.) *Changing Patterns of Military Politics.* New York: Free Press, 1962. Pp. 150-189.

106. BARNETT, C. "The Education of Military Elites." J. of Contemporary History, 1967, 2 (3): 15-35. Great Britain.

107. BAUR, W. Deutsche Generale: die militärischen Führungsgruppen in der Bundesrepublik und in der DDR (German generals: military elites in the Federal Republic and in the DDR). In W. Zapf (Ed.) *Beiträge zur Analyse der deutschen Oberschicht.* Munich: R. Piper, 1965. Pp. 114-135. Comparison of social profiles and careers.

108. BEERI, E. "Social Origin and Family Background of the Egyptian Officer Class." J. of Asian and African Studies, 1966, 2: 1-46. See also 740.

109. BIDERMAN, A. D. "Sequels to a Military Career: the Retired Military Professional." In M. Janowitz (Ed.) *The New Military; Changing Patterns of Organization.* New York: Russell Sage Foundation, 1964. Pp. 287-336. Employment of retired U.S. officers.

110. BOPEGAMAGE, A. "Caste, Class and the Indian Military: a Study of the Social Origins of Indian Army Personnel." In J. van Doorn (Ed.) *Military Profession and Military Regimes.* The Hague & Paris: Mouton, 1969. Pp. 127-153.

111. BOUJU, P. M., & THOMAS, J.-P. H. "Problèmes de structure et de genre de vie" (Problems of structure and mode of life). In R. Girardet (Ed.) *La crise militaire française 1945-1962: aspects sociologiques et idéologiques.* Paris: A. Colin, 1964. Pp. 73-149. Career problems in the context of stratification and mobility patterns.

112. BUSQUEST BRAGULAT, J. "El estado mayor como aristocracia militar" (The general staff as a military aristocracy). Anales de Sociologia, 1966, 1 (2): 76-99.

113. CAPITAINES, T., & A. "Capitaines, ou bas-officiers? Essai sur la structure sociale de l'armée française" (Captains or subalterns? Essay on the social structure of the French Army). Nouvelle Critique, 1959, 107: 43-84. The promotion squeeze.

114. COATES, C. H. "America's New Officer Corps." Trans-action, 1966, 3 (3): 22-24. Military careers as an avenue of social advancement.

115. CVROEK, J. "Social Changes in the Officer Corps of the Czechoslovak People's Army." In J. van Doorn (Ed.) *Military Profession and Military Regimes.* The Hague & Paris: Mouton, 1969. Pp. 94-106.

116. ENCEL, S. "The Study of Militarism in Australia." Australian and New Zealand J. of Sociology, 1967, 3: 2-18. Also in J. van Doorn (Ed.) *Armed Forces and Society.* The Hague & Paris: Mouton, 1968. Pp. 127-147.

117. FRANDEN, O. "Notes on Mobility into and out of the Swedish Officer Corps." In J. van Doorn (Ed.) *Military Profession and Military Regimes.* The Hague & Paris: Mouton, 1969. Pp. 107-126.

118. GIRARDET, R., & THOMAS, J.-P. H. "Problèmes de recrutement"

(Problems of recruitment). In R. Girardet (Ed.) *La crise militaire française 1945-1962.* Paris: Armand Colin, 1962. Pp. 11-72. Social origins and recruitment into various ranks.

119. GRACZYK, J. "Social Promotion in the Polish People's Army." In J. van Doorn (Ed.) *Military Profession and Military Regimes.* The Hague & Paris: Mouton, 1969. Pp. 82-93.

120. GRUSKY, O. "The Effects of Succession: a Comparative Study of Military and Business Organization." In M. Janowitz (Ed.) *The New Military; Changing Patterns of Organization.* New York: Russell Sage Foundation, 1964. Pp. 83-111.

121. JOHNSON, P. V., & MARCRUM, R. H. "Perceived Deficiencies in Individual Need Fulfillment of Career Army Officers." J. of Applied Psychology, 1968, 52: 457-461.

122. LEHMAN, H. "The Age of Eminent Leaders: Then and Now." American J. of Sociology, 1947, 52: 342-356. Contains data on military leaders.

123. LOVELL, J., & others. "Recruitment Patterns into the Republic of Korea Military Establishment." J. of Comparative Administration, 1970, 1: 428-454. Backgrounds of students in military schools.

124. MASLAND, J. W., & RADWAY, L. I. *Soldiers and Scholars; Military Education and Military Policy.* Princeton, N.J.: Princeton University Press, 1957. xx + 530 pp. Educational requirements and practices in the U.S. officer corps.

125. McMAHAN, C. A., & COMBS, J. W., Jr. "The Age of Military Leaders and Expansion of the Armed Forces." Southwestern Social Science Q., 1956, 36: 365-375.

126. McMAHAN, C. A., FOLGER, J. K., & FOTIS, S. W. "Retirement and Length of Life." Social Forces, 1956, 34: 234-241. U.S. Air Force officers retired between 1925 and 1948.

127. MITCHELL, V. F. "Need Satisfactions of Military Commanders and Staff." J. of Applied Psychology, 1970, 54: 282-287.

128. MODEL, H. *Der deutsche Generalstabsoffizier; seine Auswahl und Ausbildung in Reichswehr, Wehrmacht und Bundeswehr* (The German general staff officer; his selection and training in the Reichswehr, Wehrmacht, and Bundeswehr). Frankfurt/Main: Bernard & Graefe, 1968. 300 pp.

129. NOTHAAS, J. "Sozialer Auf- und Abstieg im deutschen Volk" (Social ascent and descent among the German population). *Beiträge zur Statistik Bayerns,* 1930, No. 117. Pages 65 to 73, which treat the occupational status of former German officers after World War I, translated by A. Lissance, Columbia University, 1937 (mimeo).

130. OTLEY, C. B. "Militarism and the Social Affiliations of the British Army Elite." In J. van Doorn (Ed.) *Armed Forces and Society.* The Hague & Paris: Mouton, 1968. Pp. 84-108.

131. POOL, I. de S. *The Satellite Generals: a Study of Military Elites in the Soviet Sphere.* Stanford, Cal.: Stanford University Press, 1955. vi + 165 pp.

132. RAZZELL, P. E. "Social Origins of Officers in the Indian and British Home Army: 1758-1962." British J. of Sociology, 1963, 14: 248-260.

133. REISSMAN, L. "Life Careers, Power and the Professions: the Retired Army General." American Sociological R., 1956, 21: 215-221. Employment in civilian work.

134. SCHOSSLER, D. "Militär und Gerwerkschaften: Berufsproblematik und Interessenartikulation der westdeutschen Berufssoldaten" (The military and trade unions: career problems and interest articulation of professional officers in West-Germany). Kölner Zeitschrift für Soziologie und Sozialpsychologie, 1968, 20 (Special Issue 12): 136-156.

135. SEGAL, D. R. "Selective Promotion in Officer Cohorts." Sociological Q., 1967, 8: 199-206. Service academy graduates versus others.

136. SEGAL, D. R., & WILLICK, D. H. "The Reinforcement of Traditional Career Patterns in Agencies under Stress." Public Administration R., 1968, 28 (1): 30-38. Pressure on military and foreign service for representative recruitment.

137. VAGTS, A. "Generals: Old and Young." J. of Politics, 1942, 4: 396-406.

138. VAN RIPER, P. P., & UNWALLA, D. B. "Military Careers at the Executive Level." Administrative Science Q., 1965, 9: 421-436. Importance of line and staff versus technical and support for career advancement.

139. WARNER, W. L., VAN RIPER, P. P., MARTIN, N. H., & COLLINS, O. F. *The American Federal Executive: a Study of the Social and Personal Characteristics of the Civilian and Military Leaders of the United States Federal Government.* New Haven & London: Yale University, 1963. xvii + 405 pp.

140. WHITSON, W. W. "The Concept of Military Generation: the Chinese Communist Case." Asian Survey, 1968, 8: 921-947. Intercohort differences since the revolution.

141. WIATR, J. J. "Military Professionalism and Transformation of Class Structure in Poland." In J. van Doorn (Ed.) *Armed Forces and Society.* The Hague & Paris: Mouton, 1968. Pp. 229-239.

142. WIATR, J. J. "Social Prestige of the Military: a Comparative Approach." In J. van Doorn (Ed.) *Military Profession and Military Regimes.* The Hague & Paris: Mouton, 1969. Pp. 73-80.

143. ZALD, M. N., & SIMON, W. "Career Opportunities and Commitments among Officers." In M. Janowitz (Ed.) *The New Military; Changing Patterns of Organization.* New York: Russell Sage Foundation, 1964. Pp. 257-285. Survey of U.S. officers.

    II.2 See also 156, 350, 580, 581, 598, and 737.

## II.3. Selection and socialization

144. ABRAHAMSSON, B. "Attityder och profesionell socialisering" (Attitudes and professional socialization). Sociologisk Forskning, 1967, 3: 88 pp. Effects of officer selection and socialization.

145. BORNEMANN, E. "Auslesemethoden zur Ermittlung der Führerbefähigung" (Methods of selection to determine aptitude for leadership). Soziale Welt, 1953, 4: 331-340.

146. CENTRE D'ETUDES D'INSTRUCTION PSYCHOLOGIQUES DE L'ARMEE DE L'AIR. "Attitudes et motivation des candidats aux grandes écoles militaires" (Attitudes and motivations of the candidates in the foremost military academies). Revue Française de Sociologie, 1961, 2 (2): 133-151.

147. DENBLYDEN, B. E. "Le centre de psychosociologie militaire de belgique et le perfectionnement permanent des cadres (The Belgian center for military psychosociology and the permanent improvement of the cadres). Information Psychologique, 1966, 23: 55-62.

148. DORNBUSCH, S. M. "The Military Academy as an Assimilating Institution." Social Forces, 1955, 33: 316-321. Based on participant observation in the U.S. Coast Guard Academy.

149. EISENDORFER, A., & BERGMANN, M. S. "The Factor of Maturity in Officer Selection." Psychiatry, 1946, 9: 73-79.

150. GAYLORD, R. H., & RUSSELL, E. "West Point Evaluative Measures in the Prediction of Officer Efficiency." Educational and Psychological Measurement, 1951, 2: 605-611.

151. KOERDT, H. "Die Interaktionanalyse als Instrument zur Auswahl militärischer Führer" (The analysis of group interaction as a method for selecting military leaders). Kölner Zeitschrift für Soziologie und Sozialpsychologie, 1968, 20 (Special Issue 12): 317-326.

152. LAMMERS, C. J. *Het Koninklijk Instituut voor de Marine: een sociologische Analyse van de Inlijving van Groepen Adspirant-Officieren in de Zeemacht* (The Royal Naval Institute: a sociological analysis of the assimilation of officer candidate groups in the navy). Assen: Van Gorcum & Co., 1963. xx + 685 pp. With English summary, pp. 561-590. See also 153.

153. LAMMERS, C. J. "Midshipmen and Candidate Reserve Officers at the Royal Netherlands Naval College. A Comparative Study of a Socialization Process." Sociologia Neerlandica, 1965, 2: 98-122. Survey findings of degree of acceptance of Navy culture by the two groups.

154. LOVELL, J. P. "The Professional Socialization of the West Point Cadet." In M. Janowitz (Ed.) *The New Military; Changing Patterns of Organization.* New York: Russell Sage Foundation, 1964. Pp. 119-157. Based on comparison of freshmen and upperclassmen.

155. LYONS, G., & MASLAND, J. W. *Education and Military Leadership: a Study of the R.O.T.C.* Princeton, N.J.: Princeton University Press, 1959. 283 pp.

156. MICHELAT, G., & THOMAS, J.-P. "Contribution à l'étude du recrutement des écoles d'Officiers de la Marine, 1945-1960" (Contribution to the study of recruitment into Naval officer academies, 1945-1960). Revue Française de Sociologie, 1968, 9: 51-70. Predominance of recruits from traditionalist families during the decolonization period.

157. MORRIS, B. S. "Officer Selection in the British Army, 1942-1945" Occupational Psychology, 1949, 23: 219-234.

158. NUBER, H. *Wahl des Offizierberufs; eine charakterologische Untersuchung von Persönlichkeit und Berufsethos* (Choice of the officer profession; a characterological study of personality and professional ethos). Heidelberg & Berlin: K. Vowinckel, 1935. xi + 190 pp.

159. PETERSEN, P. B., & LIPPITT, G. L. "Comparison of Behavioral Style Between Entering and Graduating Students in Officer Candidate School" J. of Applied Psychology, 1968, 52: 66-70.

160. RANDELL, S. "On Some Social Influences of the Military Organization" Acta Sociologica, 1967, 10: 258-274. Study of change in occupational imagery in an officer training academy.

161. VON WIESE, L. *Kindheit: Erinnerungen aus meinen Kadettenjahren* (Childhood: reminiscences of my years in the cadet corps). Hanover: P. Steegemann, 1924. 95 pp.

162. VON WIESE, L. "Uber militärische Erziehung" (On military education). In *Spätlese.* Köln & Opladen: Westdeutscher Verlag, 1954. Pp. 39-50.

163. WARREN, R. L. "The Naval Reserve Officer: a Study in Assimilation." American Sociological R., 1946, 11: 202-211. Factors favoring successful transformation of U.S. civilians in World War II.

164. WILLIAMS, S. B., & LEAVITT, H. J. "Group Opinion as a Predictor of Military Leadership." J. of Consulting Psychology, 1947, 11: 283-291.

165. WILLIAMS, S. B., & LEAVITT, H. J. "Methods of Selecting Marine Corps Officers." In G. A. Kelley (Ed.) *New Methods in Applied Psychology.* College Park, Md.: University of Maryland, 1947. Pp. 96-99.

II.3  See also 185, 327, 358, and 558.

## II.4. Professional role, ideology, and self-image

166. ABRAHAMSSON, B. "The Ideology of an Elite: Conservatism and National Insecurity; Some Notes on the Swedish Military." In J. van Doorn (Ed.) *Armed Forces and Society.* The Hague & Paris: Mouton, 1968. Pp. 71-83.

167. ABRAHAMSSON, B. "Military Professionalization and Estimates on the Probability of War." In J. van Doorn (Ed.) *Military Profession and Military Regimes.* The Hague & Paris: Mouton, 1969. Pp. 35-51.

168. ABRAMS, P. "The Late Profession of Arms: Ambiguous Goals and Deteriorating Means in Britain." Archives Européennes de Sociologie, 1965, 6: 238-261.

169. BELL, D. "The Dispossessed—1962." In D. Bell (Ed.) *The Radical Right.* New York: Doubleday, 1963. Pp. 1-38. Includes military officers among sources of support for militant conservative movement.

170. COLLINET, M. "Le Saint-Simonism et l'armée" (Saint-Simonism and the army). Revue Française de Sociologie, 1961, 2 (2): 38-47. View of the armed forces as an instrument of progress.

171. CROWLEY, J. B. "Japanese Army Factionalism in the Early 1930's." J. of Asian Studies, 1962, 21: 309-326.

172. DAVIS, A. K. "Bureaucratic Patterns in the Navy Officer Corps." Social Forces, 1948, 27: 143-153.

173. DOGAN, M. "Les Officers dans la Carrière Politique: du Maréchal MacMahon au Général de Gaulle" (Officers in political careers: from Marshal MacMahon to General de Gaulle). Revue Française de Sociologie, 1961, 2 (2): 88-99. Study of 350 officers who became members of parliament or held cabinet posts.

174. ENDRES, F. C. "Soziologische Struktur und ihr entsprechende Ideologien des deutschen Offizierskorps vor dem Weltkrieg" (The German officer corps before the first world war: its sociological structure and its corresponding ideology). Archiv Sozialwissenschaft und Soziologie, 1927, 58: 282-319.

175. FELD, M. D. "Military Self-Image in a Technological Environment." In M. Janowitz (Ed.) *The New Military; Changing Patterns of Organization.* New York: Russell Sage Foundation, 1964. Pp. 159-188. Documentation of 20-year trend by an analysis of service journals.

176. FELD, M. D. "Professionalism, Nationalism, and the Alienation of the Military." In J. van Doorn (Ed.) *Armed Forces and Society.* The Hague & Paris: Mouton, 1968. Pp. 55-70.

177. GINSBURGH, R. N. "The Challenge to Military Professionalism." Foreign Affairs, 1964, 42: 255-268. Civilian intervention into purely military functions.

178. GIRARDET, R. "Problemes moreaux et ideologiques" (Moral and ideological problems). In R. Girardet (Ed.) *La crise militaire française 1945-1962: aspects sociologiques et idéologiques.* Paris: A. Colin, 1964. Pp. 151-217.

179. HAMON, A. *Psychologie de militaire professionnel* (Psychology of the professional military). Paris: Tresse & Stock, 1904. lxxvii + 216 pp. An antimilitarist perspective.

180. HENRY, A. F., MASLAND, J. W., & RADWAY, L. I. "Armed Forces

Unification and the Pentagon Officer." Public Administration R., 1955, 15: 173-180. Development of perspectives beyond the service viewpoint.

181. JACKSON, J. A. "The Irish Army and the Development of the Constabulary Concept." In J. van Doorn (Ed.) *Armed Forces and Society.* The Hague & Paris: Mouton, 1968. Pp. 109-126.

182. KOLKOWICZ, R. "The Impact of Modern Technology on the Soviet Officer Corps." In J. van Doorn (Ed.) *Armed Forces and Society.* The Hague & Paris: Mouton, 1968. Pp. 148-168.

183. KOLKOWICZ, R. "The Impact of Modern Technology on the Soviet Officer Corps." Orbis, 1967, 11: 378-393.

184. KRAKOWSKI, K., & SOBOLSKI, K. "Spoleczne i swiatopogladowe postawy polskich oficerów—jeńców przebywajacych w czasie drugie j wojny światowej w wojskowych obozach w Niemczech" (Social and ideological attitudes of Polish officers—POW's in Germany during World War II). Studia Socjologiczno-Polityczne, 1963, 14: 57-112.

185. LAWRENCE, W. G. "The Greater Degree of Specialization Demanded by Modern Weapons, its Effects on the Training of Officers, and How the Opposing Requirements of Specialization and Wide Experience Can Best be Resolved." J. of the Royal United Service Institution, 1955, 100: 90-103.

186. LOVELL, J. P., SOK, M. H., & LEE, Y. H. "Professional Orientation and Policy Perspectives of Military Professionals in the Republic of Korea." Midwest J. of Political Science, 1969, 13: 415-438. A Survey.

187. LUCKHAM, A. R. "The Nigerian Military: Disintegration or Integration." In S. K. Panter-Brick (Ed.) *Nigerian Politics and Military Rule: Prelude to the Civil War.* London: Athlone Press, 1970. Pp. 58-77. Composition and cleavages.

188. MAITRE, J. "Le Catholisme d'extrême droite et la croisade anti-subversive" (Extreme right wing Catholicism and the antisubversive crusade). Revue Française de Sociologie, 1961, 2 (2): 106-117. Connections between officers and the Catholic right.

189. NEEDLER, M. C. "The Latin American Military: Predatory Reactionaries or Modernizing Patriots? J. of Inter-American Studies, 1969, 11: 237-244.

190. OCHOA DE EGUILEOR, J., & BELTRAN, V. R. *Las fuerzas armadas hablan* (The armed forces speak). Buenos Aires, Paidos, 1968. 223 pp. Social and political attitudes of the Argentine armed forces during the critical years 1943 to 1963.

191. PLANCHAIS, J. "Crise de modernisme dans l'armée (Modernization crisis in the army). Revue Française de Sociologie, 1961, 2 (2): 118-123.

192. SOLOMON, D. N. "The Soldierly Self and the Peace-Keeping Role: Canadian Officers in Peace-Keeping Forces." In J. van Doorn (Ed.) *Military Profession and Military Regimes.* The Hague & Paris: Mouton, 1969. Pp. 52-69.

193. VAN GILS, M. R. *Het officierskorps: de krisis in een professie* (The officer corps: crisis in a profession). Teppel, Netherlands: J. A. Boom en Zoon, 1969. 32 pp. Address before the Royal Naval Institute.

194. VAN RIPER, P. P., & UNWALLA, D. B. "Voting Patterns among High-Ranking Military Officers." Political Science Q., 1965, 80: 48-61. Electoral participation.

195. WIATR, J. J. "Ekspert i polityk: rozbiezne aspekty spolecznej roli wojskowego." Stud. socjol.-polit., 1964, 17: 63-73. Translated as "Expert and Politican; the Divergent Aspects of the Social Role of the Army Man." Polish Sociological B., 1964, 1 (9): 44-53. Officer roles.

196. WOLFE, T. W. "Political Primacy vs. Professional Elan." Problems of Communism, 1964, 13 (3): 44-52. Conflicting imperatives among Soviet officers.

197. ZUCKERMAN, S. "Judgment and Control in Modern Warfare." Foreign Affairs, 1962, 40: 196-212. Technology causes shift of locus away from military. Reprinted in S. Zuckerman. *Scientists at War.* London: Hamish Hamilton, 1966. Pp. 101-121.

II.4 See also 84, 85, 246, 358, 697, 701, 736, 739, 851, 946, 958, and 974.

## III. MILITARY ORGANIZATION AS SOCIAL STRUCTURE
(also 41, 50, 52, 53, 56, and 63)

### III.1. General characteristics of military environment

198. ANONYMOUS. "Civilt och miliärt" (Civilian and military). In *Social Arsbok, 1950-51*. Stockholm: Kooperativa Förbundets Förlag, 1951.

199. BIGLER, R. R. *Der einsame Soldat; eine soziologische Deutung der militarischen Organisation* (The lonely soldier; a sociological interpretation of military organization). Frauenfeld: Verlag Huber, 1963. 266 pp.

200. BREPOHL, W. "Das Heerwesen-kultursoziologish gesehen" (Army life from the viewpoint of sociology of culture). Soziale Welt, 1953, 4: 317-324.

201. BROTZ, H., & WILSON, E. K. "Characteristics of Military Society." American J. of Sociology, 1946, 51: 371-375. As refracted through U.S. Army basic training experience.

202. EATON, W. H. "The Military Environment." Social Forces, 1947, 26: 88-94.

203. ETZIONI, A. *A Comparative Analysis of Complex Organizations.* New York: Free Press, 1961. 366 pp. Includes a discussion of military organization within framework of a broader theory.

204. FREEMAN, F. D. "The Army as a Social Structure." Social Forces, 1948, 27: 78-83.

205. GUTTE, R. "Die Mentalität unserer Armee; Analyse von Bundeswehr-Publikationen" (The mentality of our army; analysis of Bundeswehr publications). Frankfurter Hefte, 1966, 21: 6-16. Themes in information sheets to enlisted men (Information für die Truppe).

206. LANG, K. "Military Organizations." In J. G. March (Ed.) *Handbook of Social Organizations.* Chicago: Rand-McNally, 1964. Pp. 838-878.

207. LEHOUCK, F. "Armia a biurokracja" (The army and bureaucracy). Studia Socjologiczno-Polityczne, 1968, 25: 147-175. Comparison of army and other organizations.

208. MOSKOS, C. C., Jr. *The American Enlisted Man.* New York: Russell Sage Foundation, 1970. x + 274 pp. Field observations of U.S. forces overseas.

209. ROSE, A. M. "The Social Structure of the Army." American J. of Sociology, 1946, 51: 361-364. Fusion of American democratic tradition, feudal archaisms, and formal regulations.

210. SOLOMON, D. N. "Sociological Research in a Military Organization." Canadian J. of Political Science and Economics, 1954, 20: 531-541. Reprinted in B. R. Blishen et al. (Eds.) *Canadian Society: Sociological Perspectives.* (1st Ed.) New York: Free Press, 1961. Pp. 275-285. Tradition and change in authority and internal environment.

211. SPINDLER, G. D. "American Character as Revealed by the Military." Psychiatry, 1948, 11: 275-281.

212. SPINDLER, G. D. "The Military—a Systematic Analysis." Social Forces, 1948, 27: 83-88.

213. VAN DOORN, J. "Militärische und industrielle Organisation: ein soziologischer Vergleich" (Military and industrial organization: a comparative approach). In J. Matthes (Ed.) *Soziologie und Gesellschaft in den Niederlanden.* Neuwied/Rhein & Berlin: Luchterhand, 1965. Pp. 276-300.

214. VAN DOORN, J. A. A. *Sociologie van de Organisatie: Beschouwingen over Organiseren in het bizonder Gebaseerd op een Onderzoeck van het Militaire System* (Sociology of organization: observations about organizations with special reference to military social structure). Leiden: H. E. Stenfort Kroese, 1956. xv + 338 pp.

III.1 See also 172, 309, and 505.

## III.2. Stratification

215. BORGATTA, E. F. "Attitudinal Concomitants of Military Statuses." Social Forces, 1955, 33: 342-347. Authority, discipline, and deviance as seen by officers and noncoms.

216. DOWNS, J. F. "Environment, Communication and Status Change Aboard an American Aircraft." Human Organization, 1958, 17 (3): 14-19. Impact of technology on informal structure.

217. FRANK, J. D. "Personal Problems Related to Army Rank." American J. of Psychiatry, 1946, 103: 97-104.

218. HENRY, A. F., & BORGATTA, E. F. "A Comparison of Attitudes of Enlisted and Commissioned Air Force Personnel." American Sociological R., 1953, 18: 669-671.

219. LEVI, M., TORRANCE, E. P., & PLETTS, G. O. "Sociometric Studies of Combat Air Crews in Survival Training." Sociometry, 1954, 17: 304-328. Changes in choice status.

220. LEWIS, R. "Officer-Enlisted Men's Relationships." American J. of Sociology, 1947, 52: 410-419. General observations.

221. LITTLE, R. "Rangsysteme im amerikanischen Militär" (Rank systems in the American military). Kölner Zeitschrift für Soziologie und Sozialpsychologie, 1968, 20 (Special Issue 12): 187-198. On stratification.

222. McDONAGH, E. G. "Military Social Distance." Sociology and Social Research, 1945, 29: 289-296. General observations by an enlisted man.

223. MACK, R. "The Prestige System of an Air Base: Squadron Rankings and Morale." American Sociological R., 1954, 19: 281-287.

224. MERTON, R. K. & KITT, ALICE. "Contributions to the Theory of Reference Group Behavior." In R. K. Merton & P. F. Lazarsfeld (Eds.) Continuities in Social Research: Studies in the Scope and Methods of "The American Soldier." New York: Free Press, 1950. Pp. 40-105. Aspirations and adjustment among U.S. troops in World War II.

225. MOSER, M. "Neue Probleme der militärischen Führung" (New problems of military leadership). Soziale Welt, 1953, 4: 325-330. Effect of new orientations among enlisted men.

226. MURDOCK, G. P. "The Military Hierarchy and 'Caste' Divisions." In. R. H. Williams (Ed.) Human Factors in Military Operations. Chevy Chase, Md.: Operations Research Office, Johns Hopkins University, 1954. Pp. 371-379. Military rank structure and its lack of congruence with the civilian occupational and skill structure.

227. NELSON, P. D., & BERRY, N. H. "Change in Sociometric Status during Military Basic Training Related to Performance Two Years Later." J. of Psychology, 1965, 61: 251-255.

228. PORTER, L. W., & MITCHELL, V. F. "Comparative Study of Need Satisfactions in Military and Business Hierarchies." J. of Applied Psychology, 1967, 51: 139-144. Based on self-administered questionnaires for different ranks.

229. SPEIER, H. " 'The American Soldier' and the Sociology of Military Organization." In R. K. Merton and P. F. Lazarsfeld (Eds.) *Continuities in Social Research: Studies in the Scope and Method of 'The American Soldier.'* New York: Free Press, 1950. Pp. 106-132. Also in H. Speier, *Social Order and the Risks of War.* New York: Stewart, 1952. Pp. 295-319. Cleavage and consensus between officers and men.

230. STONE, R. C. "Status and Leadership in a Combat Fighter Squadron." American J. of Sociology, 1946, 51: 388-394. Based on participant observation.

231. WACHTEL, S. B., & FAY, L. C. "Allocation of Grades in the Army Air Forces." American J. of Sociology, 1946, 51: 395-403. A rationale.

III.2 See also 249, 254, 309, 395, 401, 406, 574, 580, 581, and 582.

### III.3. Authority structure and work relations

232. DANIELS, ARLENE K., & CLAUSEN, R. E. "Role Conflicts and their Ideological Resolution in Military Psychiatric Practice." American J. of Psychiatry, 1966, 123: 280-287. Professional versus organizational commitments.

233. DE GREGORI, T., & PI-SUNYER, O. "Technology, Traditionalism and Military Establishments." Technology and Culture, 1966, 7: 402-407.

234. FELD, M. D. "Information and Authority: the Structure of Military Organization." American Sociological R., 1959, 24: 15-22. Flow of information and commands between tactical units and higher echelons.

235. FLEISHMAN, E. A. "Differences between Military and Industrial Organizations." In R. M. Stogdill & C. L. Shartle (Eds.) *Patterns of Administrative Performance.* Ohio State University Bureau of Business Research Monographs, No. 81, 1956. Pp. 31-38. Executive behavior in four naval and four industrial organizations.

236. GETZELS, J. W., & GUBA, E. G. "Role Conflict and Personality." J. of Personality, 1955, 24: 365-370. Study of instructional staff at U.S. Air University.

237. GOETZINGER, C., & VALENTINE, M. "Communication Patterns, Interactions and Attitudes of Top-Level Personnel in the Air Defense Command." J. of Communication, 1963, 13: 54-57.

238. GROSS, E. "Some Functional Consequences of Primary Controls in

Formal Work Organizations." American Sociological R., 1953, 18: 368-373. Study of U.S. Air Force base.

239. HALPIN, A. W. "The Leader Behavior and Leadership Ideology of Educational Administrators and Air-Craft Commanders." Harvard Educational R., 1955, 25: 18-31. Responsibility, authority, and delegation scores.

240. HALPIN, A. W. "The Leadership Ideology of Aircraft Commanders." J. of Applied Psychology, 1955, 39: 82-84. Responsibility, authority, and delegation.

241. HALPIN, A. W. "The Observed Leader Behavior and Ideal Leadership Behavior of Aircraft Commanders and School Superintendents." In R. M. Stogdill & A. E. Coons (Eds.) *Leadership Behavior: its Description and Measurement.* Ohio State University Bureau of Business Research Monographs, No. 88, 1957. Pp. 65-68. Managerial leadership studies series.

242. HEISELER, J. H. von. "Militär und Technik; Arbeitssoziologische Studien zum Einfluss der Technisierung auf die Sozialstruktur des modernen Militärs" (Military and technology; studies in the sociology of work on the influence of technological complexity on the social structure of the modern military). In G. Picht (Ed.) *Studien zur politischen und gesellschaftlichen Situation der Bundeswehr.* Witten & Berlin: Eckart-Verlag, 1965-1966. Pp. 66-158.

243. HENRY, A. F., BORGATTA, E. F., & STOUFFER, S. A. "Role Conflict as a Factor in Organizational Effectiveness." In R. V. Bowers (Ed.) *Studies in Organizational Effectiveness.* Washington, D.C.: Air Force Office of Scientific Research, 1962. Pp. 5-27. Staff and command relations under conditions of technological change.

244. JANOWITZ, M. "Changing Patterns of Organizational Authority: the Military Establishment." Administrative Science Q., 1959, 3: 473-493. The impact of technology.

245. JANOWITZ, M. "The Military Establishment: Organization and Disorganization." In R. K. Merton & R. A. Nisbet (Eds.) *Contemporary Social Problems.* New York: Harcourt, Brace & World, 1966. Pp. 515-552.

246. KATZENBACH, E. L. "The Horse Cavalry in the Twentieth Century: a Study in Policy Response." *Public Policy; Yearbook of the Graduate School of Public Administration, Harvard University,* Vol. 7, 1958. Pp. 120-149. Case study of cultural lag.

247. LEIGHTON, R. M. "Allied Unity of Command in the Second World War: a Study in Regional Military Organization." Political Science Q., 1952, 67: 399-425. Problems of hierarchical authority in coalition warfare.

248. MARWALD, A. "The German General Staff: Model of Military Organization." Orbis, 1959, 3: 38-62. Organizational practices and performance.

249. MITCHELL, V. F., & PORTER, L. W. "Comparative Managerial Role Perceptions in Military and Business Hierarchies." J. of Applied Psychology, 1967, 51: 449-452. Based on word lists.

250. MOSEN, W. *Eine Militärsoziologie; technische Entwicklung und Autoritätsprobleme in modernen Armeen* (Military sociology; technological development and authority structure in modern armies). Neuwied & Berlin: Luchterhand, 1967. 148 pp.

251. PAGE, C. H. "Bureaucracy's Other Face." Social Forces, 1946, 25: 88-94. Informal structure.

252. PURKRABEK, M. "Influence of Social Changes and the Modern Military Technology on Discipline: Some Remarks on the Sociological Model of a Socialist Military Discipline." In *Current Issues of Military Discipline. Proceedings of the Conference on the Disciplinary Training of Soldiers.* Prague: VPA KG, 1966. Pp. 29-56. In Czech.

253. RADWAY, L. I. "Military Behavior in International Organization—NATO's Defense College." In S. P. Huntington (Ed.) *Changing Patterns of Military Politics.* New York: Free Press, 1962. Pp. 102-120.

254. SADLER, P. J. "Technical Change and Military Social Structure." In F. A. Geldard (Ed.) *Defence Psychology.* New York: Pergamon Press, 1962. Pp. 312-317. Some effects of recent developments on rank and authority system.

255. SCHON, D. A. "Champions for Radical New Innovations." Harvard Business R., 1963, 41 (2): 77-86. Resistance to change in military organization and the pattern of success.

256. SCOTT, E. L. *Leadership and Perceptions of Organization.* Ohio State University Bureau of Business Research Monographs, No. 82, 1956. 122 pp. Study of work groups in the U.S. Navy.

257. SHARTLE, C. L. "Studies in Naval Leadership: Part I." In H. A. Guetzkow (Ed.) *Groups, Leadership and Men.* Pittsburgh: Carnegie, 1951.

Pp. 119-133. Summary of Ohio State University studies on responsibility, authority, and delegation.

258. STOGDILL, R. M. "Studies in Naval Leadership: Part II." In H. A. Guetzkow (Ed.) *Groups, Leadership and Men.* Pittsburgh: Carnegie, 1951. Pp. 134-145.

259. SUOJANEN, W. W. "Military Management and the General Staff." Academy of Management J., 1961, 4: 115-122.

260. THOMPSON, J. D. "Authority and Power in 'Identical' Organizations." American J. of Sociology, 1956, 62: 290-301. Discrepancies between formal and informal structure in Air Force wings.

261. TURNER, R. H. "The Naval Disbursing Officer as Bureaucrat." American Sociological R., 1947, 12: 342-348.

III.3 See also III.5(2) and 52, 210, 216, 263, 266, 407, and 417.

### III.4. Discipline and the management of deviance

262. AHRENFELDT, R. H. *Psychiatry in the British Army in the Second World War.* New York: Columbia University Press, 1958. xiii + 312 pp.

263. BURCHARD, W. W. "Role Conflicts of Military Chaplains." American Sociological R., 1954, 19: 523-535.

264. CALDWELL, N. W. "Welfare Organization in the Luftwaffe." Social Forces, 1946, 25: 53-60.

265. COULET, W. "Le nouveau règlement de discipline générale dans les armées" (The new regulation with regard to general discipline in the armed forces). Revue du Droit Public et de la Science Politique en France et à l'Etranger, 1968, 84: 1-82. Limits of military jurisdiction considered in connection with social and organizational factors.

266. DANIELS, ARLENE K. "The Captive Professional: Bureaucratic Limitations in the Practice of Military Psychiatry." J. of Health and Human Behavior, 1969, 10: 255-265. Conflict between therapeutic and control functions.

267. EVAN, W. "Due Process of Law in Military and Industrial Organization." Administrative Science Q., 1962, 7: 187-207. Focus on appeal system.

268. GREGORY, W. E. "Chaplain and Mental Hygiene." American J. of Sociology, 1947, 52: 420-423.

269. HADLEY, E. E. "Military Psychiatry: a Note on Social Status." Psychiatry, 1943, 6: 203-216.

270. HARRIS, F. G., & LITTLE, R. W. "Military Organization and Social Psychiatry." In *Symposium on Preventive and Social Psychiatry.* Washington, D.C.: Walter Reed Army Institute of Research, 1957. Pp. 173-184.

271. HUNT, W. A. "An Investigation of Naval Neuropsychiatric Screening Procedures." In H. Guetzkow (Ed.) *Groups, Leadership and Men.* Pittsburgh: Carnegie Press, 1951. Pp. 245-256.

272. LITTLE, R. W. "The 'Sick' Soldier and the Medical Ward Officer." Human Organization, 1956, 15 (1): 22-24. Participant observation.

273. McDONAGH, E. G. "Military Social Controls." Sociology and Social Research, 1945, 29: 197-205. Participant observations on how the army controls its men.

274. MANDELBAUM, D. G. "Psychiatry in Military Society." Human Organization, 1954, 13 (3): 5-15, and 1955, 13 (4): 19-25.

275. PORTER, W. C. "The Functions of a Neuropsychiatrist in an Army General Hospital." Psychiatry, 1942, 5: 321-329.

276. ROSE, A. M. " 'Official' vs. 'Administrative' Criteria for Classification of Combat Breakdown Cases." Administrative Science Q., 1958, 3: 185-194. Operating criteria for determining evacuation of U.S. ground troops in world war.

277. STRANGE, R. E., & ARTHUR, R. J. "Hospital Ship Psychiatry in a War Zone." American J. of Psychiatry, 1967, 124: 281-286.

278. UYEKI, S. "Organizational Behavior and Preventive Intervention." Human Organization, 1964, 23 (1): 11-15. Authority structure and coping with deviance.

279. VAN GILS, M. R. *De militaire Straf- en Tuchtklasse; in het Depot voor Discipline to Nieuwersluis* (Military punishment and disciplinary classes in the disciplinary barracks at Nieuwersluis). s'Gravenhage: J. A. Boom en Zoon, 1963. 174 pp.

280. WHITE, H. B. "Military Morality." Social Research, 1946, 13: 410-440. Interpretation of deviance based on participant observation.

281. ZAHN, G. *The Military Chaplaincy: a Study of Role Tension in the Royal Air Force.* Toronto: University of Toronto Press, 1969. 310 pp.

III.4 See also 215, 218, 232, 252, 349, 350, 426, 427, 450, and 706.

**III.5. Transition from civilian to military life** (also 57)

5(1) Problems and processes of adjustment

282. ABRAHAMSSON, B. *Anpassning och avgängsbenägenhet blant militärt befäl* (Adjustment and retention among military personnel). Halmstad: Bull's, 1965. 341 pp. Summary of data on the social and attitudinal concomitants of adaptation to military life collected by the Militärpsykoliska Institutet, Offical Report No. 37.

283. BJORKLUND, E. "Social anpassning under militärtjänsten" (Social adjustment during military service). Tidskrift i sjovasendet, 1963, 126: 404-417. Delinquency among enlisted personnel.

284. CANTER, F. M., & CANTER, A. N. "Authoritarian Attitudes and Adjustment in a Military Situation." U.S. Armed Forces Medical Journal, 1957, 8: 1201-1207. Mean F-scores of delinquents, psychiatric patients, and unselected service troops.

285. CLARK, J. H. "The Adjustment of Army AWOL's." J. of Abnormal Psychology, 1949, 44: 394-401.

286. CLARK, R. A. "Aggressiveness and Military Training." American J. of Sociology, 1946, 51: 423-432. Problems of adjustment.

287. CUBER, J. F. "The Adjustment of College Men to Military Life: Case Data." Sociology and Social Research, 1943, 27: 267-276.

288. DATEL, W. E., & LIFRAK, S. T. "Expectations, Affect Change, and Military Performance in the Army Recruit." Psychological Reports, 1969, 24: 855-879. Psychological impact of basic combat training.

289. DAVENPORT, R. K. "The Negro in the Army: a Subject of Research." J. of Social Issues, 1947, 3 (4): 32-39.

290. EKBLAD, M. *A Psychiatric and Sociological Study of a Series of Swedish Naval Conscripts.* Copenhagen: E. Munkgaard, 1948. 200 pp.

291. FIRESTONE, R. W. "Social Conformity and Authoritarianism in the Marine Corps." Dissertation Abstracts, 1959, 20, 394.

292. FOX, H. M. "A Variety of Furlough Psychosis." Psychiatry, 1944, 7: 207-213.

293. FRENCH, R. L. "Sociometric Status and Individual Adjustment among Naval Recruits." J. of Abnormal and Social Psychology, 1951, 46: 64-72.

294. GIBBS, D. N. "The National Serviceman and Military Delinquency." Sociological R., 1957, 5 (New Series): 255-263.

295. GROSS, E., & MILLER, D. C. "The Impact of Isolation on Worker Adjustment in Military Installations in the United States and Japan." Estudios Sociológicos (Mexico), 1961, 1: 70-83.

296. HOLLINGSHEAD, A. B. "Adjustment to Military Life." American J. of Sociology, 1946, 51: 439-447.

297. HORTON, MILDRED M. "Women in the United States Army." American J. of Sociology, 1946, 51: 448-450.

298. HUSEN, T. Militärt och Civilt (Military and civilian). Stockholm: Norstedts, 1956. 352 pp. Discipline, delinquency, and recruitment patterns under conscription.

299. JANIS, I. L. "Psychodynamic Aspects of Adjustment to Army Life." Psychiatry, 1945, 8: 159-176.

300. KIEV, A., & GIFFEN, M. B. "Some Observations on Airmen Who Break Down during Basic Training." American J. of Psychiatry, 1965, 122: 184-188.

301. McCALLUM, M. R. "The Study of the Delinquent in the Army." American J. of Sociology, 1946, 51: 479-482.

302. McDONAGH, E. G. "Social Adjustments to Militarism." Sociology and Social Research, 1945, 29: 449-457.

303. McDONAGH, E., & McDONAGH, L. "War Anxieties of Soldiers and their Wives." Social Forces, 1945, 24: 195-200.

304. MASKIN, M. H. "Something about a Soldier." Psychiatry, 1946, 9: 187-191.

305. MASKIN, M. H., & ALTMAN, L. L. "Military Psychodynamics: Psychological Factors in the Transition from Civilian to Soldier." Psychiatry, 1943, 6: 263-269.

306. PRATTIS, P. L. "The Morale of the Negro in the Armed Services of the United States." J. of Negro Education, 1943, 12: 355-363.

307. SHAINBERG, D. "Motivations of Adolescent Military Offenders." Adolescence, 1967, 2: 243-255.

308. SPENCER, J. C. *Crime and the Services.* London: Routledge & Kegan Paul, 1954. xii + 306 pp. Contains chapters on adjustment to service life in World War II and on the readjustment of ex-POWs.

309. STOUFFER, S. A., et al. *The American Soldier.* Vol. 1. *Adjustment during Army Life.* Princeton, N.J.: Princeton University Press, 1949. xii + 599 pp. Study of World War II conscripts.

310. VAN VELTHOVEN, G. M. *Attitudes van Meisjes in militaire Vrouwenafdelingen* (Attitudes of women in military service). Nijmegen: Dekker & van de Vegt, 1963. 184 pp.

311. VYROUBAL, M. *Cultural and Aesthetic Concerns of Soldiers.* Prague: UDA, 1964. 48 pp. In Czech.

312. WEINBERG, S. K. "Problems of Adjustment in Army Units." American J. of Sociology, 1945, 50: 271-278.

313. WIEDMANN, TEN. CEL. L., & FELIPPE, S. "Adjustamento do convocado civil ao grupo militar" (Adjustment of the civilian to the military group). Sociologia (Brasil), 1959, 21: 23-46.

314. WILLIAMS, M. J. "A Socio-Economic Analysis of the Functions and Attitudes of War-Time Youths." Social Forces, 1945, 24: 200-210.

   5(1) See also IV.2(2) and 217, 224, 363, 387, 564, 568, and 571.

5(2) Leadership, cohesion, and morale

315. BARABANTCHIKOV, A. V., GLOTOCHKIN, A. D., FEDENKO, H. S., & SHELIAG, V. V. *Psikhologiia Voinskogo Kollektiva* (Psychology of a military collective). Moskow: Voenzidat, 1967. 251 pp. Social psychological study of the basis of morale.

316. BASSAN, M. E. "Some Factors Found Valuable in Maintaining Morale on a Small Combatant Ship." B. of the Menninger Clinic, 1947, 11: 33-42.

317. CAMPBELL, D. T. *Leadership and its Effect upon the Group.* Ohio State University Bureau of Business Research. No. 83, 1953. 92 pp. Morale measures of submarine crews related to characteristics of commanders.

318. CHRISTNER, CHARLOTTE A., & HEMPHILL, J. K. "Leader Behavior of B-29 Commanders and Changes in Crew Members' Attitudes toward the Crew." Sociometry, 1955, 18: 82-87. Consideration and initiating structure.

319. DAVIS, F. J. "Conceptions of Official Leader Roles in the Air Force." Social Forces, 1954, 32: 253-258. Congruity and adjustment.

320. DICKS, H. V., SHILS, E. A., & DINERSTEIN, H. S. *Service Conditions and Morale in the Soviet Armed Forces: a Pilot Study.* U.S. Air Force Project Rand. Santa Monica, Ca.: Rand Corporation, August 25, 1951 (R-213) Vol. 1. *The Soviet Army.* v + 367 pp.

321. FRENCH, R. L. "Morale and Leadership." In *Human Factors in Undersea Warfare.* Washington, D.C.: National Research Council, 1949. Pp. 463-488.

322. GROSS, E. "Primary Functions of the Small Group." American J. of Sociology, 1954, 60: 24-29. Basis of informal groups in the U.S. Air Force.

323. GROSS, E. "Symbiosis and consensus as integrative factors in small groups." American Sociological R., 1956, 21: 174-179. Informal relations on a military base.

324. GUETZKOW, H. (Ed.) *Groups, Leadership and Men.* Pittsburgh: Carnegie, 1951. ix + 293 pp. Papers from U.S. Navy conference held by its Human Relations Advisory Panel, Sept., 1950. Includes studies on naval leadership by Stogdill and Shartle.

325. HALL, R. L. "Social Influence on the Aircraft Commander's Role." American Sociological R., 1955, 20: 292-298.

326. HESSE, K. *Der Feldherr Psychologos* (The combat leader psychologos). Berlin: E. S. Mittler & Sohn, 1922. xvi + 209 pp. Observations on the future military leadership in Germany.

327. HOLLANDER, E. P. "Authoritarianism and Leadership Choice in a Military Setting." J. of Abnormal and Social Psychology, 1954, 49: 365-370. Groups of aviation cadets.

328. HOLLOMAN, C. R. "The Perceived Leadership Role of Military and Civilian Supervisors in a Military Setting." Personnel Psychology, 1967, 20: 199-210. Work relations at an Air Force installation.

329. HOMANS, G. C. "The Small Warship." American Sociological R., 1946, 11: 294-300.

330. HUTCHINS, E. B., & FIEDLER, F. E. "Task-Oriented and Quasi-Therapeutic Role Functions of the Leader in Small Military Groups." Sociometry, 1960, 23: 393-406.

331. IL'IN, S. K. *Moral'nyi faktor v sovremennoi voine* (The moral factor in modern warfare). Moscow: Boeh, 1967. 125 pp. The structure of morale in the Soviet army.

332. JOSEPHSON, E. "Irrational Leadership in Formal Organizations." Social Forces, 1952, 31: 109-117.

333. KIPNIS, DOROTHY. "Interaction between Members of Bomber Crews as a Determinant of Sociometric Choice." Human Relations, 1957, 10: 263-270.

334. KORPI, W. "A Note on the Ability of Military Leaders to Assess Opinions in their Units." Acta Sociologica, 1965, 8: 293-303.

335. LOETHER, H. J. "Propinquity and Homogeneity as Factors in the Choice of Best Buddies in the Air Force." Pacific Sociological R., 1960, 3: 18-22.

336. MARKS, A. "A Factor Analytic Study of Military Leadership." Dissertation Abstracts, 1959, 20: 1452-1458.

337. MEDALIA, N. Z. "Authoritarianism, Leader Acceptance, and Group Cohesion." J. of Abnormal and Social Psychology, 1955, 51: 207-213.

338. MEDALIA, N. Z. "Unit Size and Leadership Perception." Sociometry, 1954, 17: 64-67.

339. MESSINEO, A. "Sociologia e diritto di fronte al problema morale della guerra" (Sociology and front command as related to war morale). Civilita Cattolica, Roma, 1964, 4: 433-445.

340. NELSON, P. D., & BERRY, N. H. "Cohesion in Marine Recruit Platoons." J. of Psychology, 1968, 68: 63-71. Performance in basic training.

341. PATERSON, T. T. *Morale in War and Work; an Experiment in the Management of Men.* London: M. Parrish, 1955. 256 pp.

342. ROGHMANN, K., & SODEUR, W. "Führerschaft im Militär" (Leadership in the military). Kölner Zeitschrift für Soziologie und Sozialpsychologie, 1968, 20 (Special Issue 12): 221-238. Authoritarianism and peer cohesion.

343. ROTGER CANAVES, M. "Estructura de los grupos primeros en el ejercito Español" (The structure of primary groups among Spanish military recruits). Revista del Instituto de Ciencias Sociales, 1968-1969, 12-13: 357-376.

344. ROTGER CANAVES, M. "Sociograma de una compania" (Sociogram of a company). Revista del Instituto de Ciencias Sociales, 1968-1969, 12-13: 377-388.

345. SANFORD, F. H. "Research on Military Leadership." In J. C. Flanagan (Ed.) Current Trends: Psychology in a World Emergency. Pittsburgh: University of Pittsburgh Press, 1949. Pp. 17-74. A review of the literature.

346. SELVIN, H. C. The Effects of Leadership. New York: Free Press, 1960. ix + 270 pp. Leadership styles and their effect on off duty behavior of U.S. Army enlisted men.

347. SODEUR, W. "Führungsstile, Spannungen und Spannungsbewältigung in militärischen Gruppen" (Leadership styles, tensions, and the mastery of tension in military groups). Kölner Zeitschrift für Soziologie und Sozialpsychologie, 1968, 20 (Special Issue 12): 300-316.

348. SPECTOR, A. J., CLARK, R. A., & GLICKMAN, A. S. "Supervisory Characteristics and Attitudes of Subordinates." Personnel Psychology, 1960, 13: 301-316.

349. WALDMAN, E. The Goose Step Is Verboten; the German Army Today. New York: Free Press, 1964. xi + 294 pp. Also published in German as Soldat im Staat. Boppard am Rhein: H. Boldt, 1963. 294 pp. Evaluation of new forms of indoctrination and leadership.

350. WANG, E. Huai-chun Chih (On the army of the Huai). Academy Sinica (Institute of Modern History, Taipei), 1967, No. 22. 456 pp. Organization, training, morale, and background of leaders.

351. WHERRY, R. H., & FRYER, D. "Buddy Ratings: Popularity Contest or Leadership Criteria? " Personnel Psychology, 1949, 2: 147-159.

352. ZELENY, L. D. "Selection of Compatible Flying Partners." American J. of Sociology, 1947, 52: 424-431.

353. ZENTNER, H. "Morale: Certain Theoretical Implications of Data in The American Soldier." American Sociological R., 1951, 16: 297-307.

5(2) See also III.6(1), III.6(2) and 205, 219, 227, 238, 293, 363, 365, and 473.

5(3)  Assimilation of norms

354. ANONYMOUS. "The Making of the Infantryman." American J. of Sociology, 1946, 51: 376-379. Morale and esprit de corps.

355. BENAD, G. "Die Eingliederung des Einzelnen in soziale Organismen" (Assimilation of the individual into social organisms). Soziale Welt, 1953, 4: 341-346. Military socialization.

356. BLOOM, L. "Militarization as a Research Field." Sociology and Social Research, 1944, 28: 194-199. Socializing influences.

357. BRAMSON, L. "The Armed Forces Examining Station: a Sociological Perspective." In T. Shibutani (Ed.) *Human Nature and Collective Behavior: Papers in Honor of Herbert Blumer.* Englewood Cliffs, N.J.: Prentice-Hall, 1970. Pp. 367-387. Preinduction impact.

358. CAMPBELL, D. T., & McCORMACK, THELMA H. "Military Experience and Attitudes toward Authority." American J. of Sociology, 1957, 62: 482-490. Authoritarianism among officers.

359. CHRISTIE, R. "Changes in Authoritarianism as Related to Situational Factors." American Psychologist, 1952, 7: 307-308. Abstract of *An Experimental Study of Modification in Factors Influencing Recruits' Adjustment to the Army.* Research Center for Human Relations, New York University, 1953 (mimeo). Based on observations before and after six months of infantry training.

360. DEDEK, J. "Implications of the Attitudes of Recruits toward Military Service for Disciplinary Training." In *Current Issues of Military Discipline. Proceedings of the Conference on the Disciplinary Training of Soldiers.* Prague: VPA KG, 1966. Pp. 129-137. In Czech.

361. FRENCH, E. G., & ERNEST, R. R. "The Relationship between Authoritarianism and the Acceptance of Military Ideology." J. of Personality, 1955, 24: 181-191.

362. GAGE, R. W. "Patriotism and Military Discipline as a Function of Degree of Military Training." J. of Social Psychology, 1964, 64 (1): 101-111.

363. HARNQVIST, K. *Adjustment: Leadership and Group Relations in a Military Training Situation.* Stockholm: Almqvist & Wiksell, 1956. 214 pp. Study of Swedish conscripts.

364. JONES, F. E. "The Socialization of the Infantry Recruit." In B. R. Blishen et al. (Eds.) *Canadian Society: Sociological Perspectives.* (3rd Ed.) Toronto: Macmillan of Canada, 1968. Pp. 353-365. Techniques and sanctions employed by officers and noncoms.

365. KORPI, W. *Social Pressures and Attitudes in Military Training.* Stockholm: Almqvist & Wiksell, 1964. 336 pp. Field study of Swedish army conscripts.

366. MARLOWE, D. H. "The Basic Training Process." In K. L. Artiss (Ed.) *The Symptom as Communication in Schizophrenia.* New York: Grune & Stratton, 1959. Pp. 75-98.

367. ROUCEK, J. S. "Social Attitudes of the Soldier in War Time." J. of Abnormal Social Psychology, 1935-1936, 30: 164-174. General observations.

368. SOLOMON, D. N. "Civilian to Soldier: Three Sociological Studies of Infantry Recruit Training." Canadian J. of Psychology, 1954, 8: 87-94.

369. VIDICH, A. J., & STEIN, M. R. "The Dissolved Identity in Military Life." In M. R. Stein, A. J. Vidich, & D. M. White (Eds.) *Identity and Anxiety: Survival of the Person in Mass Society.* New York: Free Press, 1960. Pp. 493-506.

370. ZURCHER, L. A., Jr. "The Naval Recruit Training Center: a Study of Role Assimilation in a Total Institution." Sociological Inquiry, 1967, 37: 85-98.

5(3)  See also II.3.

### 5(4) Integration of multi-ethnic and multi-national forces

371. BERKUN, M., & MEELAND, T. "Sociometric Effects of Race and of Combat Performance." Sociometry, 1958, 21: 145-149. Patterning of choices during the earlier years of racial integration in the U.S. armed forces.

372. BOGART, L. (Ed.) *Social Research and the Desegregation of the U.S. Army.* Chicago: Markham Publishing Co., 1969. vii + 393 pp. Two 1951 field reports on utilization of Negro troops.

373. COHEN, S. P. "The Untouchable Soldier: Caste, Politics, and the Indian Army." J. of Asian Studies, 1969, 28: 453-468. Changes in stratification since independence. See also 110.

374. COX, J. A., & KRUMHOLTZ, J. C. "Racial Bias in Peer Ratings of Basic Airmen." Sociometry, 1958, 21: 292-299.

375. DICKS, H. V. "National Loyalty, Identity, and the International Soldier." International Organization, 1963, 17: 425-443. Lessons learned from morale problems of national armed forces applied to international constabulary. Reprinted in L. P. Bloomfield (Ed.) *International Military Forces; the Question of Peacekeeping in an Armed and Disarmed World.* Boston: Little, Brown, 1964. Pp. 236-256.

376. EVANS, J. C., & LANE, D. A., Jr. "Integration in the Armed Services." A. of the American Academy of Political and Social Science, 1956, 304: 78-85. A chronology of events.

377. HALL, E. T., Jr. "Race Prejudice and Negro-White Relations in the Army." American J. of Sociology, 1947, 52: 401-409.

378. MOSKOS, C. C. "Racial Integration in the Armed Forces." American J. of Sociology, 1966, 72: 132-148. Assignment of Negroes and degree of integration in on duty and off duty behavior.

379. ROSE, A. M. "Army Policies towards Negro Soldiers: a Report on a Success and a Failure." J. of Social Issues, 1947, 3 (4): 26-31.

380. STAR, SHIRLEY, WILLIAMS, R. M., Jr., & STOUFFER, S. A. "Negro Infantry Platoons in White Companies." In E. E. Maccoby, T. M. Newcomb, & E. L. Hartley (Eds.) *Readings in Social Psychology.* (3rd Ed.) New York: Holt, 1958. Pp. 596-601. Evaluation of an early field experiment in racial integration.

381a. STILLMAN, R. J., II. *Integration of the Negro in the U.S. Armed Forces.* New York: Praeger, 1968. 167 pp.

381b. STILLMAN, R. "Negroes in the Armed Forces." Phylon, 1969, 30: 139-159. Further advancement of integration remains limited by prevailing social structure.

382. TALBERT, R. H. "Race Relations in the United States Army: an Example of Integration." Social Forces, 1950, 28: 317-322.

383. WEIL, F. E. G. "The Negro in the Armed Forces." Social Forces, 1947, 26: 95-98.

5(4) See also 192, 569, 585, 1320, and 1321.

5(5) Subcultural accommodations

384. ANONYMOUS. "Informal Social Organization in the Army." American J. of Sociology, 1946, 51: 365-370.

385. BERGER, M. "Law and Custom in the Army." Social Forces, 1946, 25: 82-87.

386. BERKMAN, P. L. "Life Aboard an Armed-Guard Ship." American J. of Sociology, 1946, 51: 380-387.

387. BIDWELL, C. E. "The Young Professional in the Army: a Study of Occupational Identity." American Sociological R., 1961, 26: 360-372. Experiences of peacetime draftees.

388. CAPLOW, T. "Rumors in War." Social Forces, 1947, 25: 298-302. Participant observation in the U.S. armed forces.

389. COHEN, G. B. "De Militaire Parade." Mens en Maatschappij, 1956, 31: 282-288. The world of existence (levenswereld) of the military organization considered phenomenologically by reference to the military parade.

390. DANIELS, ARLENE K. "The Social Construction of Military Psychiatric Diagnoses." In H. Dreitzel (Ed.) Patterns of Communicative Behavior. New York: Macmillan, 1970. Pp. 181-205.

391. ELKIN, F. "The Soldier's Language." American J. of Sociology, 1946, 51: 414-422.

392. ELKIN, H. "Aggressive and Erotic Tendencies in Army Life." American J. of Sociology, 1946, 51: 408-413.

393. LINTON, R. "Totemism and the A.E.F." American Anthropologist, 1924, 26: 296-300.

394. MULLAN, H. "The Regular-Service Myth." American J. of Sociology, 1948, 53: 276-281.

395. ROOS, P. D. "Jurisdiction: an Ecological Concept." Human Relations, 1968, 21: 75-84. Spatial and social relations on a U.S. Navy ship.

396. SCHNEIDER, D. M. "The Culture of the Army Clerk." Psychiatry, 1946, 9: 123-129.

397. UYEKI, E. S. "Draftee Behavior in the Cold-War Army." Social Problems, 1960, 8: 151-158. Participant observation.

398. ZURCHER, L. A., Jr. "The Sailor Aboard Ship: a Study of Role Behavior in a Total Institution." Social Forces, 1965, 43: 389-399.

5(5) See also 208, 429, and 433.

### III.6. Organizational effectiveness (also 120)

#### 6(1) Group factors in unit performance

399. ADAMS, S. "Effect of Equalitarian Atmospheres upon the Performance of Bomber Crews." American Psychologist, 1952, 7: 398.

400. ADAMS, S. "Social Climate and Productivity in Small Military Groups." American Sociological R., 1954, 19: 421-425. Equalitarianism and bomber crew effectiveness.

401. ADAMS, S. "Status Congruity as a Variable in Small Group Performance." Social Forces, 1953, 32: 16-22.

402. AMIR, Y. "The Effectiveness of the Kibbutz-Born Soldier in the Israel Defence Forces." Human Relations, 1969, 22: 333-344. Group cohesion and national service.

403. BERKOWITZ, L. "Group Norms among Bomber Crews: Patterns of Perceived Crew Attitudes, 'Actual' Crew Attitudes, and Crew Liking Related to Air Crew Effectiveness in Far Eastern Combat." Sociometry, 1956, 19: 141-153.

404. BOWERS, R. V. "Members' Perceptions and Evaluations as Measures of Organizational Effectiveness." In R. V. Bowers (Ed.) Studies in Organizational Effectiveness. Washington, D.C.: Air Force Office of Scientific Research, 1962. Pp. 115-179.

405. BOWERS, R. V. (Ed.) Studies in Organizational Effectiveness; Contributions to Military Sociology from the 1949-1954 Contract Research Program of the Human Resources Research Institute, Air University. Washington, D.C.: Air Force Office of Scientific Research, Office of Aerospace Research, 1962 (mimeo). ix + 326 pp. Includes studies of various air force organizations by A. F. Henry, E. F. Borgatta, S. A. Stouffer; E. K. Karcher, Jr.; D. C. Miller, N. Z. Medalia, G. C. McCann; R. V. Bower et al.; and H. Baumgarten, F. C. Mann.

406. CLARK, R. A. Analyzing the Group Structure of Combat Rifle Squads. American Psychologist, 1953, 8: 333. Précis of a HumRRO report.

407. FIEDLER, F. E. "The Influence of Leader-Keyman Relations on Combat Crew Effectiveness." J. of Abnormal and Social Psychology, 1955, 51: 227-235.

408. GETZELS, J. W., & GUBA, E. G. "Role and Role Conflict and Effectiveness: an Empirical Study." American Sociological R., 1954, 19: 164-175.

409. GOODACRE, D. M. "Group Characteristics of Good and Poor Performing Combat Units." Sociometry, 1953, 16: 168-179.

410. GOODACRE, D. M. "The Use of a Sociometric Test as a Predictor of Combat Unit Effectiveness." Sociometry, 1951, 14: 148-153.

411. HALPIN, A. W. "The Leader Behavior and Effectiveness of Aircraft Commanders." In R. M. Stogdill & A. Coons (Eds.) Leader Behavior: its Description and Measurement. Columbus: Bureau of Business Research, Ohio State University, No. 88, 1957. Pp. 65-68.

412. HALPIN, A. W. "The Leadership Behavior and Combat Performance of Airplane Commanders." J. of Abnormal Social Psychology, 1954, 49: 19-22.

413. HAVRON, M. D., & McGRATH, J. E. "The Contributions of the Leader to the Effectiveness of Small Military Groups." In L. Petrullo & B. M. Bass (Eds.) Leadership and Interpersonal Behavior. New York: Holt, Rinehart & Winston, 1961. Pp. 167-178.

414. JENKINS, W. O. "A Review of Leadership Studies with Particular Reference to Military Problems." Psychological B., 1947, 44: 54-79. Comment by D. E. BAIER. Note on "Review of Leadership Studies with Particular Reference to Military Problems." Ibid., pp. 466-467.

415. KARCHER, E. K., Jr. "Role Ambiguity as a Factor in Organizational Effectiveness." In R. V. Bowers (Ed.) Studies in Organizational Effectiveness; Contributions to Military Sociology from the 1949-1954 Contract Research Program of the Human Resources Research Institute, Air University. Washington, D.C.: Air Force Office of Scientific Research, Office of Aerospace Research, 1962. Pp. 28-85. Perceptions of the role of the Air Force first sergeant.

416. LANGE, C. J. "Leadership in Small Military Units." In F. A. Geldard (Ed.) Defence Psychology. New York: Pergamon Press, 1962. Pp. 286-299. Platoon leaders' behavior related to performance and morale in training situation.

417. LOFLAND, J. "Priority Inversion in an Army Reserve Company." Berkeley J. of Sociology, 1964, 9: 1-15.

418. MEDALIA, N. Z., & MILLER, D. C. "Human Relations Leadership and the Association of Morale and Efficiency in Work Groups: a Controlled Study with Small Military Units." Social Forces, 1955, 33: 348-352.

419. MILLER, D. C., & MEDALIA, N. Z. "Leadership and Morale in Small Organizations." Sociological R., 1955, 3 (New Series): 93-107. Effect of human relations-minded leadership on air site efficiency and morale.

420. MILLER, D. C., MEDALIA, N. Z., McCANN, G. C., AND OTHERS. "Morale and Human Relations as Factors in Organizational Effectiveness: an Experimental Study of Data from Fifty Comparable Squadrons." In R. V. Bowers (Ed.) *Studies in Organizational Effectiveness; Contributions to Military Sociology from the 1949-1954 Contract Research Program of the Human Resources Research Institute, Air University.* Washington, D.C.: Air Force Office of Scientific Research, Office of Aerospace Research, 1962. Pp. 86-114.

421. TORRANCE, E. P. "Group Decision-Making and Disagreement." Social Forces, 1957, 35: 314-318. A review of several studies of military groups.

422. WILLIAMS, R. H. "The Military Group." In. R. H. Williams (Ed.) *Human Factors in Military Operations.* Chevy Chase, Md.: Operations Research Office, Johns Hopkins University, 1954. Pp. 351-370.

6(1) See also III.5(2) and 219.

**6(2) Combat motivations**

423. ARDANT du PICQ, C. J. J. J. *Etudes sur le Combat; Combat Antique et Combat Moderne.* (Rev. Ed.) Paris: Chapelot, 1903. xliii + 379 pp. English translation *Battle Studies; Ancient and Modern Battle.* New York: Macmillan, 1921. xxx + 273 pp. Classic observations on leadership and group morale.

424. CHESLER, D. J., VAN STEENBERG, N. J., & BRUECKEL, JOYCE E. "Effect on Morale of Infantry Team Replacement and Individual Replacement System." Sociometry, 1955, 18: 331-341.

425. COLEMAN, J. V. "The Group Factor in Military Psychiatry." American J. of Orthopsychiatry, 1946, 16: 222-225.

426. GEORGE, A. L. *The Chinese Communist Army in Action; the Korean War*

*and its Aftermath.* New York: Columbia University Press, 1967. 255 pp. Techniques for maintaining motivation and effectiveness in combat.

427. GRINKER, R. R., & SPIEGEL, J. W. *Men under Stress.* Philadelphia: Blakiston, 1945. xii + 484 pp. Observations on air combat crews in World War II.

428. HARKABI, Y. "Basic Factors in the Arab Collapse during the Six-Day War." Orbis, 1967, 11: 677-691. Cultural impediments against trust and group loyalties.

429. LITTLE, R. W. "Buddy Relations and Combat Performance." In M. Janowitz (Ed.) *The New Military; Changing Patterns of Organization.* New York: Russell Sage Foundation, 1964. Pp. 195-223. Based on field observations in the Korean War.

430. MANDELBAUM, D. G. *Soldier Groups and Negro Soldiers.* Berkeley & Los Angeles: University of California Press, 1952. viii + 142 pp. Combat effectiveness.

431. MARSHALL, S. L. A. *Men against Fire.* Washington, D.C.: Infantry Journal, 1947. 215 pp. Observations on combat effectiveness of infantry in World War II.

432. MARSHALL, S. L. A. *Sinai Victory.* New York: Morrow, 1958. 280 pp. Account of the basis of Israeli troop morale.

433. PIPPING, K. *Kompaniet som samhälle: iakttagelser i ett finsk front-vörband,* 1941-1944 (Company of soldiers: study of a Finnish combat unit, 1941-1944). Acta Academiae Aboensis Humaniora XVI. 1. Abo Akademi, 1947. 279 pp. English summary in S. B. Sells. *Military Small Group Performance under Isolation and Stress—an Annotated Bibliography.* Arctic Aeromedical Laboratory, Fort Wainwright, Alaska, 1961, 1: 7-9.

434. MOSKOS, C., Jr. Eigeninteresse, Primärgruppen und Ideologie; eine Untersuchung der Kampfmotivation amerikanischer Truppen in Vietnam (Self-interest, primary groups, and ideology; a study of combat motivation among American troops in Viet Nam). Kölner Zeitschrift für Soziologie und Sozialpsychologie, 1968, 20 (Special Issue 12): 199-220.

435. ROSE, A. "Social and Psychological Effects of Physical Deprivation." J. of Health and Human Behavior, 1960, 1: 285-289. Relation of hunger and sleeplessness of combat enlisted men to internalization of norms.

436. SEATON, R. W. "Deterioration of Military Work Groups under Deprivation Stress." In M. Janowitz (Ed.) *The New Military; Changing Patterns of Organization.* New York: Russell Sage Foundation, 1964. Pp. 225-248. Field experiment in Greenland with U.S. military personnel as subjects.

437. SHILS, E. A. "Primary Groups in the American Army." In R. K. Merton and P. F. Lazarsfeld (Eds.) *Continuities in Social Research: Studies in the Scope and Method of The American Soldier.* New York: Free Press, 1950. Pp. 16-39.

438. SHILS, E. A., & JANOWITZ, M. "Cohesion and Disintegration of the Wehrmacht in World War II." Public Opinion Q., 1948, 12: 280-315.

439. WEINSTEIN, E. A. "The Function of Interpersonal Relations in the Neurosis of Combat." Psychiatry, 1947, 10: 307-314.

    6(2)  See also 208, 443, 445, 470, 473, 1146, and 1192.

#### 6(3)  Reactions to stress in training, battle, and captivity

440. BASOWITZ, H., PERSKY, H., KORCHIN, S. J., & GRINKER, R. *Anxiety and Stress.* New York: McGraw-Hill, 1955. xv + 320 pp. Study of troops undergoing airborne training.

441. BIDERMAN, A. D. "Effects of Communist Indoctrination Attempts: Some Comments Based on Air Force Prisoner-of-War Study." Social Problems, 1959, 6: 304-313.

442. BIDERMAN, A. D. *March to Calumny; the Story of American POW's in the Korean War.* New York: Macmillan, 1963. 326 pp.

443. BOURNE, P. G. *Men, Stress, and Vietnam.* Boston, Little, Brown, 1970. xi + 233 pp. Investigation of psychological and endocrinological reactions of Special Forces and helicopter crews, also including observations on group behavior.

444. BOURNE, P. G. "Some Observations on the Psychosocial Phenomena Seen in Basic Training." Psychiatry, 1967, 30: 187-196.

445. BOURNE, P. G., COLI, W. M., & DATEL, W. E. "Affect Levels of Ten Special Forces Soldiers under Threat of Attack." Psychological Reports, 1968, 52: 177-183. Includes participant observation of U.S. combat troops in Vietnam.

446. BOURNE, P. G., & SAN, N. G. "A Comparative Study of Neuropsychiatric Casualties in the United States Army and the Army of the Republic of Vietnam." Military Medicine, 1967, 132: 904-909.

447. COSTE, C. *La psychologie du combat* (The psychology of combat). Nancy: Berger-Levrault, 1928. xxviii + 240 pp.

448. DOLLARD, J. *Fear in Battle.* New York: The Infantry Journal, 1943. vii + 64 pp. Survey of 300 American veterans of the Spanish civil war.

449. GLASS, A. J. "Observations upon the Epidemiology of Mental Illness in Troops during Warfare." In *Symposium on Preventive and Social Psychiatry.* Washington, D.C.: Walter Reed Army Institute of Research, 1957. Pp. 185-197.

450. GLASS, A. J. "Principles of Combat Psychiatry." Military Medicine, 1955, 117: 27-33. Social and situational factors in combat breakdown and organizational responses.

451. GRAMLICH, F. W. "Psychological Study of Stress in Service." J. of General Psychology, 1949, 41: 273-296.

452. GURFEIN, M. I., & JANOWITZ, M. "Trends in Wehrmacht Morale." Public Opinion Q., 1946, 10: 78-84.

453. LIDZ, T. "Psychiatric Casualties from Guadalcanal." Psychiatry, 1946, 9: 193-213.

454. MENNINGER, W. C. *Psychiatry in a Troubled World.* New York: Macmillan, 1948. 636 pp. Contains comprehensive summary on World War II psychiatric studies.

455. MEYERS, S. M., & BIDERMAN, A. D. (Eds.) *Mass Behavior in Battle and Captivity: the Communist Soldier in the Korean War.* Research studies directed by W. C. Bradbury. Chicago: University of Chicago Press, 1968. 416 pp. Interviews in POW camps.

456. MOLL, A. E. Psychosomatic Disease due to Battle Stress. In E. D. Wittkower & R. A. Cleghorn (Eds.) *Recent Developments in Psychiatric Medicine.* Philadelphia: Lippincott, 1954. Pp. 436-454.

457. PETTERA, R. L., JOHNSON, B. M., & ZIMMER, R. "Psychiatric Management of Combat Reactions with Emphasis on a Reaction unique to Vietnam." Military Medicine, 1969, 134: 673-679. A pre-rotation reaction is replacing "combat fatigue."

458. REID, D. D. "Sickness and Stress in Operational Flying." British J. of Social Medicine, 1948, 2: 123-131.

459. ROSE, A. M. "Conscious Reactions Associated with Neuropsychiatric Breakdown in Combat." Psychiatry, 1956, 19: 87-94.

460. ROSE, A. M. "Factors in Mental Breakdown in Combat." In A. M. Rose (Ed.) *Mental Health and Mental Disorder: a Sociological Approach.* New York: W. W. Norton, 1955. Pp. 291-313.

461. ROSE, A. M. "Neuropsychiatric Breakdown in the Garrison Army and in Combat." American Sociological R., 1956, 21: 480-488.

462. ROSE, A. M. "Psychoneurotic Breakdown among Negro Soldiers in Combat." Phylon, 1956, 17: 61-69.

463. ROSE, A. M. "The Social Psychology of Desertion from Combat." American Sociological R., 1951, 16: 614-629. Study of combat AWOLs.

464. SCHEIN, E. H. "Reaction Patterns to Severe, Chronic Stress in American Army Prisoners of War of the Chinese." J. of Social Issues, 1957, 13 (3): 21-30.

465. SCHNEIDER, D. M. "The Social Dynamics of Physical Disability in Army Basic Training." Psychiatry, 1947, 10: 323-333.

466. SCHULTZ, D. P. "Panic in Organized Collectivities." J. of Social Psychology, 1964, 63: 2, 353-359. Flight behavior in military groups.

467. SCHWARTZ, S., & WINOGRAD, B. "Preparation of Soldiers for Atomic Maneuvers." J. of Social Issues, 1954, 10 (3): 42-52.

468. SEGAL, J. "Correlates of Collaboration and Resistance Behavior among U.S. Army POW's in Korea." J. of Social Issues, 1957, 13 (3): 31-40. Based on study by Human Resources Research Office, George Washington University. See *HumRRO Technical Rep.,* 1956, No. 33.

469. SHAFFER, L. W. "Fear and Courage in Aerial Combat." J. of Consulting Psychology, 1947, 11: 137-143.

470. SOBEL, R. "The Old Sergeant Syndrome." Psychiatry, 1947, 10: 315-321. Pattern of breakdown.

471. STAFFORD-CLARK, D. "Morale and Flying Experience: Results of a War-Time Study." J. of Mental Science, 1949, 95: 10-50.

472. STANDISH, A. "Crisis in Courage: I. Fighters and Nonfighters." U.S. Army Combat Forces J., 1952, 2: 13-24 (April), 33-37 (June), 31-34 (July). Based on Fighter I project conducted by the Human Resources Research Office, George Washington University. See *HumRRO Technical Rep.,* 1957, No. 44, and *HumRRO Spec. Rep.,* 1958, No. 13.

473. STOUFFER, S. A. et al. *The American Soldier.* Vol. 2. *Combat and its Aftermath.* Princeton, N.J.: Princeton University Press, 1949. 675 pp. Effectiveness and readjustment.

474. STRASSMAN, H. D., THALER, MARGARET B., & SCHEIN, E. H. "A Prisoner of War Syndrome: Apathy as a Reaction to Severe Stress." American J. of Psychiatry, 1956, 112: 998-1003.

475. TOMPKINS, V. H. "Stress in Aviation." In *The Nature of Stress Disorders; Conference held at the Royal College of Physicians, May 1958.* London: Hutchinson Medical Publications, 1959. Pp. 73-80. Different types of combat missions.

476. TORRANCE, E. P. "The Behavior of Small Groups under the Stress Conditions of 'survival'." American Sociological R., 1954, 19: 751-755. Military survival training.

477. TORRANCE, E. P. "What Happens to the Sociometric Structure of the Small Group in Emergencies and Extreme Conditions." Group Psychotherapy, 1957, 10: 212-220. Includes data based on personal accounts of military subjects as well as simulated conditions and laboratory experiments.

478. VAN MEURS, A. J. *Over de Gevechtsuitputting* (On combat performance). Rotterdam: W. L. & J. Brusse, 1955. 308 pp. An analysis of combat breakdown cases in Korea, with English summary.

479. WEINBERG, S. K. "The Combat Neuroses." American J. of Sociology, 1946, 51: 465-478.

6(3) See also 262, 288, 300, 435, 573, and 1256.

## IV. THE MILITARY SYSTEM: INTERDEPENDENCE OF ARMED FORCES AND SOCIETY (also 43 and 45)

### IV.1. Allocation of roles and missions

#### 1(1) Comparative studies

480. ABDEL-MALEK, A. "Armee und Technokratie in den Ländern der Dritten Welt" (Army and technology in the nations of the third world). Kölner Zeitschrift für Soziologie und Sozialpsychologie, 1968, 20 (Special Issue 12): 89-98.

481. ANDERSON, W. A. "Social Structure and the Role of the Military in National Disaster." Sociology and Social Research, 1969, 53: 242-253. Internal organizational and external societal factors assessed on the basis of observations of five countries.

482. ANDRESKI, S. *Military Organization and Society.* (2nd Ed.) London: Routledge & Kegan Paul, 1968. xviii + 238 pp. Propositions illustrated with historical and contemporary evidence.

483. BELL, M.J.V. *Army and Nation in Sub-Saharan Africa.* Adelphi Papers, No. 21. London: Institute for Strategic Studies, 1965. 16 pp.

484. BELTRAN, V. R. *Las fuerzas armadas como elite modernizante en algunas sociedades en transición del Medio Oriente* (The armed forces as a modernizing elite in some Middle Eastern societies in transition). Dessarollo Económico, 1964, 4: 49-68.

485. BOBROW, D. B. "The Civic Role of the Military: Some Critical Hypotheses." Western Political Q., 1966, 19: 101-111. Reprinted in D. B. Bobrow (Ed.) *Components of Defense Policy.* Chicago: Rand McNally, 1965. Pp. 272-283.

486. BRICE, B., Jr. "The Nature and Role of the Military in Sub-Saharan Africa." African Forum, 1966, 2 (1): 57-67.

487. CAZENEUVE, J. "Société industrielle et société militaire selon Spencer" (Industrial and militant society according to Spencer). Revue Française de Sociologie, 1961, 2 (2): 48-53.

488. CENTRE D'ETUDES DES RELATIONS POLITIQUES, UNIVERSITE DE DIJON. *Le role extra-militaire de l'armeé dans le tiers monde* (The extramilitary role of the army in the third world). Paris: Presses Universitaires de France, 1966. xi + 457 pp. Report edited by L. Hamon on a conference held in 1962.

489. CHANG, D. W. "The Military and Nation-Building in Korea, Burma, and Pakistan." Asian Survey, 1969, 9: 818-830.

490. COLBY, E. "Army." In *Encyclopedia of the Social Sciences.* Vol. 2. New York: Macmillan, 1937. Pp. 210-218. Outline of history of military systems.

491. EWING, L. L., & SELLERS, R. C. (Eds.) *Reference Handbook of the Armed Forces of the World.* Washington, D.C.: R. C. Sellers, 1966. Unpaged.

492. FELD, M. D. "A Typology of Military Organization." In C. J. Friedrich & S. E. Harris (Eds.) *Public Policy; Yearbook of the Graduate School of Public Administration, Harvard University,* Vol. 7, 1958. Pp. 3-40. Stratification and policy base as variables.

493. FOLTZ, W. J. "Military Influences." V. McKay (Ed.), *African Diplomacy.* New York: Praeger, 1966. Pp. 69-89. Characteristics of African armed forces.

494. GUTTERIDGE, W. *Armed Forces in New States.* London: Oxford University Press, 1962. xii + 68 pp. Deals with Africa.

495. GUTTERIDGE, W. "The Place of the Armed Forces in Society in African States." Race, 1962, 4 (1): 22-33.

496. HALPERN, M. "Middle Eastern Armies and the New Middle Class." In J. J. Johnson (Ed.), *The Role of the Military in Underdeveloped Countries.* Princeton, N.J.: Princeton University Press, 1962. Pp. 277-315.

497. HINTZE, O. Staatsverfassung und Heeresverfassung (System of government and armed forces). In *Staat un Verfassung.* (2nd Ed.) Göttingen: Vanderhoek & Ruprecht, 1962. Pp. 52-83. Interdependence of military and political system.

498. HUREWITZ, J. C. "Beginnings of Military Modernization in the Middle East: a Comparative Analysis." Middle East J., 1968, 22: 144-158.

499. LEE, J. M. *African Armies and Civil Order.* London: Chatto & Windus—
New York: Praeger, 1969. Pp. 198. Institute of Strategic Studies' report
on the structure and social composition of African security forces and
their internal tensions.

500. LEVY, M. J., Jr. "Armed Forces Organizations." In *Modernization and
the Structure of Society.* Princeton, N.J.: Princeton University Press,
1966, Vol. 2, pp. 571-605.

501. LOWRY, R. P. "Changing Military Roles: Neglected Challenge to Rural
Sociologists." Rural Sociology, 1965, 30: 219-225. Proposals for research.

502. LOWRY, R. P. "To Arms: Changing Military Roles and the Military
Industrial Complex." Social Problems, 1970, 18: 3-16. Historical comparisons based on functions and consequences of the conduct of war.

503. PICHT, W. "Die Wandlungen des Kämpfers" (The changing character of
the combatant). In *Vom Wesen des Krieges und vom Kriegswesen der
Deutschen.* Stuttgart: Friedrich Vorwerk, 1952. Pp. 119-249. Characteri-
zation of German military systems in terms of evolution of the "warrior"
type into the "soldier" type.

504. RAPOPORT, D. C. "A Comparative Theory of Military and Political
Types." In S. P. Huntington (Ed.) *Changing Patterns of Military Politics.*
New York: Free Press, 1962. Pp. 71-101. Nation-in-arms concept.

505. RAPOPORT, D. C. "Military and Civil Societies: the Contemporary
Significance of a Traditional Subject in Political Theory." Political Studies,
1964, 12: 178-201. Theoretical assumptions underlying different military
systems.

506. RUSSETT, B. M. "Measures of Military Effort." American Behavioral
Scientist, 1964, 7 (6): 26-29. An international comparison.

507. SPENCER, H. *The Principles of Sociology.* Vol. 2. New York: D.
Appleton, 1898. Pp. 568-642. Militant versus industrial societies.

508. VAN DEN BERGHE, P. L. "The Role of the Army in Contemporary
Africa." Africa Report, 1965, 10 (3): 12-17. Reprinted in W. C.
McWilliams (Ed.) *Garrisons and Government; Politics and the Military in
New States.* San Francisco: Chandler Publishing Co., 1967. Pp. 278-287. A
typology.

509. ZHELTOV, A. S. (Ed.) *V. I. Lenin i sovetskie voorozhennye sily* (V. I. Lenin and the soviet armed forces). Moscow: Voenizdat, 1967. 445 pp. Includes discussions of the character and peculiarities of the military in socialist society.

1(1)  See also 643, 647, 648, 836, and 853.

**1(2)  Case studies**

510. ADAMS, R. N. "The Development of the Guatemalan Military." Studies in Comparative International Development, 1969, 4: 91-110.

511. BENOIST-MECHIN, J. G. P. M. *L'Histoire de l'armée allemande, 1918-1946*. 6 vols. Paris: Michel, 1964-1966. Earlier edition translated as *History of the German Army since the Armistice*. Zurich: Scientia, 1939. 2 vols.

512. BERGER, M. *Military Elite and Social Change: Egypt since Napoleon*. Princeton, N.J.: Princeton University Press, 1960. 35 pp.

513. BLUM, I. "Spoleczne role ludowego Wojska Polskiego w latach 1944-1948" (Social role of the Polish Armed Forces, 1944-1948). Kultura i Spoleczenstwo, 1965, 1: 95-108.

514. BOURRICAUD, F. "Los militares: por qué y para qué? " (The military: why and what for? ). Aportes, 1970, 16: 13-55. Characteristics and ideology of Peruvian military as influence on modernizing role.

515. BUCK, J. "The Japanese Self-Defense Forces." Asian Survey, 1967, 7: 597-613.

516. FRIED, M. H. "Military Status in Chinese Society." American J. of Sociology, 1952, 57: 347-357.

517. FUKUSHIMA, S. "Nihon no kindaika to guntai" (The modernization of Japan and the armed forces). Senshû Hôgaku Ronshû, 1966, 1: 32-52.

518. GRIFFITH, S. B., II. *The Chinese People's Liberation Army*. A volume in the series, The United States and China in World Affairs. Published for The Council on Foreign Relations. New York: McGraw-Hill, 1967. ix + 398 pp.

519. GRUE, B. Le rôle sociale de l'armée en Iran (The social role of the army in Iran). Orient, 1962, 6 (24): 49-54.

520. GUTTERIDGE, W. "The Indianisation of the Indian Army 1918-45." Race, 1963, 4 (2): 39-48.

521. HOHN, R. *Die Armee als Erziehungsschule der Nation; das Ende einer Idee* (The armed forces as the school of the nation; the end of an idea). Bad Harzburg: Verlag für Wissenschaft, Wirtschaft und Technik, 1963. xlvii + 590 pp.

522. HUREWITZ, J. C. "The Role of the Military in Society and Government in Israel." In S. N. Fisher (Ed.) *The Military in the Middle East: Problems in Society and Government.* Columbus: State University Press, 1963. Pp. 89-104.

523. KATZENBACH, E. L. "The French Army." Yale R., 1956, 45: 498-513. Post-World War II.

524. KEHR, E. Zur Genesis des Königlich Preussischen Reserveoffizier (On the genesis of the royal Prussian reserve officer). Die Gesellschaft, 1929, 6: 253-274. Reprinted in E. Kehr, *Der Primat der Innenpolitik.* Berlin: Walter de Gruyter, 1965. Pp. 53-63. Instrument for the ideological reconciliation between bourgeoisie and military monarchy.

525. LISSAK, M. "Social Change, Mobilization, and Exchange of Services Between the Military Establishment and Civil Society: the Burmese Case." Economic Development and Cultural Change, 1964, 13: 1-19.

526. MONTEILHET, J. *Les institutions militaires de la France, 1814-1932* (The military institutions of France, 1814-1932). (2nd Ed.) Paris: F. Alcan, 1932. xxiv + 472 pp.

527. MOORE, R. A., Jr. "The Army as a Vehicle for Social Change in Pakistan." J. Developing Areas, 1967, 2: 57-73.

528. MOORE, R. A., Jr. "Use of the Army in Nation-Building: the Case of Pakistan." Asian Survey, 1969, 9: 447-456.

529. REDLICH, F. *The Germany Military Enterpriser and his Work Force.* Wiesbaden: Franz Steiner Verlag, 1964-65. 2 Vols. xv + 532 pp. and viii + 322 pp. His rise and demise between 1350 and 1800.

530. ROGHMANN, K. *Soziologische Analyse von Militär und Gesellschaft in der Bundesrepublik Deutschland* (Sociological analysis of military and society and the Federal Republic of Germany). Bundesministerium für Verteidigung, Schriftenreihe Innere Führung, Wehrsoziologische Studien No. 2, 1967. 64 pp.

531. WIATR, J. J. Kierunki rozwoju socjologii wojska w Polsche (Development trends of the sociology of the army in Poland). Studia Socjologiczno-Polityczne, 1967, 24: 7-16.

532. WIATR, J. "Sozio-politische Besonderheiten und Funktionen von Streit-kräften in sozialistischen Ländern" (Sociopolitical peculiarities and functions of armed forces in the socialist countries). Kölner Zeitschrift für Soziologie und Sozialpsychologie, 1968, 20 (Special Issue 12): 99-121.

533. ZHILIN, P. "The Armed Forces of the Soviet State: Fifty Years of Experience in Military Construction." In J. van Doorn (Ed.) *Military Profession and Military Regimes.* The Hague & Paris: Mouton, 1969. Pp. 157-174.

   1(2)  See also V.2(4) and 684 and 696.

## IV.2.  Military service (also 44)

### 2(1)  Manpower procurement

534. CARMICHAEL, L., & MEAD, L. C. *The Selection of Military Manpower; a Symposium.* Washington, D.C.: National Academy of Sciences–National Science Foundation, 1951. Publ. 209. 269 pp. Deals with selection and classification.

535. CHALLENER, R. D. *The French Theory of the Nation in Arms, 1866-1939.* New York: Columbia University, 1955. 305 pp. Ideological influences on the organization and effectiveness of French forces.

536. CHANDESSAIS, COL. "Observations sur un symposium de psychologie de la defense" (Observations on a symposium on the psychology of defense). Revue Française de Sociologie, 1961, 2 (2): 124-132. For full proceedings see F. A. Geldard (Ed.) *Defense Psychology.* New York: Pergamon Press, 1962. vii + 354 pp.

537. CUNIS, R. "Rekrutierungsmodelle im demokratischen Gesellschaftssystem" (Recruitment models in a democratic social system). Kölner Zeitschrift für Soziologie und Sozialpsychologie, 1968, 20 (Special Issue 12): 122-135.

538. DAVIS, J. W., Jr., & DOLBEARE, K. M. *Little Groups of Neighbors: the Selective Service System.* Chicago: Markham Publishing Co., 1968. xv + 276 pp. Military manpower policy and its implementation.

539. DAVIS, J. W., Jr., & DOLBEARE, K. M. "Selective Service and Military Manpower Procurement: Induction and Deferment Policies in the 1960s." In A. Ranney (Ed.) *Political Science and Public Policy.* Chicago: Markham Publishing Co., 1968. Pp. 83-122. See also 538.

540. DAVIS, J. W., Jr., & DOLBEARE, K. M. "A Social Profile of Local Draft Board Members: the Case of Wisconsin." In R. W. Little (Ed.) *Selective Service and American Society.* New York: Russell Sage Foundation, 1969. Pp. 53-82. See also 538.

541. DEDEK, J. *The Attitudes of Youth Toward Military Service.* Prague: *Politická Správa,* 1966. 198 pp. In Czech.

542. DEUTSCH, K., & WEILENMANN, H. "Die militärische Bewährung eines sozialen Systems: die schweizer Eidgenossenscaft im 14. Jahrundert" (The military worth of a social system: the Swiss Confederation in the 14th century). Kölner Zeitschrift für Soziologie und Sozialpsychologie, 1968, 20 (Special Issue 12): 38-58.

543. EATON, J. W. "National Service and Forced Labor." J. of Conflict Resolution, 1968, 12: 129-134.

544. FOOT, M. R. D. *Men in Uniform: Military Manpower in Modern Industrial Societies.* New York: Praeger, 1961. x + 161 pp. A survey under the auspices of the Institute for Strategic Studies, London.

545. FORD, F. F., & TOLLISON, R. "Notes on the Color of the Volunteer Army." Social Science Q., 1969, 50: 544-547. Forecast of Negro dominated force in the United States.

546. FORWARD, R., & REECE, B. (Eds.) *Conscription in Australia.* Australia: University of Queensland Press, 1968. 284 pp.

547. GALLAGHER, M. P. "Military Manpower: a Case Study." Problems of Communism, 1964, 13 (3): 53-58 & 60-62. Procurement in the Soviet Union.

548. ISAMBERT-JAMATI, VIVIANE. "Remarques sur le service militaire" (Remarks on military service). Revue Française de Sociologie, 1961, 2 (2): 100-105. Attitudes and reactions among French youth.

549. KREIDBERG, COL. M. A., & HENRY, LT. M. G. *History of Military Mobilization in the United States Army: 1775-1945.* Washington, D.C.: Department of the Army, 1955. 721 pp. Treatment of manpower aspects of military mobilization.

550. LITTLE, R. W. (Ed.) *Selective Service and American Society.* New York: Russell Sage Foundation, 1969. xvi + 220 pp. With an introductory essay "Procurement of Manpower: an Institutional Analysis" and a conclusion by the editor.

551. MILLIS, W. *Arms and men: a Study in American Military History.* New York: G. P. Putnam's Sons, 1956. 382 pp.

552. MOSKOS, C. C., Jr. "The Negro and the Draft." In R. W. Little (Ed.) *Selective Service and American Society.* New York: Russell Sage Foundation, 1969. Pp. 139-162.

553. NEWTON, I. G. "Negro and the National Guard." Phylon, 1962, 23: 18-28.

554. NORMAN, E. H. *Soldier and Peasant in Japan; the Origins of Conscription.* New York: Institute of Pacific Relations, 1943. xiv + 76 pp.

555. PALMER, J. McA. *America in Arms: the Experience of the U.S. with Military Organization.* New Haven: Yale University, 1941. 215 pp. Critical history of manpower policies.

556. PALMER, R. R., WILEY, B. I., & KEAST, M. R. "The Procurement and Training of Ground Combat Troops." In *U.S. Army in World War II.* Washington, D.C.: Historical Division, Department of Army, 1948. xi + 696 pp.

557. ROGGEN, I. Soldats-citoyens et citoyens-miliciens (Soldier citizens and citizen soldiers). Res Publica, 1965, 7: 231-253.

558. SMITH, R. J., & RAMSEY, C. E. "Attitudes of Japanese High School Seniors toward the Military." Public Opinion Q., 1962, 26: 249-253. Occupational prestige of an officer career.

559. SUCHMAN, E. A., WILLIAMS, R. M., & GOLDSEN, ROSE K. "Student Reaction to Impending Military Service." American Sociological R., 1953, 18: 293-304.

560. TAX, S. (Ed.) *The Draft; a Handbook of Facts and Alternatives.* Chicago & London: University of Chicago Press, 1967. xiii + 497 pp. Report of a conference, including papers, held at the University of Chicago, Dec. 4-7, 1966.

561. WAMSLEY, G. L. Decision-Making in Local Boards: a Case Study. In R. W. Little (Ed.) *Selective Service and American Society.* New York: Russell Sage Foundation, 1969. Pp. 83-108. Activities of U.S. draft boards. See also 562.

562. WAMSLEY, G. L. *Selective Service and a Changing America.* Columbus:

Charles E. Merrill, 1969. ix + 295 pp. A study of the institution in its environment.

2(1) See also 110, 118, and 271.

### 2(2) Patterns of utilization and performance

563. BAIER, D. E. "The Marginally Useful Soldier." American J. of Mental Deficiency, 1943, 48: 62-66. Utilization and performance.

564. BERRY, N. H., & NELSON, P. D. "The Fate of School Dropouts in the Marine Corps." Personnel Guidance J., 1966, 45: 20-23.

565. BIDERMAN, A. D. "What is Military? " In S. Tax (Ed.) The Draft; Handbook of Facts and Alternatives. Chicago: University of Chicago Press, 1967. Pp. 122-137. Positions in which civil-military disparities in occupational activities are greatest.

566. BIDERMAN, A. D., & SHARP, LAURE M. " The Convergence of Military and Civilian Occupational Structures: Evidence from Studies of Military Retired Employment." American J. of Sociology, 1968, 73: 381-399.

567. DAILEY, J. T. "Prediction of First-Cruise Reenlistment Rate." Operations Research, 1958, 6: 686-692.

568. DRESSLER, D. "Men on Parole as Soldiers in World War II." Social Service R., 1946, 20: 537-550.

569. DWYER, R. J. "The Negro in the United States Army: his Changing Role and Status." Sociology and Social Research, 1953, 38: 103-112.

570. FOX, V. "A Study of the Promotion of Enlisted Men in the Army." J. of Applied Psychology, 1947, 31: 298-305.

571. GINZBERG, E. "The Occupational Adjustment of 1000 Selectees." American Sociological R., 1943, 8: 256-263.

572. GINZBERG, E., & BRAY, D. W. The Uneducated. New York: Columbia University Press, 1953. 246 pp. Effectiveness of an educational program in making this group acceptable for military service.

573. GINZBERG, E., et al. The Ineffective Soldier; Lessons for Management and the Nation. 3 vols. New York: Columbia University Press, 1959. Vol. 1: The Lost Divisions. xx + 225 pp. Vol. 2: Breakdown and Recovery. xvii + 284 pp. Vol. 3: Patterns of Performance. xix + 340 pp.

574. GUNDERSON, E. K., & NELSON, P. D. "Socio-economic Status and Navy Occupations." Personnel Guidance J., 1965, 44: 263-266.

575. HADLEY, E. E., et al. "An Experiment in Military Selection." Psychiatry, 1942, 5: 371-402.

576. HASTIE, W. H. "The Negro in the Army Today." A. of the American Academy of Political and Social Science, 1942, 223: 55-59.

577. HUNT, W. A., WITTSON, C. L., & HUNT, E. B. "The Serviceability of Military Personnel of Low Intelligence." J. of Clinical Psychology, 1954, 10: 286-288.

578. KARPINOS, B. D. "Fitness of American Youth for Military Service." Milbank Memorial Fund Q., 1960, 38: 213-247.

579. KOCHS, S. C., & IRLE, K. W. "Prophesying Army Promotion." J. of Applied Psychology, 1920, 4: 73-87.

580. LANG, K. " 'Career-Management': Formen organisatorischer Anpassung an den technischen Wandel in den amerikanischen Streitkräften" (Career management: Forms of organizational adaptation to technological change in the U.S. armed forces). Kölner Zeitschrift für Soziologie und Sozialpsychologie, 1968, 20 (Special Issue 12): 157-186.

581. LANG, K. "Technology and Career Management in the Military Establishment." In M. Janowitz (Ed.) The New Military; Changing Patterns of Organization. New York: Russell Sage Foundation, 1964. Pp. 39-81. Impact of new skill requirements on U.S. armed forces.

582. MAYER, A. J., & HOULT, T. E. "Social Stratification and Combat Survival." Social Forces, 1955, 34: 155-159.

583. MONTMOLLIN, M. de "Le niveau intellectuel des recrues du contingent" (The intellectual level of new draftees). Population, 1958, 13: 259-268.

584. MONTMOLLIN, M. de "Le niveau intellectuel des recrues du contingent: répartition géographique pour certaines professions" (The intellectual level of new draftees: regional and professional breakdown). Population, 1959, 14: 233-252.

585. MUELLER, W. R. "The Negro in the Navy." Social Forces, 1945, 24: 110-115.

586. OWENS, A. G. "Job Satisfaction and Re-Engagement Among Australian Regular Army Soldiers." Australian J. of Psychology, 1969, 21: 137-144.

587. RYAN, F. J. *Relation of Performance to Social Background Factors among Army Inductees.* Washington, D.C.: Catholic University of America Press, 1958. 124 pp.

588. SOKOLOV, P. V. *Voɪnai liudskie resursy* (The war and manpower resources). Moscow: Boeh, 1961. 187 pp.

589. U.S. PRESIDENT'S COMMISSION ON VETERANS PENSIONS. *Veterans' Benefits in the United States.* Washington, D.C.: U.S. G.P.O., 1956. Appendix 4. Conditions of military service in the United States since the Civil War, including occupational structure and battle deaths.

590. VERNON, P. E., & PARRY, J. H. *Personnel Selection in the British Forces.* London: University of London Press, 1949. 324 pp. Includes data on occupational structure.

591. VIMONT, C., & BAUDOT, J. "Les causes d'inaptitude au service militaire" (Causes for disqualification from military service). Population, 1964, 19: 55-78.

592. VIMONT, C., & BAUDOT, J. "Etude des caractéristiques sanitaires et sociales des jeunes du contingent" (A study of the health and social characteristics of young military draftees). Population, 1963, 18: 499-530.

593. VLEUGEL, E. S. van der. *Begaafdheidsonderzoek en intelligentiespreiding: methoden en uitkomsten van het med. en psycholog. onderzoek bij de Keuring voor de militaire dienstplicht* (Aptitude studies and intelligence testing: methods and results of the medical and psychological investigations by Keuring prior to compulsory military service). Utrecht: Demologisch Instituut, 1951. iv + 79 pp.

594. WOOL, H. "Military and Civilian Occupational Structures." Monthly Labor R., 1966, 88: 29-33. Comparisons of historical trends and current structures.

595. WOOL, H. *The Military Specialist; Skilled Manpower for the Armed Forces.* Baltimore: Johns Hopkins University Press, 1968. xiii + 216 pp.

2(2) See also II.3 and 226, 231, 373, 378, and 379.

### IV.3. Social and political impact of military activities

596. BELTRAN, V. R. "Estrategia, armes y cambio social en América latina" (Strategy, arms, and social change in Latin America). Mundo nuevo, 1968, No. 28: 13-26. The military as modernizing agent.

597. BIDERMAN, A. D. "The Prospective Impact of Large-Scale Military Retirement." Social Problems, 1959, 7: 84-90. In the United States.

598. BIDERMAN, A. D. "Relationships between Active Duty and Post-Retirement Careers." In N. A. B. Wilson (Ed.) *Manpower research.* London: English Universities Press, 1969. Pp. 426-441. "Second careers" of officers and enlisted men.

599. BOBROW, D. B. "Soldiers and the Nation-State." A. of the American Academy of Political and Social Science, 1965, 358: 65-76. How to measure the inputs of the military into political development.

600. BRANDT, G. "Diverging Functions of Military Armament: the Case of the Federal Republic of Germany." In J. van Doorn (Ed.) *Armed Forces and Society.* The Hague & Paris: Mouton, 1968. Pp. 185-201.

601. BRANDT, G. "Socio-Economic Aspects of German Rearmament." Archives Européennes de Sociologie, 1965, 6: 294-308. See also 600.

602. CONGRESSIONAL QUARTERLY. "The Military-Industrial Complex; a Problem for the Secretary of Defence." Congressional Q. Weekly Report, May 24, 1968 (Special Report No. 21). Pp. 1155-1178.

603. COOK, F. J. *The Warfare State.* New York: Macmillan, 1962. viii + 376 pp. Develops the thesis that the "military-industrial complex" affects virtually all major institutions and associations in the United States.

604. DARLING, F. C. "The Impact of American Military Aid on Political Systems in Asia." Rocky Mountain Social Science J., 1963, 1: 20-30.

605. DRAPER, JEAN A., STROTHER, G. B., & GARRETT, DORIS E. "The Effect of Training and Previous Experience on the Employment of Military Retirees." J. of Gerontology, 1963, 18: 71-79.

606. FERGUSON, T., & CUNNISON, J. "The Impact of National Service." British J. of Sociology, 1959, 10: 283-290.

607. FRIED, M. H. "Warfare, Military Organization, and the Evolution of Society." Anthropologica, 1961, 3: 134-147. Its relation to stratification and the state.

608. HACKETT, R. F. "The Military; Japan." In R. E. Ward & D. A. Rustow (Eds.) *Political Modernization in Japan and Turkey.* Princeton, N.J.: Princeton University Press, 1964. Pp. 328-351. Impact of military service and professionalization on political development.

609. IANNI, O. Los Estados Unidos y el militarismo latinoamericano (The United States and Latin American militarism). Revista Mexicana de Sociologia, 1968, 30: 511-524. Impact of assistance on internal politics and the role of the armed forces.

610. JANOWITZ, M. "American Democracy and Military Service." Transaction, 1967, 4 (4): 5-11, 57-59. Implications of manpower procurement policies.

611. KATENBRINK, I. G., Jr. "Military Service and Occupational Mobility." In R. W. Little (Ed.) Selective Service and American Society. New York: Russell Sage Foundation, 1969. Pp. 163-190.

612. KERSTING, A. "Der Einfluss des Kriegswesens auf die Gesamtkultur" (The influence of military affairs on the total culture). In P. Hinneberg (Ed.) Kultur der Gegenwart. Part 4, Vol. 12. Technik des Kriegswesens edited by M. Schwarte. Berlin & Leipzig: B. G. Teubner, 1913. Pp. 774-871.

613. KLINGEMANN, H. "Wirtschaftliche und soziale Probleme der Auf- und Abrüstung. Volkswirtschaftliche Konsequenzen der Rüstung in der Bundesrepublik Deutschland" (Economic and social problems of armament and disarmament; the economic problems of defense in the Federal Republic of Germany). Kölner Zeitschrift für Soziologie und Sozialpsychologie, 20 (Special Issue 12): 239-269.

614. LERNER, D., & ROBINSON, R. D. "Swords and Ploughshares: the Turkish Army as a Modernizing Force." World Politics, 1960, 13: 19-44.

615. LITTLE, R. W. "Basic Education and Youth Socialization in the Armed Forces." American J. of Orthopsychiatry, 1968, 38: 869-876.

616. McNEIL, J. S., & GIFFEN, M. B. "Social Impact of Military Retirement." Social Casework, 1965, 46: 203-207. Job market experiences.

617. MARANTZ, M. "Dépenses d'armaments et économie nationale" (Armaments expenditures and the national economy). Revue Française de Sociologie, 1961, 2 (2): 54-65.

618. MERTON, R. K. "Science and Military Technique." Scientific Monthly. Dec. 1935: 542-545. Military problems influenced the direction of scientific inquiry in 17th century England.

619. PATTEN, T. H., Jr. "Social Class and the 'old soldier'." Social Problems, 1960, 8: 263-271.

620. PIRES PINTO, O. "El proceso de aculturacion del hijo del immigrante en las fuerzas armadas Brasileñas" (The process of acculturation of the immigrant son in the Brazilian armed forces). Revista Mexicana de Sociologia, 1956, 18: 585-608.

621. POWELL, J. D. "Military assistance and militarism in Latin America." Western Political Q., 1965, 18: 382-392. Comparison of nations wherein military is "always" dominant, "occasionally" dominant, and "never" dominant.

622. PYE, L. W. "Armies in the process of political modernization." Archives Européennes de Sociologie, 1961, 2: 82-92. Reprinted in J. J. Johnson (Ed.) *The Role of the Military in Underdeveloped Countries.* Princeton, N.J.: Princeton University Press, 1962. Pp. 69-90. Military represents modern outlook.

623. RUSTOW, D. A. "The Military; Turkey." In R. E. Ward & D. A. Rustow, *Political Modernization in Japan and Turkey.* Princeton, N.J.: Princeton University Press, 1964. Pp. 352-388.

624. SCHLEH, E. P. A. "Post-War Careers of Ex-Servicemen in Ghana and Uganda." J. of Modern African Studies, 1968, 6: 203-220.

625. SHARPE, LAURE M., & BIDERMAN, A. D. "Out of Uniform: the Employment Experience of Retired Servicemen Who Seek a Second Career." Monthly Labor R., 1967, 90: 15-21.

626. SOMBART, W. *Studien zur Entwicklungsgeschichte des modernen Kapitalismus.* Vol. 2. *Krieg und Kapitalismus* (War and capitalism). Munich & Leipzig: Duncker & Humblot, 1913. viii + 232 pp. Expansionist tendency of modern army and growing standardization as impetus toward capitalist production.

627. SPENCER, D. L. "On External Military Presence, Technological Transfer, and Structural Change." Kyklos, 1965, 18: 451-473.

628. SUBUR, R. "The Organizational Role of the Military in the Modernization-Process." Mens en Maatschappij, 1966, 41: 310-328. Indonesia.

629. TRAPHAGEN, W. "Militärdienst und Volkserziehung" (Military service and public education) Soziale Welt, 1953, 4: 346-356.

630. VAERTING, M. T. "Soziologische und tiefensoziologische Ursachen der Expansions des Militärs" (Sociological and depth sociological causes for

the expansion of the military). Zeitschrift für die gesamte Staatswissenschaft, 1962, 9 (3): 16-18.

631. VAN DOORN, J. A. A. "Enkele sociologische en sociaal-psychologische functies van de militaire training" (Some social and social psychological functions of military training). Mens en Maatschappij, 1954, 29: 278-292.

632. VILMAR, F. *Rüstung und Abrüstung im Spätkapitalismus; eine sozioökonomische Analyse des Militarismus in unserer Gesellschaft* (Armament and Disarmament in late capitalism; a socioeconomic analysis of militarism in our society). (3rd Ed.) Frankfurt/Main: Europaische Verlagsanstalt, 1967. 401 pp. The bearing of economic, social, and political factors on the level of military expenditures.

633. VOGT, E. *Navaho Veterans; a Study of Changing Values.* Cambridge, Mass.: Peabody Museum, 1951. xix + 223 pp.

634. VON FRIEDEBURG, L. Rearmament and Social Change: Observations on Civil-Military Relations in Western Germany. In J. Van Doorn (Ed.) *Armed Forces and Society.* The Hague & Paris: Mouton, 1968. Pp. 171-184.

635. WINDLE, E., & VALLANCE, T. R. "Optimizing Military Assistance Training." World Politics, 1962, 15: 91-107. U.S. Military Aid program as a potential modernizing force.

636. WOLF, C. "The Political Effects of Military Programs; Some Indications from Latin America." Orbis, 1965, 8: 871-893.

637. WOOL, H. "The Armed Services as a Training Institution." In E. Ginzberg (Ed.) *The Nation's Children.* Vol. 2. New York: Columbia University Press, 1959. Pp. 158-185. Value of service schools for future civilian occupations.

IV.3  See also VI.3 and 109, 129, 133, 663, 664, and 1053.

## V. CIVIL-MILITARY RELATIONS (also 42, 54, 58, 61, and 62)

### V.1. Civil-military polities

638. ARON, R. La mitraillette, le char d'assaut et l'idée (Machine gun, tank, and idea). Archives Européennes de Sociologie, 1961, 2: 92-111. Military versus civil power in old and new states.

639. BORRERO, F. L. Problemas de politica militar: la estructura social y las posibilidades orgánicas (Problems of military politics: social structure and its organic potentialities). Revista de Estudios Politicos, 1957, 95: 39-70.

640. COLES, H. L. (Ed.) *Total War and Cold War: Problems in Civilian Control of the Military.* Columbus: Ohio State University Press, 1962. xii + 300 pp. Papers read at a conference on civil-military relations held under the auspices of the Mershon National Security Program on Feb. 27-28, 1959. Papers deals with the Allied and Nazi high command in American government since 1900, and generals and party leaders in communist states.

641. DAALDER, H. *The Role of the Military in the Emerging Countries.* Publications of the Institute of Social Studies, Series Minor Vol. 1. 's Gravenhage: Mouton, 1962. 25 pp.

642. DOWSE, R. E. "The Military and Political Development." In C. Leys (Ed.) *Politics and Change in Developing Countries: Studies in the Theory and Practice of Development.* Cambridge: Cambridge University Press, 1969. Pp. 213-246. An analysis based on Nigeria and Ghana.

643. DUPREE, L. "Democracy and the Military Base of Power." Middle East J., 1968, 22: 29-44. Six phase model of transition from tribal nation or colony to representative government.

644. FELDBERG, ROSLYN L. "Political Systems and the Role of the Military." Sociological Q., 1970, 2: 206-218.

645. FISHER, S. N. (Ed.) *The Military in the Middle East: Problems in Society and Government.* Columbus: Ohio University Press, 1963. 138 pp. Case studies of Turkey, Iraq, Syria, Egypt, and Israel with several general essays on the role of the military in the Near East and in emerging nations.

646. FOX, W. T. R. "Civil-Military Relations Research: the SSRC Committee and its Research Survey." World Politics, 1954, 6: 278-288.

647. GUTTERIDGE, W. F. *The Military in African Politics.* London: Methuen—New York: Barnes & Noble, 1969. vii + 166 pp.

648. GUTTERIDGE, W. F. *Military Institutions and Power in the New States.* New York: Praeger, 1965. viii + 182 pp.

649. HOOPES, T. "Civilian Military Balance." Yale R., 1954, 93: 218-234.

650. HOPKINS, K. "Civil-Military Relations in Developing Countries." British J. of Sociology, 1966, 17: 165-182. A world perspective.

651. HOWARD, M. "Civil-Military Relations in Europe and the United States: a Bibliographical Note." Archives Européennes de Sociologie, 1961, 2: 112-116.

652. HOWARD, M. "Civil-Military Relations in Great Britain and the U.S., 1945-1958." Political Science Q., 1960, 75: 35-46.

653. HOWARD, M. "Introduction: the Armed Forces as a Political Problem." In M. Howard (Ed.) *Soldiers and Governments: Nine Studies in Civil-Military Relations.* Bloomington, Indiana: Indiana University Press, 1962. Pp. 9-24.

654. HOWARD, M. (Ed.) *Soldiers and Governments: Nine Studies in Civil-Military Relations.* Bloomington, Indiana: Indiana University Press, 1962. 192 pp. Historical studies of several European nations, United States, Japan, and Latin America.

655. HUNTINGTON, S. P. "Civil-Military Relations." In *International Encyclopedia of the Social Sciences.* Vol. 2. New York: Macmillan & Free Press, 1968. Pp. 487-494.

656. HUNTINGTON, S. P. "The New Military Politics." In S. P. Huntington (Ed.) *Changing Patterns of Military Politics.* New York: Free Press, 1962. Pp. 13-16.

657. HUNTINGTON, S. P. *The Soldier and the State; the Theory and Politics of Civil-Military Relations.* Cambridge, Mass.: Harvard University Press, 1957. xiii + 534 pp. Emergence of professionalism in Western Europe and the United States.

658. JANOWITZ, M. "Military Elites and the Study of War." J. of Conflict Resolution, 1957, 1: 9-18. Emerging patterns of civil-military relations.

659. JANOWITZ, M. "The Military in the Political Development of New Nations." B. of the Atomic Scientists, 1964, 20: 6-10. Reprinted in W. C. McWilliams (Ed.) *Garrisons and Government; Politics and the Military in New States.* San Francisco: Chandler Publishing Co., 1967. Pp. 67-79. See also 660.

660. JANOWITZ, M. *The Military in the Political Development of New Nations: an Essay in Comparative Analysis.* Chicago: University of Chicago Press, 1964. vii + 134 pp. Role of the military in 51 new nations of Africa and Asia classified into 5 types of civil-military relations and related to internal organization and external conditions.

661. JOHNSON, J. J. (Ed.) *The Role of the Military in Underdeveloped Countries.* Princeton, N.J.: Princeton University Press, 1962. viii + 427 pp. Contains general essays by E. A. Shils and L. W. Pye and area studies by a variety of contributors.

662. KOSSOK, M. "Zur Politischen Funktion der Armee in Lateinamerika" (On the political function of the armed forces in Latin America). Zeitschrift für Militärgeschichte, 1968, 2: 149-166. Role vis-à-vis liberation movements.

663. LASSWELL, H. D. "The Garrison State." American J. of Sociology, 1941, 46: 455-468. Developmental model of growing role of military in governing elite.

664. LASSWELL, H. D. "The Garrison State Hypothesis Today." In S. P. Huntington (Ed.) *Changing Patterns of Military Politics.* New York: Free Press, 1962. Pp. 51-70.

665. LISSAK, M. "Modernization and Role Expansion of the Military in Developing Countries." Comparative Studies in Society and History, 1967, 9: 233-255.

666. McALISTER, L. N. "Changing Concepts of the Role of the Military in Latin America." A. of the American Academy of Political and Social Science, 1965, 360: 85-98. A review article.

667. McALISTER, L. N. "Civil-Military Relations in Latin America." J. of Inter-American Studies, 1961, 3: 341-350. A plea for comparative study.

668. McWILLIAMS, W. C. (Ed.) *Garrisons and Government: Politics and the Military in New States.* San Francisco: Chandler Publishing Co., 1967. ix + 340 pp. Previously published essays together with an introduction (pp. 1-41) by the editor.

669. PERLMUTTER, A. "The Praetorian State and the Praetorian Army: toward a Taxonomy of Civil-Military Relations in Developing Polities." Comparative Politics, 1969, 1: 382-404.

670. RALSTON, D. B. (ed.) *Soldiers and States; Civil-Military Relations in Modern Europe.* Boston: Heath, 1966. x + 218 pp. Readings on the dynastic state, the national state, and the age of totalitarianism.

671. RIDDLEBERGER, P. B. *Military Roles in Developing Countries: an Inventory of Past Research and Analysis.* Washington, D.C.: Special Operations Research Office, American University, 1965. v + 182 pp.

672. RONNEBERGER, F. "Militärdiktaturen in den Entwicklungsländern; ein Beitrag zur politischen Formenlehre" (Military dictatorships in developing countries; a contribution to political morphology). Jahrbuch für Sozialwissenschaft, 1965, 16: 13-49. Uniformity and diversity in the development of new nations.

673. ROUQUIE, A. Le rôle politique des forces armées en Amerique Latine; états des travaux (The political role of armed forces in Latin America; state of the literature). Revue Française de Science Politique, 1969, 19: 862-885.

674. SHILS, E. "The Military in the Political Development of the New States." In J. J. Johnson (Ed.) *The Role of the Military in Underdeveloped Countries.* Princeton, N.J.: Princeton University Press, 1962. Pp. 7-67. Social basis of the antipolitical mentality among elites.

675. VAN DOORN, J. "Armed Forces and Society: Patterns and Trends." In J. van Doorn (Ed.) *Armed Forces and Society.* The Hague & Paris: Mouton, 1968. Pp. 39-51.

676. VON DER MEHDEN, F. R., & ANDERSON, C. W. "Political Action by the Military in the Developing Areas." Social Research, 1961, 28: 459-479. A typology of regimes and the determinants.

V.1 See also IV.4(1) and 86, 733, 734, 740, 741, 745, 783, 787, 808, 825, 896, and 898.

V.2. "Militarism" (also II.4)

### 2(1) Civilian controls

677. ANDRESKI, S. "Militarism." In J. Gould & W. L. Kolb (Eds.) *A Dictionary of the Social Sciences.* New York: Crowell-Collier, 1964. Pp. 429-430.

678. ARMACOST, M. H. *The Politics of Weapons Innovation: the Thor-Jupiter Controversy.* New York: Columbia University Press, 1969. x + 304 pp.

679. BRZEZINSKI, Z. K. "Party Controls in the Soviet Army." J. of Politics, 1952, 14: 565-591. Reprinted in Z. K. Brzezinski (Ed.) *Political Controls in the Soviet Army: a Study Based on Reports by Former Soviet Officers.* New York: Research Program on the U.S.S.R., 1954. viii + 93 pp. Description of effort and techniques used to insure political loyalty of members of the armed forces.

680. BUSCH, O. *Militärsystem und Sozialleben im alten Preussen* (Military system and social life in old Prussia). Berlin: Walter de Gruyter, 1962. xiv + 203 pp. The beginnings of the militarisation of Prussian-German society.

681. BURNS, C. D. "Militarism." In *Encyclopedia of the Social Sciences.* Vol. 10. New York: Macmillan, 1933. Pp. 446-450.

682. BUTWELL, R. "Civilians and Soldiers in Burma." In R. K. Sakai (Ed.) *Studies in Asia.* Lincoln: University of Nebraska Press, 1961. Pp. 74-85.

683. CALDWELL, N. W. "Political Commissars in the Luftwaffe." J. of Politics, 1947, 9: 57-79.

684. CLIFFORD-VAUGHAN, MICHALINA. "Changing Attitudes to the Army's Role in French Society." British J. of Sociology, 1964, 15: 338-349. Historical survey from Revolution to Fifth Republic.

685. COHEN, S. P. "Rulers and Priests: a Study in Cultural Control." Comparative Studies in Society and History, 1964, 6: 199-216. Traditional Indian (pre-Muslim) role of the military.

686. DAVIS, V. *Politics of Innovation Patterns in Navy Cases.* University Graduate School of International Studies, 1967. 69 pp. U.S. Navy.

687. de EVIAO, S. "Un militarismo especial" (A special militarism). Panoramas, 1964, 2 (10): 73-83. Brazilian militarism.

688. DUPUY, T. N. "Burma and its Army: a Contrast in Motivation and Characteristics." Antioch R., 1960/61, 20: 428-440.

689. EHMKE, H. "Militärischer Oberbefehl und parlamentarische Kontrolle" (Military high command and parliamentary control). Zeitschrift für Politik, 1954, 1: 337-356.

690. EKIRCH, A. A., Jr. "The Civilian and the Military: A History of the American Anti-Militarist Tradition." New York: Oxford University Press, 1956. 340 pp. Sympathetic history and interpretation of antimilitarism in the United States.

691. FEDOTOFF-WHITE, D. D. *The Growth of the Red Army.* Princeton, N.J.: Princeton University Press, 1944. xiv + 486 pp. Internal and civil-military conflicts.

692. FICK, H. E. *Der deutsche Militarismus der Vorkriegszeit: ein Beitrag zur Soziologie des Militarismus* (German militarism of the prewar era; an inquiry into the sociology of militarism). Potsdam: Alfred Protte, 1932. 103 pp. Army and society before World War I.

693. FUKUSHIMA, S. "Soviet Union ni okeru Gumbu no chii" (The relationship between the Army and the Party in the Soviet Union). Hôgaku Ronsô (Kyôto), 1959, 64: 1-25; 1959, 65: 23-53.

694. FURNISS, E. S. *De Gaulle and the French Army; a Crisis in Civil-Military Relations.* New York: Twentieth Century Fund, 1964. x + 331 pp.

695. GESEK, J. T., SZOSTKIEWICZ, S., & WIATR, J. J. "Z badań opinii spoleczeństwa of wojsku" (Studies of public attitudes toward the armed forces). Studia Socjologiczno-Polityczne, 1962, 13: 97-142.

696. GITTINGS, J. *The Role of the Chinese Army.* London: Oxford University Press, 1967. xix + 331 pp. Transformation of a revolutionary force into a regular army.

697. HONG, S. C. "Political Diagnosis of Korean Society: a Survey of Military and Civilian Values." Asian Survey, 1967, 7: 329-340.

698. HUNTINGTON, S. P. "Civilian Control of the Military: a Theoretical Statement." In H. Eulau, S. J. Eldersveld & M. Janowitz (Eds.) *Political Behavior.* New York: Free Press, 1956. Pp. 380-384.

699. HUNTINGTON, S. P. "Interservice Competition and the Political Roles of

Armed Services." American Political Science R., 1961, 55: 40-52. Reprinted in H. L. Coles (Ed.) *Total War and Cold War.* Columbus: Ohio State University Press, 1962. Pp. 178-210. Crisscrossing conflicts diminish the probability of direct civil-military confrontations. See also 936.

700. JOFFE, E. "The Conflict between Old and New in the Chinese Army." China Q., 1964, 18: 118-140. Reprinted in W. C. McWilliams (Ed.) *Garrisons and Government; Politics and the Military in New States.* San Francisco: Chandler Publishing Co., 1967. Pp. 101-129. Problems of civil-military relations in the transition from guerrilla army to modern army.

701. JOFFE, E. "Party and Army: Professionalism and Political Control in the Chinese Officer Corps, 1949-1964." Harvard University East Asian Monographs, 1965, No. 19. xii + 198 pp.

702. KAMINSKI, A. *Militaryzm niemiecki; glowne zagadnienia spoleczne i polityczne* (German militarism; social and political problems). Warsaw: Wydawnictwo Ministerstwa Obrony Narodowej, 1962.

703. KEHR, E. "Zur Soziologie der Reichswehr" (On the sociology of the Reichswehr). Neue Blätter für den Sozialismus, 1930, 1: 156-164. Reprinted in E. Kehr, *Der Primat der Innenpolitik.* Berlin: Walter de Gruyter, 1965. Pp. 235-243. Diagnosis of the social isolation of the armed forces during the Weimar Republic.

704. KERWIN, J. G. (Ed.) *Civil-military Relationships in American Life.* Chicago: University of Chicago Press, 1948. xi + 181 pp. Essays on role of the military.

705. KILLINEN, K. "Polittisen ja sotilaallisen johdon suhteesta demokratiassa" (On the relations between political and military direction in a democracy). Valtio Ja Yhteiskunta, 1956, 16: 20-33.

706. KLAUSENITZER, F. A. "Die Diskussion um die innere Führung; zum Verhältnis von Bundeswehr und Offentlichkeit" (The discussion concerning the "innere Führung"; on the relationship between Bundeswehr and the public). In G. Picht (Ed.) *Studien zur politischen und gesellschaftlichen Situation der Bundeswehr.* Witten & Berlin: Eckart-Verlag, 1965-1966. Pp. 159-246.

707. KLUCKHOHN, C. "American Culture and Military Life." *Report of the Working Group on Human Behavior under Conditions of Military Service.* Washington, D.C.: Department of Defense, Research and Development Board, June 1951. Appendix No. 106.

708. KOLKOWICZ, R. "Interest Groups in Soviet Politics: the Case of the Military." Comparative Politics, 1970, 2: 445-472.

709. KUNTZ, F. *L'officier française dans la nation* (The French officer in the nation). Paris: Charles-Lavauzelle, 1960. xxii + 184 pp. Covers some aspects of social transformation and civil-military relations.

710. LAUTERBACH, A. T. "Militarism in the Western World." J. of the History of Ideas, 1944, 5: 446-478.

711. LINDESMITH, A. R. "The Need for a Sociology of Militarism." Sociology and Social Research, 1943, 27: 191-199.

712. MAZRUI, A. "Anti-Militarism and Political Power in Tanzania." J. of Conflict Resolution, 1968, 12: 269-284. Reprinted in J. van Doorn (Ed.) *Military Profession and Military Regimes.* The Hague & Paris: Mouton, 1969. Pp. 219-240. Liberation movement and attitudes toward armed forces.

713. MERRIAM, C. E., & HULL, M. D. "Security without Militarism: Preserving Civilian Control in American Political Institutions." In J. Kerwin (Ed.) *Civil-Military Relations in American Life.* Chicago: University of Chicago Press, 1948. Pp. 156-172.

714. OBERMANN, E. *Soldaten, Bürger, Militaristen; Militär und Demokratie in Deutschland* (Soldiers, citizens, militarists; armed forces and democracy in Germany). Stuttgart: J. G. Cotta'sche Buchhandlung, 1958. 328 pp. Social history.

715. OCHOCKI, K. *Bundeswehra-szkola militaryzmu niemieckiego* (Bundeswehr—school of the German militarism). Warsaw: Wojsko Ludowe, 1963. 12 pp.

716. POWELL, R. L. "The Military Affairs Committee and Party Control of the Military in China." Asian Survey, 1963, 3: 347-356.

717. RADWAY, L. I. "Militarism." In *International Encyclopedia of the Social Sciences.* Vol. 10. New York: Macmillan & Free Press, 1968. Pp. 300-304.

718. RANSOM, H. H. "The Politics of Air Power—a Comparative Analysis." In C. J. Friedrich & S. E. Harris (Eds.) *Public Policy; Yearbook of the Graduate School of Public Administration, Harvard University,* Vol. 7, 1958. Pp. 87-119. Acknowledgment of air arms independence came from civilians.

719. RIDLEY, F. "The Parliamentary Commissioner for Military Affairs in the Federal Republic of Germany." Political Studies, 1964, 12: 1-20. Institutional mechanism for the civilianization of the Bundeswehr.

720. SCHOECK, E. "Ist die amerikanische Gesellschaft 'unsoldatisch' "? –der Amerikaner und die Uniform (Is American society "unsoldierly"? –the American and the uniform). Aussenpolitik, 1955, 6: 481-488 and 561-571.

721. SECHER, H. P. "Controlling the New Germany Military Elite: the Political Role of the Parliamentary Defense Commissioner in the Federal Republic." American Philosophical Society Proceedings, 1965, 109: 63-84. Problem of civilian control over internal activities of the Bundeswehr.

722. SMITH, L. American Democracy and Military Power; a Study of Civil Control of the Military Power in the United States. Chicago: University of Chicago Press, 1951. xv + 370 pp.

723. SOHN, J. S. "Factionalism and Party Control of the Military in Communist North Korea." Koreana Q., 1967, 9 (3): 16-40. Reprinted in J. van Doorn (Ed.) Military Profession and Military Regimes. The Hague & Paris: Mouton, 1969. Pp. 269-292.

724. SPINDLER, G. D. "The Doolittle Board and Cooptation in the Army." Social Forces, 1951, 29: 305-310. Organizational response to criticism by discharged World War II soldiers.

725. SPROUT, H. "Trends in the Traditional Relation between Military and Civilian." American Philosophical Society Proceedings, 1948, 92: 264-270. A general discussion.

726. TURNER, G. B. (Ed.) A History of Military Affairs in Western Society Since the Eighteenth Century. New York: Harcourt, Brace & Co., 1953. 776 pp. Wide ranging collection.

727. VAN DOORN, J. "Political Change and the Control of the Military: Some General Remarks." In J. van Doorn (Ed.) Military Profession and Military Regimes. The Hague & Paris: Mouton, 1969. Pp. 11-32.

728. VON FRIEDEBURG, L. "Zum Verhältnis von Militär und Gesellschaft in der Bundesrepublik" (On the relation of the military and society in the Federal Republic). In G. Picht (Ed.) Studien zur politischen und gesellschaftlichen Situation des Bundeswehr. Vol. 2. Witten & Berlin: Eckart-Verlag, 1966. Pp. 10-65.

729. WIATR, J. J. "Militaryzm: pojecie i problematyka socjologiczna" (Militarism: concept and sociological problem). Studia Socjologiczno-Polityczne, 1960, 6: 33-62.

730. WIATR, J. J. O militaryzmie niemieckin (German militarism). Studia Socjologiczno-Polityczne, 1962, 12: 129-156. General sociological characteristics of German militarism; various stages of its growth and development.

731. WIATR, J. J. "Neiktore problemy socjologiczne armii socjalistyczjej" (Some sociological problems of the socialist army). Studia Socjologiczno-Polityczne, 1963, 14: 23-56.

732. WILDENMANN, R. Politische Stellung und Kontrolle des Militärs (Political opinions and control of the military). Kölner Zeitschrift für Soziologie und Sozialpsychologie, 1968, 20 (Special Issue 12): 59-88.

   2(1) See also 72, 102, 116, 130, 140, 197, 535, 538, 561, 602, 603, 812, 816, 941, 954, 971, 1139, and 1232.

### 2(2) Political role and influence of military

733. ALBA, V. El militarismo; ensayo sobre un fenómeno político-social iberoamericano (Militarism: essay concerning a politico-social phenomenon in Spanish America). México: Biblioteca de Ensayos Sociológicos, Instituto de Investigaciones Sociales, Universidad Nacional Autónoma de México, 1959. 289 pp.

734. ALBA, V. "The Stages of Militarism in Latin America." In J. J. Johnson (Ed.) The Role of the Military in Underdeveloped Countries. Princeton, N.J.: Princeton University Press, 1962. Pp. 165-183. An overview of historical trends.

735. AMBLER, J. S. The French Army in Politics, 1945-1962. Columbus: Ohio State University Press, 1966. xi + 427 pp.

736. ANDRESKI, S. "Conservatism and Radicalism of the Military." Archives Européennes de Sociologie, 1961, 2: 53-61. An examination of determinants.

737. ASTIZ, C. A. "The Argentine Armed Forces: their Role and Political Involvement." Western Political Q., 1969, 22: 862-878. Changing background of officers.

738. BARLILL, J. "Die politische Führerrolle des Militärs in Ghana" (The

political leadership role of the military in Ghana). Internationales Afrika-forum, 1968, 4: 349-360.

739. BEDARIDA, F. "L'armée et la République: les opinions politiques des officiers français en 1876-78" (The army and the Republic: political opinions of French officers in 1876-78). Revue Historiques, 1964, 232: 119-164.

740. BEERI, E. *Na-Ketsunah veha-shilton ba-'olam na'aravi.* Merhavīah: Sifrut po'alîm, 1969. 382 pp. English translation: *Army Officers in Arab Politics and Society.* Jerusalem: Israel University Press, 1970. xii + 514 pp. Social profiles and other basic data.

741. BELL, M. J. V. "The Military in the New States of Africa." In J. van Doorn (Ed.) *Armed Forces and Society.* The Hague & Paris: Mouton, 1968. Pp. 259-273.

742. BELTRAN, V. R. "The Army and Structural Changes in 20th Century Argentina: an Initial Approach." In J. van Doorn (Ed.) *Armed Forces and Society.* The Hague & Paris: Mouton, 1968. Pp. 317-341.

743. BRILL, J. A. "The Military and Modernization in the Middle East." Comparative Politics, 1969, 2: 41-62.

744. CADERNOS BRASILEIROS. "Os militares" (The armed forces). Cadernos Brasileiros, 1966, 8 (6): 1-111 (Special Issue). Militarism in Brazil by various contributors.

745. CAMPBELL, J. C. "The Role of the Military in the Middle East: Past Patterns and New Directions." In S. N. Fisher (Ed.) *The Military in the Middle East: Problems in Society and Government.* Columbis: Ohio State University Press, 1963. Pp. 105-114.

746. CANTON, D. "Notas sobres las fuerzas armadas argentinas" (Sober notes on the Argentine armed forces). Revista Latinoamericana de Sociologia, 1965, 1: 290-313.

747. CARSTEN, F. L. "Germany: from Scharnhorst to Schleicher: the Prussian Officer Corps in Politics 1806-1933." In M. Howard (Ed.) *Soldiers and Governments: Nine Studies in Civil-Military Relations.* Bloomington, Indiana: Indiana University Press, 1962. Pp. 73-98.

748. CARSTEN, F. L. *Reichswehr und Politik, 1918-1933.* Cologne: Kiepenheuer & Witsch, 1964. 484 pp. English translation: *The Reichswehr and Politics: 1918-1922.* Oxford: Clarendon Press, 1966. viii + 427 pp.

749. CHAPMAN, G. France: The French Army and Politics. In M. Howard (Ed.) *Soldiers and Governments: Nine Studies in Civil-Military Relations.* Bloomington, Indiana: Indiana University Press, 1962. Pp. 51-72.

750. CHENG, C. (Ed.) *The Politics of the Chinese Red Army.* Cal.: The Hoover Institute, 1966. vi + 776 pp.

751. CHORLEY, KATHERINE C. *Armies and the Art of Revolution.* London: Faber & Faber, 1943. 273 pp. Historical survey of the role of armed forces in revolution, for the purpose of formulating some generalization.

752. COHEN, S. P. "Subhas Chandra Bose and the Indian National Army." Pacific Affairs, 1963, 36: 411-429. Impact of INA trials on civil-military relations in India.

753. COLEMAN, J. S., & BRICE, B., Jr. "The Role of the Military in Sub-Saharan Africa." In J. J. Johnson (Ed.) *The Role of the Military in Underdeveloped Countries.* Princeton, N.J.: Princeton University Press, 1962. Pp. 359-405.

754. COWAN, L. G. "The Military and African Politics." International J., 1966, 21: 289-297.

755. CRAIG, G. A. *The Politics of the Prussian Army: 1640-1945.* New York: Oxford University Press, 1956. xx + 536 pp.

756. CRAIG, G. "Reichswehr and National Socialism: the Policy of Wilhelm Groener, 1928-32." Political Science Q., 1948, 63: 194-229.

757. DAVIS, V. *The Admirals Lobby.* Chapel Hill: The University of North Carolina Press, 1967. xviii + 329 pp. Activities during the American carrier controversy.

758. DENT, M. J. "The Military and the Politicians." In S. K. Panter-Brick (Ed.) *Nigerian Politics and Military Rule: Prelude to the Civil War.* London: Athlone Press, 1970. Pp. 78-93.

759. DERTHICK, M. "Militia Lobby in the Missile Age: the Politics of the National Guard." In S. P. Huntington (Ed.) *Changing Patterns of Military Politics.* New York: Free Press, 1962. Pp. 190-234. See also 760.

760. DERTHICK, MARTHA. *The National Guard in Politics.* Cambridge, Mass.: Harvard University Press, 1965. viii + 202 pp. Analysis of the power of the National Guard and its lobby, the National Guard Association, as a pressure group from 1879 to present.

761. DOMENACH, J. M. "The French Army in Politics." Foreign Affairs, 1961, 39: 185-195. 1958 to 1960.

762. DUDLEY, B. J. "The Military in the New States of Africa." Nigerian J. of Economic and Social Studies, 1964, 6: 351-361.

763. FERREIRA, O. S. As fôrças armadas e o desafio da revolução (The armed forces and the provocation of revolution). Rio de Janeiro: Edições GRD, 1964, 152 pp.

764. FINER, S. E. The Man on Horseback: the Role of the Military in Politics. New York: Praeger, 1962. 268 pp. Levels of intervention in different societies.

765. FINER, S. E. "Military and Society in Latin America." In Sociological Review M. No. 11. Latin American Sociological Studies edited by P. Halmos. Staffordshire, England: University of Keele, 1967. Pp. 133-152. Expanded version of an article previously published in Encounter.

766. FISHER, S. N. "The Role of the Military in Society and Government in Turkey." In S. N. Fisher (Ed.) The Military in the Middle East: Problems in Society and Government. Columbus: Ohio State University Press, 1963. Pp. 21-40.

767. FITZGIBBON, R. H. "What Price Latin American Armies? " Virginia Quarterly R., 1960, 36: 517-532. Discusses some of the conditions under which officers tend to withdraw from direct participation in decision-making.

768. GARTHOFF, R. L. "The Military in Russia, 1861-1965." In J. van Doorn (Ed.) Armed Forces and Society. The Hague & Paris: Mouton, 1968. Pp. 240-256.

769. GARTHOFF, R. L. "The Role of the Military in Recent Soviet Politics." Russian R., 1957, 16 (2): 15-24.

770. GILMORE, R. L. Caudillism and Militarism in Venezuela 1810-1910. Athens, Ohio: Ohio University Press, 1964. vi + 211 pp.

771. GLICKMAN, H. "The Military in African Politics; a Bibliographic Essay." African Forum, 1966, 2 (1): 68-75.

772. GOLDWERT, M. "Dichotomies of Militarism in Argentina." Orbis, 1966, 10: 930-939.

773. GOLDWERT, M. "The Rise of Modern Militarism in Argentina." Hispanic American Historical R., 1968, 48: 189-205.

774. GORDON, H. J. *The Reichswehr and the German Republic 1919-1926.* Princeton, N.J.: Princeton University Press, 1957. xvi + 478 pp.

775. GRANATSTEIN, J. L. "The Armed Forces Vote in Canadian General Elections; 1940-1968." J. of Canadian Studies, 1969, 4: 6-16.

776. GRUNDY, K. W. "The Negative Image of Africa's Military." R. of Politics, 1968, 30: 428-439. Its legitimacy as national leadership.

777. HADDAD, G. M. *Revolutions and Military Rule in the Middle East: the Northern Tier.* New York: Speller, 1965. iv + 251 pp. Historical studies of Turkey, Iran, Afghanistan, and Pakistan with some attempt at comparison.

778. HALPERN, B. "The Role of the Military in Israel." In J. J. Johnson (Ed.) *The Role of the Military in Underdeveloped Countries.* Princeton, N.J.: Princeton University Press, 1962. Pp. 317-357.

779. HARRIS, G. S. "Role of the Military in Turkish Politics." Middle East J., 1965, 19: 54-66, 169-176. A historical account.

780. HELGUERA, J. L. "The Changing Role of the Military in Colombia." J. of Inter-American Studies, 1961, 3: 351-358.

781. HOROWITZ, I. L. "El militarísmo en América Latina" (Militarism in Latin America). Ciencias Politicas y Sociales, 1966, 12 (45-46): 133-177.

782. HUMPHREYS, R. A. "Latin America: the Caudillo Tradition." In M. Howard (Ed.) *Soldiers and Governments: Nine Studies in Civil-Military Relations.* Bloomington, Indiana: Indiana University Press, 1962. Pp. 149-165.

783. HUNTINGTON, S. P. *Political Order in Changing Societies.* New Haven, Conn.: Yale University Press, 1968. xi + 488 pp. Chapter 4, "Praetorianism and Political Decay," deals with sources of military intervention.

784. JOHNSON, J. J. "The Latin-American Military as a Politically Competing Group in Transitional Society." In J. J. Johnson (Ed.) *The Role of the Military in Underdeveloped Countries.* Princeton, N.J.: Princeton University Press, 1962. Pp. 91-129.

785. JOHNSON, J. J. *The Military and Society in Latin America.* Stanford,

Cal.: Stanford University Press, 1964. xi + 308 pp. Social and political activities of officers in the past and present.

786. KELLY, G. A. "The French Army Re-Enters Politics, 1940-1955." Political Science Q., 1961, 76: 367-392.

787. KELLY, G. A. "Global Civil-Military Dilemma." R. of Politics, 1963, 25: 291-308. Achieving accommodation within the state structure of the needs of national defense.

788. KELLY, G. A. *Lost Soldiers; the French Army and Empire in Crisis 1947-1962.* Cambridge, Mass.: M.I.T. Press, 1965. x + 404 pp.

789. KERCHE, C. O. "Militarens roll i amerikansk politik av i dag" (The role of the military in American politics today). Statsvetenskaplig Tidskrift, 1960, 63: 54-68.

790. KHADDURI, M. "The Role of the Military in Iraqi Society." In S. N. Fisher (Ed.) *The Military in the Middle East: Problems in Society and Government.* Columbus: Ohio State University Press, 1963. Pp. 41-51.

791a. KHADDURI, M. "The Role of the Military in Middle Eastern Politics." American Political Science R., 1953, 47: 511-524.

791b. KLING, M. "Towards a Theory of Power and Political Instability in Latin America." Western Political Q., 1956, 9: 21-31. Reprinted in O. Feinstein (Ed.) *Two Worlds of Change.* Garden City, N.Y.: Doubleday-Anchor, 1964.

792. KOSSOK, M. "Armee und Politik in Lateinamerika" (Army and politics in Latin America). In *Die nationale Freiheitsbewegung 1965; Bilanz, Berichte, Chronik.* Leipzig: Karl-Marx-Universität, 1966. Pp. 135-161.

793. LA GORCE, P. M. de *La Republic et son armée.* Paris: Fayard, 1963. 708 pp. English translation: *The French Army: a Military-Political History.* New York: Braziller, 1963. 568 pp.

794. LA SOUCHERE, E. de "Los militares en el Brasil" (The military in Brazil). Mundo Nuevo, 1967, 15: 71-95.

795. LEV, D. S. "Political Role of the Army in Indonesia." Pacific Affairs, 1963, 36: 349-364. Reprinted in W. C. McWilliams (Ed.) *Garrisons and Government; Politics and the Military in New States.* San Francisco: Chandler Publishing Co., 1967. Pp. 150-170.

796. LEVINE, D. N. "The Military in Ethiopian Politics: Capabilities and Constraints." In H. Bienen (Ed.) *The Military Intervenes; Case Studies in Political Development.* New York: Russell Sage Foundation, 1968. Pp. 5-34.

797. LIEUWEN, E. *Arms and Politics in Latin America.* (Rev. Ed.) New York: Praeger, 1961. xvi + 335 pp. Part I deals with armed forces; part II with military aspects of U.S. policy in Latin America.

798. LIEUWEN, E. *Generals versus Presidents: Neo-Militarism in Latin America.* New York: Praeger, 1964. 160 pp. Chapter 6 contains a comparative analysis of seven coups during the early 1960's.

799. LIEUWEN, E. "Militarism and Politics in Latin America." In J. J. Johnson (Ed.) *The Role of the Military in Underdeveloped Countries.* Princeton, N.J.: Princeton University Press, 1962. Pp. 131-163.

800. LIEUWEN, E. "The Military: a Revolutionary Force." A. of the American Academy of Political and Social Science., 1961, 334: 30-40.

801. LOVELL, J., & KIM, C. "The Military and Political Change in Asia." Pacific Affairs, 1967, 40: 113-123.

802. McALISTER, L. N. "The Military." In J. J. Johnson (Ed.) *Continuity and Change in Latin America.* Stanford, Cal.: Stanford University Press, 1964. Pp. 136-160. An overview of functions and activities of the military in various countries and over time.

803. McALISTER, L. "Recent Research and Writings on the Role of the Military in Latin America." Latin American Research R., 1966, 2 (1): 5-33.

804. MEYNAUD, J. "Les militaires et le pouvoir" (Military men and power). Revue Française de Sociologie, 1961, 2 (2): 75-87.

805. MORNER, M. "Caudillos y militares en evolución hispanoamericana" (Caudillos and military in Latin American development). J. of Inter-American Studies, 1960, 2: 295-310.

806. NOBECOURT, J., & PLANCHAIS, J. *Une histoire politique de l'armée* (A political history of the army). Paris: Editions du Seuil, 1967. 2 vols. Volume 1 from Pétain to Pétain, 1919-1942; Volume 2 from de Gaulle to de Gaulle, 1940-1967.

807. NORTH, L. *Civil-Military Relations in Argentina, Chile, and Peru.* University of Calfornia (Berkeley) Institute for International Studies. Political Modernization Series, No. 2, 1966. 86 pp.

808. ODA, H. "Gendai Africa no seiji to gonbu" (Political and the military in contemporary Africa). Hôgaku Kenkyû (Tokyo), 1967, 40: 110-150.

809. OLIVEIRA TORRES, J. C. de "As fôrças armadas conio fôrça politica" (The armed forces as a political force). Revista Brasileira de Estudos Politicos, 1966, 20: 39-47.

810. PAUKER, G. J. "The Role of the Military in Indonesia." In J. J. Johnson (Ed.) *The Role of the Military in Underdeveloped Countries.* Princeton, N.J.: Princeton University Press, 1962. Pp. 185-230.

811. PERLMUTTER, A. "The Arab Military Elite." World Politics, 1970, 22: 269-300. A review article.

812. PERLMUTTER, A. "The Israeli Army in Politics: the Persistence of the Civilian over the Military." World Politics, 1968, 20: 606-643. See also 813.

813. PERLMUTTER, A. *Military and Politics in Israel: Nation-Building and Role Expansion.* New York: Praeger, 1969. xiv + 161 pp.

814. POTASH, R. A. "The Changing Role of the Military in Argentina." J. of Inter-American Studies, 1961, 3: 571-578.

815. RALSTON, D. B. "The Army of the Republic; the Place of the Military in the Political Revolution of France, 1871-1914." Cambridge, Mass.: M.I.T. Press, 1967. xiii + 395 pp.

816. RAU, V. G., SCHULZE, K., & STUBER, E. "Das Problem des Militarismus und die Armeen der beiden deutschen Staaten" (The problem of militarism and armies in the two Germanys). In R. Schulz & H. Steiner (Eds.) *Soziologie und Wirklichkeit: Beiträge zum VI. Weltkongress für Soziologie.* Berlin: VEB Deutscher Verlag der Wissenschaften, 1966. Pp. 118-136.

817. REMOND, R. "Les anciens combattants et la politique" (Veterans and politics). Revue Française de Science Politique, 1955, 5: 267-290.

818. RITTER, G. *Staatskunst und Kriegshandwerk; das Problem des "Militarismus" in Deutschland.* 3 vols. (The art of state and the profession of arms; the problem of "militarism" in Germany). Munich: R. Oldenburg, 1954-1960. A historical study.

819. RUDOLPH, L. J., & RUDOLPH, SUSANNE H. "Generals and Politicians in India." Pacific Affairs, 1964, 37: 5-19. Reprinted in W. C. McWilliams (Ed.) *Garrisons and Government; Politics and the Military in New States.* San Francisco: Chandler Publishing Co., 1967. Pp. 130-149. Noninvolvement of military in politics.

820. RUSTOW, D. A. "The Military in Middle Eastern Society and Politics." In S. N. Fisher (Ed.) *The Military in the Middle East: Problems in Society and Government.* Columbus: Ohio State University Press, 1963. Pp. 3-20.

821. SCHMITT, K. M. "The Role of the Military in Contemporary Mexico." In A. C. Wilgus (Ed.) *The Caribbean: Mexico Today.* Gainesville: University of Florida Press, 1964. Pp. 52-62. Its power in the political structure.

822. SETON-WATSON, G. H. N. "Russia: Army and Autocracy." In M. Howard (Ed.) *Soldiers and Governments: Nine Studies in Civil-Military Relations.* Bloomington, Indiana: Indiana University Press, 1962. Pp. 99-114.

823. SPIRO, H. J. "The Military in Sub-Saharan Africa." In W. C. McWilliams (Ed.) *Garrisons and Government: Politics and the Military in New States.* San Francisco: Chandler Publishing Co., 1967. Pp. 264-272.

824. VATIKIOTIS, P. J. *Politics and the Military in Jordan: a Study of the Arab Legion, 1921-1957.* New York: Praeger, 1967. 169 pp.

825. WELCH, C. E. "Soldier and State in Africa." J. of Modern African Studies, 1967, 5: 305-322.

826. WIARDA, H. "The Politics of Civil-Military Relations in the Dominican Republic." J. of Inter-American Studies, 1965, 7: 465-484.

827. WIATR, J. J. *Militaryzm a demokracja; szkice o politycznej roli armii w powojennej Francji* (Militarism versus democracy; sketch of the political role of the army in postwar France). Warsaw: Wydawnictwo Ministerstwa Obrony Narodowej, 1966. 351 pp.

828. WOOTTON, G. "Ex-Servicemen in Politics." Political Q., 1958, 29: 28-39.

829. WOOTTON, G. *The Politics of Influence: British Ex-Servicemen, Cabinet Decisions and Cultural Change (1971-1957).* Cambridge, Mass.: Harvard University Press, 1963. xiv + 301 pp.

2(2) See also V.2(4) and 82, 98, 100, 173, 187, 189, 499, 514, 522, 662, and 1118.

2(3) Military coups and takeovers

830. BIENEN, H. (Ed.) The Military Intervenes; Case Studies in Political Development. New York: Russell Sage Foundation, 1968. xxiii + 175 pp.

831. BIENEN, H. "Public Order and the Military in Africa: Mutinies in Kenya, Uganda, and Tanganyika." In H. Bienen (Ed.) *The Military Intervenes; Case Studies in Political Development.* New York: Russell Sage Foundation, 1968. Pp. 35-69.

832. BRILL, W. H. *Military Intervention in Bolivia: the Overthrow of Paz Estenssoro and the MNR.* Political Studies Series, No. 3. Washington, D.C.: Institute for the Comparative Study of Political Systems, 1967. iii + 68 pp.

833. CANTON, D. "Military Interventions in Argentina: 1900-1966." In J. van Doorn (Ed.) *Military Profession and Military Regimes.* The Hague & Paris: Mouton, 1969. Pp. 241-268.

834. CHALLENER, R. D. "The French Army: from Obedience to Insurrection." World Politics, 1967, 19: 678-691. Civil-military conflicts leading to the Algerian uprising.

835. CROZIER, B. *The Rebels: a Study of Post-War Insurrections.* London: Chatto & Windus, 1960. 256 pp. Includes officers who overthrew civilian regimes.

836. DESPRADEL, L. "Les fonctions des armées en Amerique latine et les causes de leurs interventions politiques" (The functions of armies in Latin America and the causes for their political intervention). Revue de l'Institute de Sociologie, 1969, 4: 689-709.

837. FEIT, E. "Military Coups and Political Development—Some Lessons from Ghana and Nigeria." World Politics, 1968, 20: 179-193.

838. FIDEL, K. "Military Organization and Conspiracy in Turkey." Studies in Comparative International Development, 1970-71, 6 (2): 19-43.

839. FINER, S. E. "The Military Take-Over Bidders." New Society, 1965, No. 162: 7-9. Incidence of military regimes.

840. FOSSUM, E. "Factors Influencing the Occurrence of Military Coups d'Etat in Latin America." J. of Peace Research, 1967, 4: 228-251.

841. GERMANI, G., & SILVERT, K. "Politics, Social Structure and Military Intervention in Latin America." Archives Européennes de Sociologie,

1961, 2: 62-81. Reprinted in W. C. McWilliams (Ed.) *Garrisons and Government; Politics and the Military in New States.* San Francisco: Chandler Publishing Co., 1967. Pp. 227-248.

842. GIRARDET, R. Pouvoir civil et pouvoir militaire dans la France contemporaine (Civil and military power in the Fourth Republic). Revue Française de Science Politique, 1960, 10: 5-38. Translation in S. P. Huntington (Ed.) *Changing Patterns of Military Politics.* New York: Free Press, 1962. Pp. 121-149. The Algerian uprising of 1958.

843. GREENE, F. "Toward understanding Military Coups." Africa Report, 1966, 11 (2): 10-11, 14.

844. GUILLEN, F. Militarismo y golpes de estado en américa latina (Militarism and coup d'état in Latin America). Cuadernos Americanos, 1965, 24 (3): 7-19. Mexico.

845. HANDMAN, M. "Bureaucratic Culture Pattern and Revolution." American J. of Sociology, 1933, 39: 301-313. Patronage distribution.

846. HIRSCH, E. E. Rationale Legitimierung eines Staatsstreiches als soziologisches Problem. Erläutert am Beispiel des türkischen Umsturzes vom 27. Mai 1960 (Rational legitimation of a coup d'état as a sociological problem: the Turkish takeover of 27th of May 1960). Kölner Zeitschrift für Soziologie und Sozialpsychologie, 1965, 17: 632-646.

847. HOROWITZ, I. L. "The Norm of Illegitimacy: toward a General Theory of Latin American Political Development." Soundings, 1968, 51: 8-32. Some notes on the functions of golpes.

848. HOROWITZ, I. L. "The Organization and Ideology of Hemispheric Militarism." In *Three Worlds of Development; the Theory and Practice of International Stratification.* New York: Oxford University Press, 1966. Pp. 272-290. Military intervention in Latin America and the United States.

849. KELLY, G. A. "Algeria, the Army, and the Fifth Republic (1959-1961): a Scenario of Civil-Military Conflict." Political Science Q., 1964, 79: 335-359.

850. KIM, C. I. E. "The South Korean Military Coup of May, 1961: its Causes and the Social Characteristics of its Leaders." In J. van Doorn (Ed.) *Armed Forces and Society.* The Hague & Paris: Mouton, 1968. Pp. 298-316.

851. KOURVETARIS, G. A. "The Contemporary Officer Corps in Greece: an

Inquiry into its Professionalism and Interventionism." Dissertation Abstracts, 1970, 30.

852. LANG, K. "The Military Putsch in a Developed Political Culture: Confrontations of Military and Civil Power in Germany and France." In J. van Doorn (Ed.) *Armed Forces and Society.* The Hague & Paris: Mouton, 1968. Pp. 202-228.

853. LISSAK, M. "Center and Periphery in Developing Countries and Prototypes of Military Elites." Studies in Comparative International Development, 1969-70, `5: 139-150. Preconditions for intervention and the effective exercise of political power by officers.

854a. MALAPARTE, C. *Coup d'Etat: the Technique of Revolution.* New York: Dutton, 1932. 251 pp. Theory of minimal use of force.

854b. MAZRUI, A. A., & ROTHCHILD, D. "The Soldier and the State in East Africa: Some Theoretical Conclusions on the Army Mutinies of 1964." Western Political Q., 1967, 20: 82-96.

855. MEISEL, J. H. *The Fall of the Republic: Military Revolt in France.* Ann Arbor, Mich.: University of Michigan Press, 1962. 309 pp. The 1958 and 1961 putsches in Algeria.

856. MENENDEZ, J. "La rebelión de los generales" (The revolt of the generals). Revista de Politica Internacional (Madrid), 1966, 87: 57-79.

857. NEEDLER, M. C. *Anatomy of a Coup d'Etat: Equador 1963.* Washington, D.C.: Institute for the Comparative Study of Political Systems, 1964. v + 54 pp.

858. NEEDLER, M. C. "Political Development and Military Intervention in Latin America." American Political Science R., 1966, 60: 616-626. Incidence and dynamics of coups d'état.

859. NELKIN, DOROTHY. "The Economic and Social Setting of Military Takeovers in Africa." J. of Asian and African Studies, 1967, 2: 230-244.

860. NEWBURY, C. "Military Intervention and Political Change in West Africa." Africa Q., 1967, 7: 215-221. Coups in Ghana and Sierra Leone.

861. NORD, E. "Militaerkuppene i Afrika" (Military coups in Africa). Internasjonal Politikk (Bergen), 1967, 2: 85-102.

862. NUN, J. "América Latina: la crisis hegemónica y el golpe militar" (Latin America: the supremacy crisis and the military coup). Dessarollo Económico, 1966, 6: 355-415. Also published in Sociologie du Travail, 1967, 9: 281-313.

863. NUN, J. "A Latin American Phenomenon: the Middle Class Military Coup." In *Trends in Social Research.* Berkeley, Cal.: Institute for International Studies, University of California, 1965. Pp. 55-99.

864. PASSOS, A. S. "Developmental Tensions and Political Instability: Testing Some Hypotheses Concerning Latin America." J. of Peace Research, 1968, 5: 70-86.

865. PAYNE, J. "Peru: the Politics of Structured Violence." J. of Politics, 1965, 27: 362-374. Reprinted in W. C. McWilliams (Ed.) *Garrisons and Government; Politics and the Military in New States.* San Francisco: Chandler Publishing Co., 1967. Pp. 249-263.

866. PERLMUTTER, A. "From Obscurity to Rule: the Syrian Army and the Ba'ath Party." Western Political Q., 1969, 22: 827-845.

867. PUTNAM, M. C. J. "Toward Explaining Military Intervention in Latin American Politics." World Politics, 1967, 20: 83-110. A quantitative study of coups.

868. RAPOPORT, D. C. "Political Dimensions of Military Usurpation." Political Science Q., 1968, 83: 551-572. Emphasis on civilian loyalties.

869. ROTHSCHILD, J. "Military Background of Pilsudski's Coup d'Etat." Slavic R., 1962, 21: 241-260.

870. ROUCEK, J. "Der Aufstand der Militäre in Schwarzafrika" (The revolt of the military in Black Africa). Europa-Archiv, 1966, 21: 359-368.

871. SPRINGER, P. B. "Disunity and Disorder: Factional Politics in the Argentine Military." In H. Bienen (Ed.) *The Military Intervenes; Case Studies in Political Development.* New York: Russell Sage Foundation, 1968. Pp. 145-168.

872. RUSTOW, D. A. "The Army and the Founding of the Turkish Republic." World Politics, 1959, 11: 513-552. A case study of intervention and disengagement.

873. SOHN, J. S. "Political Dominance and Political Failure: The Role of the Military in the Republic of Korea." In H. Bienen (Ed.) *The Military Intervenes; Case Studies in Political Development.* New York: Russell Sage Foundation, 1968. Pp. 103-121.

874. SPRINGER, P. B. "Social Sources of Political Behavior of Venezuelan Military Officers: an Exploratory Analysis." Il Politico, 1965, 30: 348-355.

875. STUPAK, R. J. "Military's Ideological Challenge to Civilian Authority in Post-World War II France." Orbis, 1968, 12: 582-604.

876. TIXIER, G. "Les coups d'état militaires en Afrique de l'Ouest" (The military coups d'etat in West Africa). Revue du Droit Public et de la Science Politique en France et à l'Etranger, 1966, 82: 1116-1132. Also in Revue Juridique et Politique, 1967, 21: 559-576.

877. TOMAC, V. "Uzroci i karakter oojnih udara u Zapadnoj i Centralnój Africi" (Causes and features of military seizures of power in West and Central Africa). Socijalizam, 1966, 9: 983-1004.

878. VERMIER, B. *Armée et politique au Moyen-Orient* (Army and politics in the Middle East). Paris: Payot, 1966. 252 pp. Chronological accounts with a brief summary chapter.

879. WEIKER, W. F. *The Turkish Revolution 1960-1961: Aspects of Military Politics.* Washington, D.C.: Brookings Institution, 1963. 172 pp.

880. WHEELER-BENNETT, J. W. *The Nemesis of Power; the German Army in Politics, 1918-1945.* (2nd Ed.) New York: St. Martin's Press, 1964. xxii + 831 pp.

881. WYCKOFF, T. "The Role of the Military in Latin American Politics." Western Political Q., 1960, 13: 745-763. Conditions associated with different levels of intervention.

882. YALMAN, N. "Intervention and Extrication: the Officer Corps in the Turkish Crisis." In H. Bienen (Ed.) *The Military Intervenes; Case Studies in Political Development.* New York: Russell Sage Foundation, 1968. Pp. 127-144.

883. YOSHIHASHI, T. *Conspiracy at Mukden; the Rise of the Japanese Military.* New Haven: Yale University Press, 1963. xvi + 274 pp.

884. ZOLBERG, A. R. "Military Intervention in the New States of Tropical Africa: Elements of Comparative Analysis." In H. Bienen (Ed.) *The Military Intervenes; Case Studies in Political Development.* New York: Russell Sage Foundation, 1968. Pp. 71-98.

2(3)  See also 39, 178, 642, 764, and 798.

2(4) Military regimes

885. ABDEL-MALEK, A. *Egypte, société militaire.* Paris: Editions du Seuil, 1962. 379 pp. English translation: *Egypt—Military Society: the Army Regime, the Left and Social Change under Nasser.* New York: Random House, 1968. xlii + 456 pp. Tr. by C. L. Markmann.

886. ALAVI, H. "Armée et administration au Pakistan" (Army and administration in Pakistan). Revista Internacional de Sociologia (Madrid), 1966, 3 (14): 151-185.

887. AL-QAZAZZ, A. "Military Regimes and Political Stability in Egypt, Iraq and Syria." Berkeley J. of Sociology, 1967, 12: 44-54.

888. AL-QAZAZZ, A. "Political Order, Stability and Officers: a Comparative Study of Iraq, Syria, and Egypt from Independence till June 1967." Middle East Forum, 1969, 45 (2): 31-51.

889. ANDERSON, C. W. "El Salvador: the Army as Reformer." In M. C. Needler (Ed.) *Political Systems in Latin America.* Princeton, N.J.: Van Nostrand, 1964. Pp. 53-72.

890. BADGLEY, J. "Burma's Military Government: a Political Analysis." Asian Survey, 1962, 2 (6): 24-31. Reprinted in W. C. McWilliams (Ed.) *Garrisons and Government; Politics and the Military in New States.* San Francisco: Chandler Publishing Co., 1967. Pp. 171-182.

891. BADGLEY, J. H. "Two Styles of Military Rule: Thailand and Burma." Government and Opposition, 1969, 4: 100-117.

892. BEDREGAL, G. "El problema militar en Bolivia" (The military problem in Bolivia). Política (Caracas), 1966, 5 (54): 27-41.

893. CARR, A. R. M. "Spain: Rule by Generals." In M. Howard (Ed.) *Soldiers and Governments: Nine Studies in Civil-Military Relations.* Bloomington, Ind.: Indiana University Press, 1962. Pp. 133-148.

894. DUDLEY, B. J. "The Military and Politics in Nigeria: Some Reflections." In J. van Doorn (Ed.) *Military Profession and Military Regimes.* The Hague & Paris: Mouton, 1969. Pp. 203-218.

895. FAVRE, H. "Réformisme civil et réformisme militaire au Perou" (Civil and military reform moves in Peru). Politique Etrangère, 1969, 34: 349-372. Contradictory pressures on military rulers.

896. FEIT, E. "The Rule of the 'Iron Surgeons': Military Government in Spain and Ghana." Comparative Politics, 1969, 1: 485-498.

897. GRACZK, K. "Rzady zowodowych wojskowych w Egipcie, Syrii, Iraku" (The rule of professional military men in Egypt, Syria and Iraq). Stud. socjol.-polit., 1967, 24: 249-294.

898. IORDANSKIJ, VE. "O haraktere voennyh diktatur v tropičeskoj Afrika" (The character of the military dictatorships in tropical Africa). Narody Azii I Afrika, 1967, 4: 22-37.

899. KIRK, G. "The Role of the Military in Society and Government: Egypt." In S. N. Fisher (Ed.) *The Military in the Middle East: Problems in Society and Government.* Columbus: Ohio State University Press, 1963. Pp. 71-88.

900. LISSAK, M. "The Military in Burma: Innovation and Frustration." Asian and African Studies, 1969, 5: 133-163.

901. MOORE, R. A., Jr. "The Role of the Army in Pakistan." Political Science, 1968, 19 (2): 28-35.

902. PAGET, R. K. "The Military in Indonesian Politics: the Burden of Power." Pacific Affairs, 1967-68, 40: 294-314.

903. PAYNE, S. G. *Politics and the Military in Modern Spain.* Stanford University Press, 1967. xiii + 574 pp.

904. PYE, L. W. "The Army in Burmese Politics." In J. J. Johnson (Ed.) *The Role of the Military in Underdeveloped Countries.* Princeton, N.J.: Princeton University Press, 1962. Pp. 231-251.

905. SALOMON, J. "Les dictatures militaires républicaines" (Republican military dictatorships). Politique, 1958, 2: 97-146.

906. SAYEED, K. B. "The Role of the Military in Pakistan." In J. van Doorn (Ed.) *Armed Forces and Society.* The Hague & Paris: Mouton, 1968. Pp. 274-297.

907. SHARABI, H. B. "Parliamentary Government and Military Autocracy in the Middle East." Orbis, 1960, 4: 338-355. Reprinted in W. C. McWilliams (Ed.) *Garrisons and Government; Politics and the Military in New States.* San Francisco: Chandler Publishing Co., 1967. Pp. 183-202.

908. TORREY, G. H. "The Role of the Military in Society and Government in

Syria and the Formation of the U.A.R." In S. N. Fisher (Ed.) *The Military in the Middle East: Problems in Society and Government.* Columbus: Ohio State University Press, 1963. Pp. 53-69.

909. TORREY, G. H. *Syrian Politics and the Military.* Columbus: Ohio State University Press, 1964. 438 pp.

910. VATIKIOTIS, P. J. *"The Egyptian Army in Politics: Pattern for New Nations?"* Bloomington, Ind.: Indiana University Press, 1961. 300 pp.

911. WEAVER, J. "La elite politica de un regimen dominado por militares: el ejemplo de Gautemala" (The political elite of a military dominated regime: the case of Guatemala). Revista Latinoamericana de Sociologia, 1969, 5: 21-40.

912. WEAVER, J. L. "Las fuerza armadas guatemáltecas en la politica" (The Guatemalan armed forces in politics). Aportes, 1969, No. 13: 133-146.

913. WEAVER, J. L. "The Military Elite and Political Control in Guatemala, 1933-1966." Social Science Q., 1969, 50: 127-136.

914. WEAVER, J. L. "The Political Style of the Guatemalan Military Elite." Studies in Comparative International Development, 1969-70, 5.

915. WILSON, D. A. "The Military in Thai Politics." In J. J. Johnson (Ed.) *The Role of the Military in Underdeveloped Countries.* Princeton, N.J.: Princeton University Press, 1962. Pp. 253-276.

916. ZOLBERG, A. R. "Military Rule and Political Development in Tropical Africa: a Preliminary Report." In J. van Doorn (Ed.) *Military Profession and Military Regimes.* The Hague & Paris: Mouton, 1969. Pp. 175-202.

2(4) See also IV.1(2) and V.2(2) and 621.

### V.3. The policy process

917. ALMOND, G. A. "Public Opinion and National Security Policy." Public Opinion Q., 1956, 20: 371-378. A survey of political attitudes in the United States.

918. BLAKE, R. "Great Britain: the Crimean War to the First World War." In M. Howard (Ed.) *Soldiers and Governments: Nine Studies in Civil-Military Relations.* Bloomington, Ind.: Indiana University Press, 1962. Pp. 25-50.

919. BROGAN, D. W. "The United States: Civilian and Military Power." In M.

Howard (Ed.) *Soldiers and Governments: Nine Studies in Civil-Military Relations.* Bloomington, Ind.: Indiana University Press, 1962. Pp. 167-185.

920. CARALEY, D. *The Politics of Military Unification; a Study of Conflict and the Policy Process.* New York: Columbia University Press, 1966. xiii + 345 pp. The U.S. defense establishment.

921. COHEN, B. C. "The Military Policy Public." Public Opinion Q., 1966, 30: 200-211. Characteristics and size.

922. DAVIS, V. *Post-War Defense Policy and the U.S. Navy, 1943-46.* Chapel Hill: University of North Carolina Press, 1966. 371 pp. Emergence of new patterns of behavior and strategic judgments.

923. DAWSON, R. H. "Congressional Innovation and Intervention in Defense Policy: Legislative Authorization of Weapons Systems." American Political Science R., 1962, 56: 42-57. Use of purse strings to control military policy.

924. DeWEERD, H. A. "Civilian and Military Elements in Modern War." In J. D. Clarkson & T. C. Cochran (Eds.) *War as a Social Institution.* New York: Columbia University Press, 1941. Pp. 95-112.

925. EDINGER, L. J. "Military Leaders and Foreign Policy-Making." American Political Science R., 1963, 57: 392-405. A paradigm and inventory of analytic problems.

926. EKIRCH, A. E. "The Popular Desire for Peace as a Factor in Military Policy." In H. L. Coles (Ed.) *Total War and Cold War.* Columbus: Ohio State University Press, 1962. Pp. 161-177.

927. ERICKSON, J. *The Soviet High Command: a Military-Political History, 1918-1941.* New York: St. Martin's Press, 1962. 889 pp. Soviet military institutions and military-political relations.

928. FOX, W. T. R. "Civilians, Soldiers, and American Military Policy." World Politics, 1955, 7: 402-418.

929. FOX, W. T. R. "Representativeness and Efficiency: Dual Problem of Civil-Military Relations." Political Science Q., 1961, 76: 354-366.

930. GARTHOFF, R. L. *Soviet Military Policy; a Historical Analysis.* London: Faber & Faber, 1966. viii + 276 pp. See especially Chapter 2—"The Military as a Sociopolitical Force in Russia, 1861-1965"—of which an

earlier version appeared in C. E. Block (Ed.) *The Transformation of Russian Society since 1861.* Cambridge, Mass.: Harvard University Press, 1960.

931. GEORGE, A. L. "American Policy Making and the North Korean Aggression." World Politics, 1955, 7: 209-232.

932. GORDON, B. K. "The Military Budget: Congressional Phase." J. of Politics, 1961, 23: 689-710.

933. HAMMOND, P. Y. "Effects of Structure on Policy." Public Administration R., 1958, 18: 175-179. Decision-making at Department of Defense level.

934. HAMMOND, P. Y. "A Functional Analysis of Defense Department Decision-Making in the McNamara Administration." American Political Science R., 1968, 62: 57-69.

935. HAMMOND, P. Y. *Organizing for Defense.* Princeton, N.J.: Princeton University Press, 1961. xi + 403 pp. The U.S. military establishment from 1900 to 1960 and the effect of organizational forms and methods on policy.

936. HUNTINGTON, S. P. *The Common Defense: Strategic Programs in National Politics.* New York: Columbia University Press, 1961. 500 pp. Policy formation in the American system, 1945-1960.

937. HUNTINGTON, S. P. "Strategic Planning and the Political Process." Foreign Affairs, 1960, 38: 285-299. An analysis of decision-making process in the United States. See also 936.

938. HUZAR, E. *The Purse and the Sword; Control of the Army by Congress through Military Appropriations, 1933-1950.* New York: Cornell University Press, 1950. xiv + 417 pp. Emphasis on civilian control.

939. JONES, F. C. "Japan: the Military Domination of Japanese Policy, 1931-1945." In M. Howard (Ed.) *Soldiers and Governments: Nine Studies in Civil-Military Relations.* Bloomington, Ind.: Indiana University Press, 1962. Pp. 115-131.

940. KING, J. C. *Generals and Politicians; Conflict between France's High Command, Parliament and Government, 1914-1918.* Berkeley & Los Angeles: University of California Press, 1951. 294 pp.

941. KOLKOWICZ, R. *The Soviet Military and the Communist Party.* Princeton, N.J.: Princeton University Press, 1967. xvi + 429 pp.

942. KOLODZIEJ, E. A. *The Uncommon Defense and Congress, 1945-1963.* Ohio: Ohio State University Press, 1966. ix + 630 pp.

943. LYONS, G. "Exigences militaires et budgets militaires aux U.S.A." (Military requirements and military budgets in the United States). Revue Française de Sociologie, 1961, 2 (2): 66-74.

944. McLIN, J. B. *Canada's Changing Defense Policy, 1957-1963.* Baltimore: Johns Hopkins Press, 1967. ix + 251 pp.

945. MILLIS, W. (with H. C. Mansfield & H. Stein). *Arms and the State; Civil-Military Elements in National Policy.* New York: Twentieth Century Fund, 1958. 436 pp.

946. MILLS, C. W. *The Power Elite.* New York: Oxford University Press, 1956. 423 pp. Interchangeability of military and civilian elites in the United States.

947. PILISUK, M., & HAYDEN, T. "Is there a Military Industrial Complex which Prevents Peace? Consensus and Countervailing Power in Pluralistic Systems." J. of Social Issues, 1965, 21 (3): 67-117.

948. ROGERS, L. "Civilian Control of Military Policy." Foreign Affairs, 1940, 18: 280-291.

949. SAPIN, B. M., & SNYDER, R. C. *The Role of the Military in American Foreign Policy.* Garden City, N.Y.: Doubleday, 1954. viii + 84 pp.

950. SCHAFFER, B. B. "Policy and System in Defense; the Australian Case." World Politics, 1963, 15: 236-261. Role and influence of professional military.

951. SCHILLING, W. R. "Civil-Naval Politics in World War I." World Politics, 1955, 7: 572-591.

952. SCHILLING, W. R., HAMMOND, P. Y., & SNYDER, G. H. *Strategy, Politics, and Defense Budgets.* New York: Columbia University Press, 1962. viii + 532 pp.

953. SNYDER, W. P. *The Politics of British Defense Policy, 1945-1962.* Columbus: Ohio State University Press, 1964. xviii + 284 pp. Pressures on policy-making, including the role of the services.

954. SPEIER, H. German Rearmament and the Old Military Elite. World Politics, 1954, 6: 147-168. Postwar political and advisory roles of Hitler's generals.

955. STEIN, H. (Ed.) *American Civil-Military Decisions: a Book of Case Studies.* Birmingham, Ala.: University of Alabama Press, 1962, 705 pp. (Published by the Twentieth Century Fund in cooperation with the Inter-University Case Program.) Includes case studies by M. D. Reagan, A. A. Blum, M. D. Bernstein and F. L. Sloewenheim, R. J. Quinlan, P. Y. Hammond, M. Lichterman, L. W. Martin, and T. J. Lowi, with an introduction by H. Stein.

956. SWOMLEY, J. M., Jr. *The Military Establishment.* Boston: Beacon Press, 1964. xi + 266 pp. Chapters 12 and 13 are good discussions of military influence on foreign policy and its relation to the extreme right.

957. TARR, D. "Military Technology and the Policy Process." Western Political Q., 1965, 18: 135-148.

958. VAGTS, A. *Defense and Diplomacy; the Soldier and the Conduct of Foreign Relations.* New York: King's Crown Press, 1958. xv + 547 pp.

959. WIATR, J. J. *Wojsko, społeczeństwo, polityka w Stanach Zjednoczonych* (Armed forces, society, and politics in the United States). Warsaw: Wydawnictwo Ministerstwa Obrony Narodowej, 1962. 239 pp.

960. WRIGHT, Q. "The Military and Foreign Policy." In J. Kerwin (Ed.) *Civil-Military Relations in American Life.* Chicago: University of Chicago Press, 1948. Pp. 116-136.

V.3. See also V.2(1) and 88, 177, 1021, 1053, and 1286.

## V.4. Men in uniform and civilians

### 4(1) Work relations

961. BERGER, G. Hommes politiques et chefs militaire; étude psycho-sociologique (Political men and military chiefs; a psychosociological study). In Centre de Sciences Politique de l'Institute d'Etudes Juridiques de Nice (Ed.) *La défense nationale.* Paris: Presses Universitaires de France, 1958. Pp. 15-29.

962. BRANDT, G., & von FRIEDEBURG, L. *Aufgaben der Militärpublizistik in der modernen Gesellschaft* (The Tasks of Military Public Relations in Modern Society). Frankfurt/Main: Europäische Verlagsanstalt, 1966. 141 pp.

963. COATES, C. H. "The Role of the Military Sociologist in Operations Research." Sociological and Social Research, 1958, 42: 327-331.

964. DEMERATH, N. J. "Initiating and Maintaining Research Relations in a Military Organization." J. of Social Issues, 1952, 8 (3): 11-23. Obstacles and methods for overcoming them.

965. HOROWITZ, I. L. *The War Game; Studies of the New Civilian Militarists.* New York: Ballantine Books, 1963. 189 pp.

966. LANIER, L. H. "Psychological and Social Scientists in the National Military Establishment." American Psychologist, 1949, 4: 127-147.

967. LYONS, G. M. "The New Civil-Military Relations." American Political Science R., 1961, 55: 53-63.

968. LYONS, G. M., & MORTON, L. *Schools for Strategy: Education and Research in National Security Affairs.* New York: Praeger, 1965. xii + 356 pp. Response of the academic and intellectual community to closer relation between military force and policy.

969. MELTON, A. W. "Military Psychology in the United States of America." American Psychologist, 1957, 12: 740-746. Use of psychologists by the services and by agencies of military departments.

970. MICHAEL, D. N. "Some Factors Tending to Limit the Utility of the Social Scientist in Military Systems Analysis." Operations Research, 1957, 5: 90-96.

971. RADWAY, L. I. "Uniforms and Mufti: What Place in Policy? " Public Administration R., 1958, 18: 180-185. Civil-military interaction at the Pentagon.

972. SMITH, V. I. "Role Conflicts in the Position of a Military Education Advisor." Social Forces, 1961, 40: 176-178.

973. SULLIVAN, M. A., Jr., QUEEN, S. A., & PATRICK, R. C., Jr. "Participant Observation as Employed in the Study of a Military Training Program." American Sociological R., 1958, 23: 660-667.

974. VAGTS, A. *The Military Attaché.* Princeton, N.J.: Princeton University Press, 1967. 408 pp.

975. VAGTS, A. "Military Command and Military Government." Political Science Q., 1944, 59: 248-263.

976. ZINK, H. "American Civil-Military Relations in the Occupation of

Germany." In H. L. Coles (Ed.) *Total War and Cold War.* Columbus: Ohio State University Press, 1962. Pp. 211-237.

4(1)  See also 124, 155, and 1148.

### 4(2)  Garrison and host community

977. BARTH, E. A. T. "Air Force Base-Host Community Relations: a Study in Community Typology." Social Forces, 1963, 41: 260-264.

978. CONNOR, S., & FRIEDRCH, C. J. (Eds.) "Military Government." A. of the American Academy of Political and Social Science, 1950, 267: 1-200.

979. DILLARD, H. C. "Power and Persuasion: the Role of Military Government." Yale R., 1952, 42: 212-225.

980. GIMBEL, J. "American Military Government and the Education of a New German Leadership." Political Science Q., 1968, 83: 248-267.

981. GIMBEL, J. *A German Community under American Occupation: Marburg, 1945-1952.* Stanford, Cal.: Stanford University Press, 1961. vi + 259 pp.

982. GLASER, D. "The Sentiment of American Soldiers Abroad toward Europeans." American J. of Sociology, 1946, 51: 433-438.

983. HUNTER, F. Host Community and Air Force Base. Chapel Hill, N.C.: University of North Carolina Institute for Research in Social Science, 1952.

984. KYRE, M., & KYRE, JOAN. *Military Occupation and National Security.* Washington, D.C.: Public Affairs Press, 1968. vi + 198 pp.

985. RODNICK, D. *Postwar Germans: an Anthropologist's Account.* New Haven: Yale, 1948. xii + 233 pp. Responses to military occupation.

986. SMITH, T. V. "Government of Conquered and Dependent Areas." In J. Kerwin (Ed.) *Civil-Military Relations in American Life.* Chicago: University of Chicago Press, 1948. Pp. 91-115.

987. TARR, D. W. "The Military Abroad." A. of the American Academy of Political and Social Science, 1966, 368: 31-42.

988. WOLF, CHARLOTTE *Garrison Community; a Study of an Overseas American Military Colony.* Westport, Conn.: Greenwood Publishing, 1970. 344 pp. Internal social structure and relation to Turkish society.

## VI. STUDY OF WAR AND WARFARE (also 60)

### VI.1. War and conflict: general approaches

989. ANGELL, R. C. "The Sociology of Human Conflict." In E. B. McNeil (Ed.) *The Nature of Human Conflict.* Englewood Cliffs, N.J.: Prentice-Hall, 1965. Pp. 91-115. With a focus on international conflict.

990. ARAUJO, O. *Sociología de la Guerra* (Sociology of war). Biblioteca de publicaciones officiales de la Facultad de Derecho y Ciencias Sociales de la Universidad de Montevideo, 1957, seccion III-XCIII. 434 pp. War and sociology.

991. ARON, R. "Conflict and War from the Viewpoint of Historical Sociology." In *The Nature of Conflict.* Compiled by International Sociological Association, Paris: UNESCO, 1957. Pp. 177-203.

992. BERNARD, J. "Some Current Conceptualizations in the Field of Conflict." American J. of Sociology, 1965, 70: 442-454. Evaluation of utility of game theory modifications.

993. BERNARD, J. "The Theory of Games of Strategy as a Modern Sociology of Conflict." American J. of Sociology, 1954, 59: 411-424.

994. BERNARD, L. L. *War and its Causes.* New York: Holt, 1944. x + 479 pp. A wide ranging survey.

995. BOCK, K. "The Study of War in American Sociology." Sociologus, 1955, 5: 104-113.

996. BOHANNAN, P. (Ed.) *Law and Warfare; Studies in the Anthropology of Conflict.* Garden City, N.Y.: Doubleday, 1967. xvi + 441 pp. Includes discussions of warriors and armies as well as riots and raids.

997. BOULDING, K. *Conflict and Defense: a General Theory.* New York: Harper, 1962. ix + 349 pp. Conflicts among groups, organizations, and nations studied in terms of conflict models derived from economic theory.

998. BOULDING, K. E. "Towards a Pure Theory of Threat Systems." American Economic R., 1963, 53: 424-434.

999. BOUTHOUL, G. "Fonctions sociologiques des guerres" (Sociological functions of wars). Revue Française de Sociologie, 1961, 2 (2): 15-21.

1000. BOUTHOUL, G. *La guerre.* Paris: Presses universitaires de France, 1953. 119 pp. English translation: *War.* New York: Walker, 1962. 150 pp. A briefer statement of the earlier book by this author.

1001. BOUTHOUL, G. *Les guerres; éléments de polémelogic* (Wars; elements of a science of war). Paris: Payet, 1951. 550 pp. Theory of demographic equilibration.

1002. BRAMSON, L., & GOETHALS, G. W. (Ed.) *War: Studies from Psychology, Sociology, Anthropology.* New York: Basic Books, 1964. 407 pp. Includes a number of well-known previously published essays by S. Freud, E. C. Tolman, W. G. Sumner, R. E. Park, B. Malinowski, H. D. Lasswell, M. Janowitz, R. Aron, and others, plus a selected bibliography.

1003a. BUCHAN, A. *War in Modern Society.* New York: Harper & Row, 1968. xvi + 207 pp.

1003b. CHOUCRI, N., & NORTH, R. L. "The Determinants of International Violence." Peace Research Society (International) Papers, 1969, 12: 33-63.

1004. CLARKSON, J. D., & COCHRAN, T. C. (Eds.) *War as a Social Institution.* New York: Columbia University Press, 1941. xvii + 333 pp. A diverse collection of essays on many aspects.

1005. CORNEJO, M. H. *La guerre au point de vue sociologique* (War from the sociological point of view). Paris: M. Giard, 1930. 47 pp.

1006. COSER, L. A. *The Functions of Social Conflict.* New York: Free Press, 1956. 188 pp.

1007. DAVIE, M. R. *The Evolution of War.* New Haven: Yale University Press, 1929. x + 391 pp.

1008. DELBEZ, L. "La notion sociologique de guerre" (The sociological conception of war). Revue Génerale du Droit International Public, 1952, 56: 5-33. Functions, causes, magnitude, and effects of war.

1009. ERMOLENKO, D. "Sociologija i nakotorije problemy mezdunarodnogo konflikta" (Sociology and some problems of military conflict). Meždunarodnaja Zizn, 1968, No. 8: 67-76.

1010. FEDOSEEV, P. N. "Sovremennye sociologiceskie teorii o vojne i mire" (Present-day sociological theories on war and peace). In J. P. Francev (Ed.) *Istoriceskij materializm i social'naja filosofija sovremennoj burzuazii.* Moscow: Socekgiz, Akademija Nauk USSR, Institut Filosofii, 1960. Pp. 540-581.

1011. FRAGA, I. M. "Guerra y conflicto social en la segunda mitad del siglo XX" (War and social conflict in the second half of the twentieth century). Revista del Instituto de Ciencias Sociales, 1967, 10: 45-74.

1012. FRAGA, I. M. *La guerra y la teoría del conflicto social* (War and the theory of social conflict). Madrid: Real academia de ciencias morales y políticas, 1962. 160 pp.

1013. FRIED, M. H., HARRIS, M. & MURPHY, R. *War; the Anthropology of Armed Conflict and Aggression.* Garden City, N.Y.: Published for the American Museum of Natural History by the Natural History Press, 1968. 262 pp. Papers delivered at a symposium of the American Anthropological Association, November 30, 1967.

1014. GINI, C. *Problemi sociologici della guerra* (Sociological problems of war). Bologne: N. Zanichelli, 1921. vi + 390 pp.

1015. GORIELY, G. "Conflits nationaux et conflits sociaux" (National and social conflicts). Revue de l'Institute de Sociologie, 1967, 2-3: 469-483.

1016. GUMPLOVICZ, L. *Der Rassenkampf* (War among races). Innsbruck: Wagnersche Univer.-buchhandlung, 1883. viii + 376 pp. Classic exposition of the conflict school of sociology.

1017. INSTITUT INTERNATIONAL DE SOCIOLOGIE. *Annals.* Vol. 16. *Sociologie de la guerre et de la paix* (Sociology of war and peace). Paris: Marcel Giard, 1932. 318 pp. Papers given at the 10th Congress, held at Geneva, Oct. 1930.

1018. INTERNATIONAL SOCIOLOGICAL ASSOCIATION. *The Nature of Conflict; Studies on the Sociological Aspects of International Tensions.* UNESCO Tensions and Technology Series. Paris, 1957. 314 pp. Contains four essays including those by J. Bernard and R. Aron.

1019. JOHNSON, A. "War". In *Encyclopedia of the Social Sciences.* Vol. 15. New York: Macmillan, 1942. Pp. 331-341.

1020. KELLER, A. G. "Perspective on War." American Sociological R., 1945, 10: 12-17.

1021. KRIESBERG, L. (Ed.) *Social Processes in International Relations.* New York: John Wiley, 1968. xi + 577 pp. Includes articles on military policy, conflict regulation, and patterns of war.

1022. LAGORGETTE, J. *Le rôle de la guerre: étude de sociologie générale* (The Role of War: General Sociological Study). Paris: V. Giard & E. Briere, 1906. xi + 700 pp.

1023. MACK, R. W., & SNYDER, R. C. "The Analysis of Social Conflict— toward an Overview and Synthesis. J. of Conflict Resolution, 1957, 1: 212-248.

1024. McNEIL, E. B. (Ed.) *The Nature of Human Conflict.* Englewood Cliffs, N.J.: Prentice-Hall, 1965. xvi + 315 pp. Includes articles on the psychology, sociology, and history of armed conflict.

1025. MALINOWSKI, B. "An Anthropological Analysis of War." American J. of Sociology, 1941, 46: 521-550. Reprinted in L. Bramson & G. W. Goethals (Eds.) *War.* New York: Basic Books, 1964. Pp. 245-268.

1026. OECONOMO, C. "Guerres et sociologues" (Wars and sociologists). Revue Française de Sociologie, 1961, 2 (2): 22-37.

1027. PARK, R. E. "The Social Functions of War: Observations and Notes." American J. of Sociology, 1941, 46: 551-570. Reprinted in L. Bramson & G. W. Goethals (Eds.) *War.* New York: Basic Books, 1964. Pp. 229-244.

1028. PRUITT, D. G., & SNYDER, R. C. *Theory and Research on the Causes of War.* Englewood Cliffs, N.J.: Prentice-Hall, 1969. xvi + 314 pp. A review of the literature.

1029. RAPOPORT, A. *Fights, Games, and Decisions.* Ann Arbor, Mich.: University of Michigan, 1960. xvi + 400 pp. A mathematical approach to conflict and war.

1030. RAPOPORT, A. *Strategy and Conscience.* New York: Harper & Row, 1964. xxvii + 322 pp. Games.

1031. ROBERTSON, R. "Strategic Relations between National Societies: a Sociological Analysis." J. of Conflict Resolution, 1968, 12: 16-33.

1032. ROUCEK, J. S. "La sociologia de la guerra y de la organizacion internacional" (Sociology of war and of international organization). Revista Mexicana de Sociologia, 1958, 20: 181-208.

1033. RYBKIN, E. I. *Voina i politika* (War and politics). Moscow: Boeh, 1959. 144 pp.

1034. SALOMON, G. "A propos des sociologies de la guerre" (On the sociology of war). Revista Internacional de Sociologia (Madrid), 1938, 46: 423-442.

1035. SCHELLING, T. C. *The Strategy of Conflict.* New York: Oxford University Press, 1963. x + 309 pp. The social psychological nexus of decision-making incorporated into game-theoretical models.

1036. SCHOCH, J. *Der soziologische und tiefenpsychologische Aspekt des Krieges* (The sociological and depth-psychological aspect of war). Zurich: Orell Füssle, 1955. 99 pp. Topical and pacifist.

1037. SELEZNEV, I. A. *Vojna i ideologicveskaja bor'ba* (War and ideological struggle). Moscow: Voenizdat, 1964. 238 pp.

1038. SIMMEL, G. *Conflict.* New York: Free Press, 1955. 195 pp.

1039. STEINMETZ, S. R. "Krieg" (War). In A. Vierkandt (Ed.) *Handwörterbuch der Soziologie.* Stuttgart: Ferdinand Enke, 1931. Pp. 278-284.

1040. STEINMETZ, S. R. *Soziologie des Krieges* (Sociology of War). Leipzig: Verlag von Johann Ambrosius Barth, 1929. xii + 704 pp. Discussion of functions and effects of war in terms of culture and intergroup conflict.

1041. SUMNER, W. G. "War." In *War and Other Essays.* New Haven: Yale University, 1911. Pp. 3-42.

1042. TURNEY-HIGH, H. H. *Primitive War: Its Practice and Concepts.* Columbia, S.C.: University of South Carolina Press, 1949. xi + 277 pp.

1043. VALKENBURGH, P. "Naar een socilogische Theorie van de Oorlog" (Towards a sociological theory of war). Sociologische Gids, 1962, 9: 178-192.

1044. VAN BOGAERT, E. "Polémologie et irénologie" (War and peace studies). Tijdschrift voor Sociale Wetenschappen, 1968, 13: 340-352. Sociological approach to the study of war and peace.

1045. VON WIESE, L., & HONINGSHEIM, P. *Kriegssoziologie* (Sociology of war). Stuttgart: Fischer, 1958, 8 pp.

1046. WALLER, W. (Ed.) *War in the Twentieth Century.* New York: Random

House, 1940. xi + 572 pp. Includes essays on the effects of World War I as well as on the relation of war and society.

1047. WALTZ, K. N. *Man, the State and War; a Theoretical Analysis.* New York & London: Columbia University Press, 1959. viii + 263 pp. Causes of international conflict on three levels of analysis.

1048. WITHEY, S. & KATZ, D. "The Social Psychology of Human Conflict." In E. B. McNeil (Ed.) *The Nature of Human Conflict.* Englewood Cliffs, N.J.: Prentice-Hall, 1965. Pp. 64-90. With special reference to war and peace.

1049. WRIGHT, Q. *A Study of War.* (2nd Ed. with a commentary on war since 1942.) Chicago: The University of Chicago Press, 1965. xlii + 1637 pp. A major work on the military, juridical, psychological, and sociological manifestations of war.

1050. WRIGHT, Q. "The Study of War." In *International Encyclopedia of the Social Sciences.* Vol. 16. New York: Macmillan & Free Press, 1968. Pp. 453-468.

VI.1 See also 1061 and 1273.

## VI.2. Societal conditions and war

### 2(1) Internal forces leading to war

1051. ARON, R. *War and Industrial Society.* Auguste Comte Memorial Lecture No. 3. London: Oxford University Press, 1958. 63 pp. On the relations between the two.

1052. BONGER, W. A. "De Oorlog als sociologisch Probleem" (War as a sociological problem). Mens en Maatschappij, 1940, 16: 81-83. Also in W. A. Bonger, *Verspreide geschriften.* Vol. 2. Amsterdam: De Arbeiderpers, 1950. Pp. 97-109. Points to influence of semifeudal elements as a factor in recent wars.

1053. BOULDING, K. "The Role of the War Industry in International Conflict." J. of Social Issues, 1967, 23 (1): 47-61.

1054. CHARDON, L. *Le conservatisme et la paix: relations entre la guerre et les regimes politiques* (Conservatism and peace: relations between war and political regimes). Paris: Editions du Scorpion, 1963. 191 pp.

1055. DUROSELLE, J.-B. "La nature des conflits internationaux" (The nature of international conflict). Revue Française de Science Politique, 1964, 14: 295-308. A typology.

1056. GALTUNG, J. "A Structural Theory of Aggression." J. of Peace Research, 1964, 1: 95-119. Status disequilibration is viewed as the dynamic force.

1057. GINSBURG, M. "The Causes of War." Sociological R., 1939, 31: 121-143. Socialist, liberal, and psychological interpretations.

1058. HAAS, M. "Social Change and National Aggressiveness, 1900-1960." In J. D. Singer (Ed.) *Quantitative International Politics; Insights and Evidence.* New York: Free Press, 1968. Pp. 215-244. Relationship of external stress and internal strain to the military behavior of ten European nations.

1059. HAAS, M. "Societal Approaches to the Study of War." J. of Peace Research, 1965, 2: 307-323. GNP and indicators of internal disorganization correlated with foreign policy conflict.

1060. HANKINS, F. H. "Pressure of Populations as a Cause of War." A. of the American Academy of Political and Social Science, 1938, 198: 101-108. A high standard of living increases importance of population pressure in war psychology.

1061. MALINOWSKI, B. "War—Past, Present, and Future." In J. D. Clarkson & T. C. Cochran (Eds.) *War as a Social Institution.* New York: Columbia University Press, 1941. Pp. 21-31. An anthropological approach.

1062. MILLS, C. W. *The Causes of World War Three.* New York: Simon & Shuster, 1958. 172 pp. Structural conditions leading to war.

1063. SCHUMPETER, J. "Zur Soziologie der Imperialismen" (The sociology of imperialism). Archiv für Sozialwissenschaft und Soziologie, 1918/19, 46: 275-310. Also in J. Schumpeter, *Aufsätze zur Soziologie.* Tübingen: J.C.B. Mohr (Paul Siebeck), 1953 and in J. Schumpeter, *Two Essays.* New York: Meridian Books, 1951. Pp. 1-98.

1064. SPEIER, H. "Risk, Security and Modern Hero Worship." In *Social Order and the Risk of War.* New York: G. W. Stewart, 1952. Pp. 112-128. Internal politics and war.

1065. STANLEY, M. "The Turn to Violence: a Sociological View of Insurgency." International J. of Comparative Sociology, 1967, 8: 232-244.

1066. TANTER, R. "Dimensions of Conflict Behavior within and between Nations, 1958-60." J. of Conflict Resolution, 1966, 10: 41-64.

1067. VAN HEEK, F. "The Sociological Aspects of War." International J. of Comparative Sociology, 1964, 5: 25-39. Causes of two world wars.

1068. WILKENFELD, J. "Domestic and Foreign Conflict Behavior of Nations." J. of Peace Research, 1968, 4: 56-69.

2(1) See also 1193.

#### 2(2) Patterns of violence: frequency, magnitude, and duration of war

1069. BODART, G. *Militär-historisches Kriegs-Lexikon, 1618-1905* (Military and historical encyclopedia of wars, 1618-1905). Vienna & Leipzig: C. W. Stern, 1908. 956 pp. A source book on battles, wars, size of armed forces, casualties, and peace treaties by various countries.

1070. DENTON, F. H. "Some Regularities in International Conflict, 1820-1949." Background, 1966, 9: 283-296. Trends in level of violence, using Richardson's data.

1071. DENTON, F. H., & PHILLIPS, W. "Some Patterns in the History of Violence." J. of Conflict Resolution, 1968, 12: 182-195. Wars from 1480 to 1900 to analyze periodicity of violent conflict.

1072. HAAS, M. "International Sub-Systems: Stability and Polarity." American Political Science R., 1970, 64: 98-121. Paradigm for testing stability of bipolar and multipolar systems.

1073. HORVATH, W. "A Statistical Model for the Duration of Wars and Strikes." Behavioral Science, 1968, 13: 18-29.

1074. KAPLAN, M. A. "Balance of Power, Bi-Polarity and other Models of International Systems." American Political Science R., 1957, 51: 684-695.

1075. KLINGBERG, F. L. "Predicting the Termination of War: Battle Casualties and Population Losses." J. of Conflict Resolution, 1966, 10: 129-171.

1076. LEE, J. S. "The Periodic Recurrence of Internecine Wars in China." China J., 1931, 14: 111-115.

1077. MOYAL, J. E. "Distribution of Wars in Time." J. of the Royal Statistical Society, 1949, 112: 446-458.

1078. RAPOPORT, A. "Lewis F. Richardson's Mathematical Theory of War." J. of Conflict Resolution, 1957, 1: 249-299.

1079. RICHARDSON, L. F. *Statistics of Deadly Quarrels.* Edited by Q. Wright & C. C. Lienau. Pittsburgh: The Boxwood Press—Chicago: Quadrangle Books: 1960. xlvi + 373 pp. A quantitative analysis of wars in Europe between 1820 and 1945. See also 1078 for a summary.

1080. RUMMEL, R. J. "Dimensions of Conflict Behavior within and between Nations." General Systems, 1963, 8: 1-50.

1081. RUMMEL, R. J. "Dimensions of Dyadic War, 1820-1952." J. of Conflict Resolution, 1967, 11: 176-183. A factor analytic study.

1082. SHECEROV, S. *Economic Phenomena before and after War: a Statistical Theory of Modern War.* London: Routledge—New York: Dutton, 1919. viii + 232 pp.

1083. SINGER, J. D. & SMALL, M. "Alliance Aggregation and the Onset of War, 1815-1945." In J. D. Singer (Ed.) *Quantitative International Politics; Insights and Evidence.* New York: Free Press, 1968. Pp. 247-286. Operational test of balance of power and degree of bipolarity within European state system.

1084. SOROKIN, P. A. *Social and Cultural Dynamics.* Vol. 3. *Fluctuation of Social Relationships, War, and Revolution.* New York: American Book Co., 1937. xvii + 636 pp. Abridged in the one volume edition of the same title—Boston: Porter Sargent, 1957. Pp. 534-570.

1085. TRIFONENKOV, P. I. *Ob osnovnykh zakonakh khoda i iskhoda sovremennoĭ voĭny* (The general laws governing the course and final outcome in modern warfare). Moscow: Boeh, 1962. 116 pp.

1086. WALTZ, K. N. "The Stability of a Bipolar World." Daedalus, 1964, 93: 881-909. Distinction between two blocs and two super powers.

1087. WRIGHT, Q. "The Escalation of International Conflicts." J. of Conflict Resolution, 1965, 9: 434-449. Conflicts since 1914 involving different amounts of military force.

1088. ZINNES, DINA A. "An Analytical Study of the Balance of Power Theories." J. of Peace Research, 1967, 4: 270-288. Critique of Singer and Small.

1089. ZINNES, DINA A., NORTH, R. C., & KOCH, H. E., JR. "Capability, Threat, and the Outbreak of War." In J. N. Rosenau (Ed.) *International Politics and Foreign Policy.* New York: Free Press, 1961. Pp. 469-482.

2(2)  See also 1008 and 1049.

2(3) Role of images in outbreak, intensity, and termination of war

1090. ABEL, T. "The Element of Decision in the Pattern of War." American Sociological R., 1941, 6: 853-859. Timing of decision to fight in twenty-five major wars.

1091. ALLPORT, G. W. "The Role of Expectancy." In H. Cantril (Ed.) *Tensions That Cause Wars.* Urbana, Ill.: University of Illinois Press, 1950. Pp. 43-78. Personal, ideological, and structural factors in the expectancy of war.

1092. AUERBACH, L. "Krieg und Frieden; zu einigen wehrsoziologischen Untersuchungen in Polen und der Tschechoslovakei" (War and peace; comments on some studies in military sociology in Poland and Czechoslovakia). Osteuropa, 1968, 18: 298-310. Polls on the expectation of war.

1093. BOSC, R. "Sociologie de la guerre et désarmement" (Sociology of war and disarmament). Revue Action Populaire, 1960, 136: 312-321.

1094. CALLIS, H. G. "Sociology of International Relations." American Sociological R., 1947, 12: 323-329.

1095. CAMPBELL, J. T., & CAIN, LEILA S. "Public Opinion and the Outbreak of War." J. of Conflict Resolution, 1965, 9: 318-329; comments by A. Rapoport and P. E. Converse. Pp. 329-333. An attempt to test Richardson's theory of war fevers.

1096. CANTRIL, H. *Gauging Public Opinion.* Princeton, N.J.: Princeton University, 1944. xiv + 318 pp. See Chapter 16 for changes of public opinion in response to declaration of war and other decisions.

1097. CANTRIL, H. (Ed.) *Tensions That Cause Wars.* Urbana, Ill.: University of Illinois Press, 1950. 303 pp. Contains contributions by eight social scientists, including G. W. Allport, G. Gurvich, and M. Horkheimer, to a conference held in Paris under the auspices of the UNESCO Tensions Project.

1098. CARR, L. J. "A Situational Approach to Conflict and War." Social Forces, 1946, 24: 300-303.

1099. CARTER, H. "Recent American Studies in Attitudes Towards War: a Summary and Evaluation." American Sociological R., 1945, 10: 343-352.

1100. CLARKE, I. F. "Forecasts of War in Fiction." Comparative Studies in Society and History, 1967, 10: 1-25. See also 1101.

1101. CLARKE, I. F. *Voices Prophesying War, 1763-1984.* New York: Oxford University Press, 1966. x + 254 pp. Changes in the imagery of the war to come.

1102. COSER, L. A. "The Dysfunctions of Military Secrecy." Social Problems, 1963, 11: 13-22.

1103. COSER, L. A. "The Termination of Conflict." J. of Conflict Resolution, 1961, 5: 347-353.

1104. CRAWFORD, W. R. "International Relations and Sociology." American Sociological R., 1948, 13: 263-278.

1105. DEUTSCH, M. "Trust and Suspicion." J. of Conflict Resolution, 1958, 2: 265-279.

1106. ECKHARDT, W., & NEWCOMB, A. G. "Militarism, Personality, and Other Social Attitudes." J. of Conflict Resolution, 1969, 13: 210-219.

1107. GLADSTONE, A. "The Conception of the Enemy." J. of Conflict Resolution, 1959, 3: 132-137.

1108. GRANBERG, D. "War Expectancy and the Evaluation of a Specific War." J. of Conflict Resolution, 1969, 13: 546-549. Attitudes and perceptions.

1109. HAMILTON, R. F. "A Research Note on the Mass Support for 'Tough' Military Initiatives." American Sociological R., 1968, 33: 439-445. Attitudes of preventive and preemptive intervention against China among Americans during Korean conflict.

1110. HANDMAN, M. "War, Economic Motives, and Economic Symbols." American J. of Sociology, 1939, 44: 629-648.

1111. HASSNER, P. "Violence, rationalité, incertitude: tendances apocalyptiques et iréniques dans l'étude des conflits internationaux" (Violence, rationality, uncertainty: apocalyptic and pacific tendencies in the study of international conflict). Revue Française de Science Politique, 1964, 14: 1155-1178.

1112. HOLSTI, O. R., & NORTH, R. C. "The History of Human Conflict." In E. B. McNeil (Ed.) *The Nature of Human Conflict.* Englewood Cliffs, N.J.: Prentice-Hall, 1965. Pp. 155-171. Contra Abel, tensions played a role in outbreak of World War I.

1113. HUNTINGTON, S. P. "Arms Races: Prerequisites and Results." *Public Policy; Yearbook of the Graduate School of Public Administration, Harvard University,* Vol. 7, 1958. Pp. 41-86.

1114. JOYNT, C. B. "Arms Races and the Problem of Equilibrium." Yearbook of World Affairs (London), 1964, 18: 23-40.

1115. KECSKEMETI, P. *Strategic Surrender: the Politics of Victory and Defeat.* Stanford, Cal.: Stanford University, 1958. 287 pp. Prepared as part of a research program of The Rand Corporation.

1116. KELMAN, H. C. (Ed.) *International Behavior: a Social-Psychological Analysis.* New York: Holt, Rinehart & Winston, 1965. xiv + 626 pp. Review essays on national and international images and interaction in international relations.

1117. LASSWELL, H. D. "Chinese Resistance to Japanese Invasion: the Predictive Value of Precrisis Symbols." American J. of Sociology, 1943, 48: 704-716.

1118. LASSWELL, H. D. "Sino-Japanese Crisis: the Garrison State versus the Civilian State." China Q., 1937, 11: 643-649.

1119. LENTZ, T. F. "Opinion Change in Time of War." J. of Psychology, 1945, 20: 147-156.

1120. McGUIRE, M. C. *Secrecy and the Arms Race.* Cambridge, Mass.: Harvard University Press, 1965. 245 pp. A mathematical model.

1121. MILLER, D. C. "Effects of the War Declaration on the National Morale of American College Students." American Sociological R., 1942, 7: 631-644.

1122. MILLER, D. C. "National Morale of American College Students in 1941." American Sociological R., 1942, 7: 194-213.

1123. OKAMURA, H. *Sensô wa naze okoruka—kokusai kinchû no shakai-gaku* (Why war begins—sociology of international tensions). Kyoto: Seki Shoin, 1956. 324 pp.

1124. OSGOOD, R. E. "Stabilizing the Military Environment." In D.- J. Hekhuis, G. G. McClintock, & A. L. Burns (Eds.) *International Stability: Military, Economic, and Political Dimensions.* New York: John Wiley, 1964. Pp. 83-113. Policy implications stemming from instability due to technological innovation.

1125. PUTNEY, S., & MIDDLETON, R. "Some Factors Associated with Student Acceptance or Rejection of War." American Sociological R., 1963, 27: 655-667.

1126. RICHARDSON, L. F. *Arms and Insecurity; a Mathematical Study of the Causes and Origins of War.* Edited by N. Rashevsky & E. Trucco. Pittsburgh: Boxwood Press–Chicago: Quadrangle Books, 1960. xxv + 307 pp. Mutual reactivity in arms races.

1127. ROSE, A. M. "Bases of American Military Morale in World War II." Public Opinion Q., 1945, 9: 411-417.

1128. RUSSETT, B. M. "Cause, Surprise, and no Escape." J. of Politics, 1962, 24: 3-22. Factors in accidental war.

1129. SCHELER, M. F. *Der Genius des Krieges und der deutsche Krieg* (The spirit of war and the German war). Leipzig: Verlag der Weissen Bücher, 1915. xiii + 217 pp. Somewhat tendentious tract by a major figure in sociology.

1130. SMOKER, P. "Fear in the Arms Race: a Mathematical Study." J. of Peace Research, 1964, 1: 55-63.

1131. SMOKER, P. "A Mathematical Study of the Present Arms Race." General Systems, 1963, 8: 51-59.

1132. SMOKER, P. "A Pilot Study of the Present Arms Race." General Systems, 1963, 8: 61-76.

1133. SMOKER, P. "Trade, Defence, and the Richardson Theory of Arms Races: a Seven Nation Study." J. of Peace Research, 1965, 2: 161-176.

1134. SUCHMAN, E. A., GOLDSEN, ROSE K., & WILLIAMS, R. M. Jr. "Attitudes toward the Korean War." Public Opinion Q., 1953, 17: 171-184. American students.

1135. TUCKER, R. W. *The Just War; a Study in Contemporary American Doctrine.* Baltimore: Johns Hopkins Press, 1960. vii + 207 pp. Justifications for employing force and their implications for policy.

1136. VAERTING, M. T. "Zur Soziologie und Politik des Wettrüstens" (The sociology and politics of the arms race). Zeitschrift für die Gesamte Staatswissenschaft, 1963, 10 (4): 13-15.

1137. VALKENBURGH, P. *Mensen in de koude Oorlog: sociologische Bijdrage tot onze Kennis van internationaal politieke Conflictsituaties* (People and the cold war: sociological studies on the acceptance and rejection of war). Meppel: J. A. Boom en Zoon, 1964. 300 pp.

1138. WATSON, G. (Ed.) *Civilian Morale.* Boston: Houghton-Mifflin, 1942. xii + 463 pp. Second year book of the Society for the Psychological Study of Social Issues. A symposium on civilian morale in wartime.

1139. WILLIAMS, R. M., Jr. "Are Americans and their Cultural Values Adaptable to the Concept and Techniques of Unconventional Warfare? " A. of the American Academy of Political and Social Science, 1962, 341: 82-92.

1140. WRENCH, D. "A Note on 'student acceptance or rejection of war'." American Sociological R., 1963, 28: 277-278.

1141. WRIGHT, Q. "Changes in the Conception of War." American J. of International Law, 1924, 18: 755-767.

1142. ZDIMAL, M. "Public Opinion on War and Peace." Mezinárodní politika, 1967, 1. In Czech.

       2(3)  See also 1085, 1087, 1089, and 1186.

**2(4)  Conduct of war and the forms of warfare**

1143. ALLEN, F. R. "Influence of Technology on War." In F. R. Allen et al., *Technology and Social Change.* New York: Appleton-Century-Crofts, 1957. Pp. 352-387. Effects of weapons development on conduct and cost of war.

1144. ANONYMOUS. "Psychological Warfare in Korea; an Interim Report." Public Opinion Q., 1951, 15: 65-75.

1145. ARON, R. *On War.* Garden City, N.Y.: Doubleday-Anchor, 1959. 143 pp.

1146. ASHWORTH, A. E. "The Sociology of Trench Warfare, 1914-1918." British J. of Sociology, 1968, 19: 407-423. Norms limiting offensive actions to mutually tolerable limits.

1147. BEEBE, G. W., & DE BAKEY, M. E. *Battle Casualties: Incidence, Mortality, and Logistic Considerations.* Springfield, Ill.: Charles C Thomas, 1952. xxiii + 227 pp. Study by two physicians includes neuropsychiatric ineffectiveness.

1148. BLACKETT, P. M. S. "Scientific Method and the Study of War." In *Studies of War: Nuclear and Conventional.* New York: Hill & Wang, 1962. Pp. 47-53. This article, as well as other essays, contains interesting discussions of operations research applied to tactical and strategic problems.

1149a. BLOCH, J. The Future of War in its Technical, Economic and Political Relations. Boston: Ginn, 1902.

1149b. BOHANNAN, C. T. R. "Antiguerrilla Operations." A. of the American Academy of Political and Social Science, 1962, 341: 19-29.

1150. COTTRELL, L. S., Jr. "Social Research and Psychological Warfare." Sociometry, 1960, 23: 103-119.

1151. DAUGHERTY, W. E., & JANOWITZ, M. (Eds.) *A Psychological Warfare Casebook.* Baltimore: Johns Hopkins Press, 1958. xxiii + 880 pp. Includes bibliographies.

1152. DE JONG, L. *The German Fifth Column in the Second World War.* Translated by C. M. Geyl. Chicago: University of Chicago, 1956. 308 pp. A case study in psychological warfare.

1153. DELBRUCK, H. *Geschichte der Kriegskunst im Rahmen der politischen Geschichte* (History of the art of war in the context of political history). (4 vols.) Berlin: G. Stilke, 1900-20. A standard historical work and excellent source of sociological data.

1154. DELMAS, C. "La guerre révolutionaire" (Revolutionary war). Revue Travaux de l'Académie des Sciences Morales et Politiques, 1959, 112 (1): 96-118.

1155. DYER, M. *The Weapon on the Wall; Re-Thinking Psychological Warfare.* Baltimore: Johns Hopkins Press, 1959. xxi + 269 pp.

1156. EARLE, E. M. (Ed.) Makers of Modern Strategy. Princeton, N.J.: Princeton University Press, 1943. xi + 533 pp. Essays on major strategic thinkers in relation to their times.

1157. ECKSTEIN, H. (Ed.) *Internal War; Problems and Approaches.* New York: Free Press, 1964. x + 339 pp. Essays on insurgency and violence as political instruments.

1158. FOREMAN, P. B. "Buchenwald and Modern Prisoner-of-War Detention Policy." Social Forces, 1959, 37: 289-298.

1159. FULLER, J. F. C. *The Conduct of War, 1789-1961.* New Brunswick, N.J.: Rutgers University Press, 1961. 352 pp. Influence of social and technological environment.

1160. GALLI, G. "Guerriglia e guerra atomica" (Guerrilla and atomic warfare). Studi di Sociologia, 1965, 3: 109-123.

1161. GARTHOFF, R. L. *Soviet Military Doctrine.* New York: Free Press, 1953. xviii + 587 pp.

1162. GEBKA, P. "Formy prowedzenia wojny psychologicznej w Algierii" (The forms of psychological war in Algeria). Stud. socjol. polit., 1967, 24: 167-187.

1163. GEORGE, A. L. *Propaganda Analysis; a Study of Inferences Made from Nazi Propaganda in World War II.* Evanston, Ill.: Row, Peterson, 1959. 287 pp.

1164. GROSSIN, W. "Les conditions sociales de la strategie" (The social circumstances of strategy). Cahiers Internationaux de Sociologia, 1963, 34: 69-98.

1165. HALPERIN, M. H. *Limited War in the Nuclear Age.* New York: John Wiley, 1963. ix + 191 pp. Examines increasing likelihood of limited warfare.

1166. HERZ, M. F. "Some Psychological Lessons from Leaflet Propaganda in World War II." Public Opinion Q., 1949, 13: 471-486.

1167. HILSMAN, R. "Research in Military Affairs." World Politics, 1955, 7: 490-503.

1168. HOWARD, M. (Ed.) *The Theory and Practice of War.* London: Cassell, 1965. x + 377 pp. Historical essays presented to Captain B. H. Liddell Hart on his seventieth birthday dealing with the development in different countries of strategic and tactical theory since the 18th century and its impact on the practice of war.

1169. HUNTINGTON, S. P. "Guerrilla Warfare in Theory and Policy." In F. M. Osanka (Ed.) *Modern Guerrilla Warfare.* New York: Free Press, 1962. Pp. xv-xxii.

1170. HUNTINGTON, S. P. "Patterns of Violence in World Politics." In S. P. Huntington (Ed.) *Changing Patterns of Military Politics.* New York: Free Press, 1962. Pp. 17-50.

1171. JANOS, A. C. "Unconventional Warfare: Framework and Analysis." World Politics, 1963, 15: 636-646.

1172. JOHNSON, C. A. "Civilian Loyalties and Guerrilla Conflict." World Politics, 1962, 14: 646-661. Reprinted in W. C. McWilliams (Ed.) *Garrisons and Government; Politics and the Military in New States.* San Francisco: Chandler Publishing Co., 1967. Pp. 80-98. Evaluation of their importance.

1173. JOHNSON, C. "Third Generation of Guerrilla Warfare." Asian Studies, 1968, 8: 435-447.

1174. KAHN, L. A., & ANDREWS, T. G. "A Further Analysis of the Effectiveness of Psychological Warfare." J. of Applied Psychology, 1955, 39: 368-374.

1175. KVEDER, D. "Territorial War: the New Concept of Resistance." Foreign Affairs, 1953/54, 32: 91-108.

1176. LAGOVSKII, A. N. *Strategiîa i ekonomika* (Strategy and economics). Moscow: Boeh, 1961. 262 pp. Economic influences on military activities.

1177. LASSWELL, H. D. *Propaganda Technique in the World War.* New York: Alfred A. Knopf, 1927. 233 pp. Social science analysis of psychological warfare in 1914-1918.

1178. LEMERT, E. M. "Social Participation and Totalitarian War." American Sociological R., 1943, 8: 531-536.

1179. LERNER, D. *Sykewar: Psychological Warfare against Germany, D-Day to VE-Day.* New York: G. W. Stewart, 1949. xviii + 463 pp.

1180. LINEBARGER, P. M. *Psychological Warfare.* (2nd Ed.) New York: Duell, Sloan, & Pearce, 1960. 318 pp.

1181. MALCZEWSKI, F. "Problematyka propagandy w amerykańskiej teorii wojny psychologicznej" (The problems of propaganda in the American theory of psychological warfare). Studia Socjologiczno-Polityczne, 1963, 15: 135-184.

1182. MALCZEWSKI, F. "Zarys rozwoju propagandy wojskowej; jej organizacji i skodkow" (An outline of the history of military propaganda, its organization and means of persuasion). Studia Socjologiczno-Polityczne, 1967, 24: 101-166. From the Greeks to World War II.

1183. MALINOWSKI, W. R. "The Pattern of Underground Resistance." A. of the American Academy of Political and Social Science, 1944, 232: 126-133.

1184. MEGRET, M. *L'action psychologique* (Psychological action). Paris: Librairie Arthème Fayard, 1959. 200 pp. Unconventional warfare.

1185. MEGRET, M. *La guerre psychologique* (The psychological war). (2nd Ed.) Paris: Presses Universitaires de France, 1960. 127 pp.

1186. NAVILLE, P. "Les arguments sociaux de la strategy" (The social arguments of strategy). Revue Française de Sociologie, 1961, 2 (2): 4-14.

1187. OSANKA, F. M. "Guerrilla Warfare." In *International Encyclopedia of the Social Sciences.* Vol. 7. New York: Macmillan & Free Press, 1968. Pp. 503-506.

1188. OSANKA, F. M. (Ed.) *Modern Guerrilla Warfare; Fighting Communist Guerrilla Movements 1941-1961.* New York: Free Press, 1962. xxii + 519 pp. Introduction—"Guerrilla Warfare in Theory and Policy"—by S. P. Huntington is followed by descriptive case studies.

11189. OTTERBEIN, K. F. "Internal War: a Cross-Cultural Study." American Anthropologist, 1968, 4: 91-109.

1190. PARET, P. *French Revolutionary Warfare from Indochina to Algeria; the Analysis of a Political and Military Doctrine.* New York: Praeger, 1964. vi + 163 pp.

1191. PARET, P., & SHY, J. W. *Guerrillas in the 1960's.* (2nd Ed.) New York: Praeger, 1962. 98 pp.

1192. PYE, L. W. *Guerrilla Communism in Malaya; its Social and Political Meaning.* Princeton, N.J.: Princeton University, 1956. 369 pp. Based on interviews with defectors.

1193. PYE, L. W. "The Roots of Insurgency and the Commencement of Rebellions." In H. Eckstein (Ed.) *Internal War.* New York: Free Press, 1964. Pp. 157-179.

1194. RENN, L. (pseudonym). *Warfare: the Relations of War to Society.* New York: Oxford, 1939. 276 pp.

1195. RILEY, J. W., Jr., & COTTRELL, L. S., Jr. "Research for Psychological Warfare." Public Opinion Q., 1957, 21: 147-158.

1196. RILEY, J. W., JR., & SCHRAMM, W. *The Reds Take a City.* New Brunswick, N.J.: Rutgers University Press, 1951. xiv + 210 pp. North Korean occupation of Seoul.

1197. SCHEIN, E. H. "The Chinese Indoctrination Program for Prisoners of War: a Study of Attempted 'brainwashing.' " Psychiatry, 1956, 19: 149-172.

1198. SPEIER, H. "Psychological Warfare Reconsidered." In D. Lerner & H. D. Lasswell (Eds.) *The Policy Sciences.* Stanford, Cal.: Stanford University, 1951. Pp. 252-270. Also in H. Speier, *Social Order and the Risks of War.* New York: G. W. Stewart, 1952. Pp. 433-455.

1199. SPEIER, H. "The Social Types of War." American J. of Sociology, 1941, 46: 445-454. Reprinted in *Social Order and the Risks of War.* New York: G. W. Stewart, 1952. Pp. 223-229.

1200. THOMPSON, L. S. "The Psychological Impact of Air Power." A. of the American Academy of Political and Social Science, 1955, 299: 58-66.

1201. U.S. STRATEGIC BOMBING SURVEY, MORALE DIVISION. *The Effects of Strategic Bombing on German Morale.* Washington, D.C.: U.S. G.P.O., 1947. Dates of survey: March-July, 1945.

1202. U.S. STRATEGIC BOMBING SURVEY *The U.S. Strategic Bombing Survey: Overall Report (European War).* Washington, D.C.: U.S. G.P.O., 1945. x + 109 pp.

1203. VAYDA, A. P. "Primitive War." In *International Encyclopedia of the Social Sciences.* Vol. 16. New York: Macmillan & Free Press, 1968. Pp. 468-472.

1204. WOLFE, T. W., DINERSTEIN, H. S., & GOURE, L. *Soviet Strategy at the Crossroads.* Cambridge, Mass.: Harvard University Press, 1964. 342 pp.

1205. WYLIE, J. C. *Military Strategy; a General Theory of Power Control.* New Brunswick, N.J.: Rutgers University Press, 1967. vii + 111 pp.

1206. ZAWODNY, J. K. "Civil War." In *International Encyclopedia of the Social Sciences.* Vol. 7. New York: Macmillan & Free Press, 1968. Pp. 499-502.

1207. ZAWODNY, J. K. "Guerrilla and Sabotage: Organization, Operations, Motivations, Escalation." A. of the American Academy of Political and Social Science, 1962, 341: 8-18.

1208. ZAWODNY, J. K. "Unconventional Warfare." American Scholar, 1962, 31: 384-394.

   2(4) See also III.6(2) and III.6(3) and 247, 975, and 1049.

### VI.3. Costs and consequences of war

1209. BALLARD, J. S. "Demobilization and its Impact, 1944-1947." Rocky Mountain Social Science J., 1965, 2 (2): 107-118.

1210. BARON, S. W. "The Impact of Wars on Religion." Political Science Q., 1952, 67: 534-572.

1211. BECKER, D. "The Veteran: Problem and Challenge." Social Forces, 1946, 25: 95-99.

1212. BODART, G. *Losses of Life in Modern Wars.* Oxford: Clarendon Press, 1916. x + 207 pp. War losses by Austria-Hungary, 1618-1913, and by France, 1614-1913.

1213. BOGART, E. L. *Direct and Indirect Cost of the Great World War.* New York: Oxford University Press, 1919. vi + 338 pp.

1214. BRILL, N. Q., & BEEBE, G. W. *A Follow-Up Study of War Neuroses.* Washington, D.C.: U.S. Veterans Administration Medical Monograph, 1955. xviii + 393 pp.

1215. BROMBERG, W. "The Effects of the War on Crime." American Sociological R., 1943, 8: 685-691.

1216. BROOKOVER, W. B. "The Adjustment of Veterans to Civilian Life." American Sociological R., 1945, 10: 579-586.

1217. CHISHOLM, G. B. "The Soldier's Return." Psychiatry, 1945, 8: 103-105.

1218. DUCOFF, L. J., HAGOOD, M. J., & TAEUBER, C. "Effect of the War on the Agricultural Working Force and on the Rural Farm Population." Social Forces, 1943, 21: 406-412.

1219. DUMAS, S., & VEDEL-PETERSEN, K. O. *Losses of Life Caused by War.* Oxford: Clarendon Press, 1923. 191 pp.

1220. DUNHAM, H. W. "War and Mental Disorder: some Sociological Considerations." Social Forces, 1944, 22: 137-142.

1221. EATON, W. H. "Research on Veterans' Adjustment." American J. of Sociology, 1946, 51: 483-487.

1222. EXNER, F. *Krieg und Kriminalität in Osterreich* (War and crime in Austria). Vienna: Holder-Pichler-Tempsky—New Haven: Yale University, 1927. xiii + 217 pp.

1223. FAIRCHILD, H. P. "Postwar Population Problems." Social Forces, 1944, 23: 1-6.

1224. FRAZIER, E. F. "Ethnic and Minority Groups in Wartime, with Special Reference to the Negro." American J. of Sociology, 1942, 47: 369-377.

1225. GENTILE, F. M. "The Effects of the War upon the Family and its Members." Psychiatry, 1943, 6: 37-49.

1226. HARVEY, M. L. "Standards of Living of Russian Industrial Workers." In J. D. Clarkson & T. C. Cochran (Eds.) *War as a Social Institution.* New York: Columbia University Press, 1941. Pp. 235-246. World War I.

1227. HAVIGHURST, R. J., EATON, W. H., BAUGHMAN, J. W., & BURGESS, E. W. *The American Veteran Back Home: a Study of Veteran Readjustment.* New York: Longmans, Green, 1951. xiv + 271 pp. 416 veterans in midwestern community.

1228. HAVIGHURST, R. J., & MORGAN, H. G. *The Social History of a War-Boom Community.* New York: Longmans, Green, 1951. xix + 356 pp.

1229. HAWLEY, A. H. "Land Value Patterns in Okayama, Japan, 1940 and 1952." American J. of Sociology, 1955, 60: 487-492. Impact of bomb destruction.

1230. HEBERLE, R. *The Impact of the War on Population Redistribution in the South.* Nashville, Tenn.: Vanderbilt University Press, 1945. 64 pp.

1231. HENDRY, J. B. "Economic Development under Conditions of Guerrilla Warfare: the Case of Viet Nam." J. of Asian Studies, 1962, 21: 1-12.

1232. HERRING, E. P. *The Impact of War: Our American Democracy under Arms.* New York: Farrar & Rinehart, 1941. ix + 306 pp.

1233. HERSCH, L. "Demographic Effects of Modern War." In Interparliamentary Union, *What Would Be the Character of a New War?* London: King, 1931. xviii + 411 pp.

1234. IKLE, F. C., & KINCAID, H. V. *Social Aspects of Wartime Evacuation of American Cities, with Particular Emphasis on Long-Term Housing and Reemployment.* Washington, D.C.: National Academy of Sciences, National Research Council, 1956. xii + 100 pp.

1235. IKLE, F. C. *The Social Impact of Bomb Destruction.* Norman, Okla.: University of Oklahoma, 1958. xxii + 250 pp.

1236. JANIS, I. L. *Air War and Emotional Stress.* New York: McGraw-Hill, 1951. 280 pp. Effects on civilian population.

1237. KAEMPFFERT, W. "Science, Technology, and War." In J. Kerwin (Ed.) *Civil-Military Relations in American Life.* Chicago: University of Chicago Press, 1948. Pp. 1-18.

1238. KAEMPFFERT, W. "War and Technology." American J. of Sociology, 1941, 46: 431-444.

1239. LASSETER, D. B. "The Impact of the War on the South and Implications for Post-War Developments." Social Forces, 1944, 23: 20-26.

1240. LEIGHTON, A. *Human Relations in a Changing World.* New York: E. P. Dutton, 1949. 354 pp. Observations on the use of the social sciences, largely a result of visit to Hiroshima in 1945 with U.S. Strategic Bombing Survey.

1241. LIEPMANN, M. *Krieg und Kriminalität in Deutschland* (War and crime in Germany). Stuttgart & Berlin: Deutsche Verlagsanstalt—New Haven: Yale, 1930. xiii + 197 pp.

1242. McDONAGH, E. C. "The Discharged Serviceman and his Family." American J. of Sociology, 1946, 51: 451-454.

1243. MANNHEIM, H. *War and Crime.* London: Watts & Co., 1941. ix + 208 pp.

1244. MEERWARTH, R., GUNTHER, A., & ZIMMERMANN, W. *Die Einwirkung des Krieges auf die Bevölkerungsbewegung, Einkommen und Lebenshaltung in Deutschland* (The impact of the war on migration, income and living standards in Germany). Stuttgart: Deutsche Verlagsanstalt, 1932. xv + 474 pp.

1245. MINER, J. B., & ANDERSON, J. K. "The Postwar Occupational Adjustment of Emotionally Disturbed Soldiers." J. of Applied Psychology, 1958, 42: 317-322.

1246. MORTON, L. "War, Science, and Social Change." In K. H. Silvert (Ed.) *The Social Reality of Scientific Myth.* American Universities Field Staff Conference Series, 1969. Pp. 22-57.

1247. MOWRY, G. E. "The First World War and American Democracy." In J. D. Clarkson & T. C. Cochran (Eds.) *War as a Social Institution.* New York: Columbia University Press, 1941. Pp. 170-184. Wartime controls.

1248. NEF, J. U. *War and Human Progress: an Essay on the Rise of Industrial Civilization.* Cambridge, Mass.: Harvard University, 1950. ix + 464 pp.

1249. NOTTINGHAM, E. K. "Towards an Analysis of the Effects of Two World Wars on the Role and Status of Middle Class Women in the English-Speaking World." American Sociological R., 1947, 12: 666-675.

1250. NOVICOW, J. *La guerre et ses prétendus bienfaits* (War and its alleged benefits). Paris: A. Colin, 1894. 199 pp. Critique of some assumptions of the Conflict School.

1251. PRINZING, F. *Epidemics Resulting from Wars.* Ed. by H. Westergaard. Oxford: Clarendon Press, 1916. xii + 346 pp.

1252. RADOMSKA-STRZEMECKA, HELENA. "Wplyw wojny na stosunek mlodziezy wobec rodziny" (The impact of war on the attitudes of youth toward family). Przeglad Socjologiczny, 1958, 12: 164-190.

1253. RECKLESS, W. "The Impact of War on Crime, Delinquency and Prostitution." American J. of Sociology, 1942, 47: 378-386.

1254. ROTHWELL, C. E. "War and Economic Institutions." In J. D. Clarkson & T. C. Cochran (Eds.) *War as a Social Institution.* New York: Columbia University Press, 1941. Pp. 197-211.

1255. SAENGER, G. "The Effect of War on our Minority Groups." American Sociological R., 1943, 8: 15-22. General discussion of "wedge driving" influences.

1256. SEGAL, H. A. "Initial Psychiatric Findings of Recently Repatriated Prisoners of War." American J. of Psychiatry, 1954, 111: 358-363. Korean experience.

1257. SMITH, M. "The Differential Impact of Selective Service Inductions on Occupations in the United States." American Sociological R., 1946, 11: 567-572.

1258. SOROKIN, P. A. *Man and Society in Calamity; the Effects of War, Revolution, Famine, Pestilence upon Human Mind, Behavior, Social Organization and Cultural Life.* New York: E. P. Dutton, 1942. 352 pp.

1259. SOROKIN, P. A. "A Neglected Factor of War." American Sociological R., 1938, 3: 475-486.

1260. SOROKIN, P. A. "War and Post-War Changes in Social Stratification of the Euro-American Population." American Sociological R., 1945, 10: 294-303.

1261. SPEIER, H. "Class Structure and Total War." American Sociological R., 1939, 4: 370-380. Reprinted in H. Speier, *Social Order and the Risks of War.* New York: G. W. Stewart, 1952. Pp. 253-262.

1262. SPEIER, H., & KAHLER, A. (Eds.) *War in Our Time.* New York: W. W. Norton, 1939. 362 pp. Seventeen essays by members of the New School faculty on costs and dislocations of war.

1263. TETREAU, E. D. "The Impact of War on Some Communities in the South West." American Sociological R., 1943, 8: 249-255.

1264. THOMPSON, J. W. "The Aftermath of the Black Death and the Aftermath of the Great War." American J. of Sociology, 1921, 26: 565-572.

1265. TIMASHEFF, N. S. *War and Revolution.* (Edited by J. F. Scheuer.) New York: Sheed & Ward, 1965. xii + 339 pp.

1266. U.S. PRESIDENT'S COMMISSION ON VETERANS' PENSIONS. *Findings and Recommendations.* Washington, D.C.: U.S. G.P.O., April, 1956. Readjustment of veterans of World War II.

1267. VINCENT, P. "Guerre et population" (War and population) Population, 1947, 2: 9-30. Challenge to thesis of demographic equilibration.

1268. WALLER, W. *The Veteran Comes Back.* New York: Dryden, 1944. xiii + 316 pp.

1269. WECTOR, D. "From Soldier to Citizen." In J. Kerwin (Ed.) *Civil-military Relations in American Life.* Chicago: University of Chicago Press, 1948. Pp. 19-41

1270. WERNER, V. La guerre est-elle un facteur d'acceleration de progrès? (Is war a factor of acceleration of progress? ) Res Publica, 1966, 8: 200-214.

1271. WINKLER, W. *Die Einkommensverschiebungen in Oesterreich während des Weltkrieges* (Income redistribution in Austria during the world war). Vienna: Hölder-Pichler-Tempsky, 1930. xv + 278 pp.

1272. ZNANIECKI, F. "The Impact of War on Personality Organization." Sociology and Social Research, 1943, 27: 171-180. Stratification shifts from status to the functional importance of roles.

VI.3  See also 33, 34, 38, 589, 607, 612, 1040, 1046, 1049, 1082, and 1143.

### VI.4. Strategy and bargaining in the international system

1273. ARON, R. *Paix et guerre entre les nations.* Paris: Calmann-Lévy, 1962. 797 pp. English translation: *War and Peace; a Theory of International Relations.* Garden City, N.Y.: Doubleday, 1966. xviii + 820 pp. Part I–Theory: Concepts and Systems; Part II–Sociology: Determinants and Constants; Part III–History: the Global System in the Thermonuclear Age; Part IV–Praxeology: the Antinomies of Diplomatic-Strategic Conduct.

1274. ARON, R. "Remarques sur l'evolution de la pensée stratégique (1945-1968); ascension et declin de l'analyse strategique" (Remarks on the evolution of strategic thought–1945-1968; the rise and decline of strategic analysis). Archives Européennes de Sociologie, 1968, 9: 151-179. Problems of doctrine raised by experience with deterrence.

1275. ARON, R. "Une sociologie des relations internationales" (A sociology of international relations). Revue Française de Sociologie, 1963, 4: 307-320.

1276. BRODIE, B. "Military Demonstrations and Disclosure of New Weapons." World Politics, 1953, 5: 281-301. Conditions that enjoin publicity or secrecy of advances in technology.

1277. BRODIE, B. *Strategy in the Missile Age.* Princeton, N.J.: Princeton University Press, 1959. 423 pp. New meaning of deterrence.

1278. BURNS, A. L. "From balance to deterrence: a theoretical analysis." World Politics, 1957, 9: 494-529. New weapons have produced a qualitative change in international relations.

1279. DAVISON, W. P. *The Berlin Blockade: a Study in Cold War Politics.* Princeton, N.J.: Princeton University, 1958. 423 pp.

1280. DINERSTEIN, H. S. *War and the Soviet Union: Nuclear Weapons and the Revolution in Soviet Military and Political Thinking.* New York: Praeger, 1959. 268 pp.

1281. DINERSTEIN, H. S., GOURE, L. & WOLFE, T. W. *Soviet Military Strategy.* Englewood Cliffs, N.J.: Prentice-Hall, 1963. 544 pp.

1282. ETZIONI, A. *Winning without War.* Garden City, N.Y.: Doubleday, 1965. xiii + 260 pp. Discussion of strategy by a sociologist.

1283. GALTUNG, J. "On the Future of the International System." J. of Peace Research, 1967, 4: 305-333. Diagnosis of war potential in emerging international system.

1284. GOLDHAMER, H., & SPEIER, H. "Some Observations on Political Gaming." World Politics, 1959, 12: 71-83.

1285. GRAY, R. B. (Ed.) *International Security Systems: Concepts and Models of World Order.* Itasca, Ill.: Peacock, 1969. xi + 227 pp. Essays in the application of systems theory; mostly reprints by political scientists.

1286. HILSMAN, R. *Strategic Intelligence and National Decisions.* New York: Free Press, 1956. 187 pp.

1287. HOAG, M. W. On Stability in Deterrent Races. World Politics, 1961, 13: 505-527.

1288. HOFFMANN, S. *The State of War: Essays in the Theory and Practice of International Politics.* New York: Praeger, 1965. xi + 276 pp. Viewed as operating under the continuous threat of violence.

1289. HORVATH, W. J., & FOSTER, C. C. "Stochastic Models of War Alliances." J. of Conflict Resolution, 1963, 7: 110-116. Also in General Systems, 1963, 8: 77-81.

1290. HSIEH, A. L. *Communist China's Strategy in the Nuclear Era.* Englewood Cliffs, N.J.: Prentice-Hall, 1962. 204 pp.

1291. JENSEN, L. "Military Capabilities and Bargaining Behavior." J. of Conflict Resolution, 1965, 9: 155-163. U.S. and Soviet cold war politics.

1292. KAUFMANN, W. W. "The Requirements of Deterrence." In W. W. Kaufmann (Ed.) *Military Policy and National Security.* Princeton, N.J.: Princeton University Press, 1956. Pp. 12-38.

1293. KISSINGER, H. A. *Nuclear Weapons and Foreign Policy.* Garden City, N.Y.: Doubleday-Anchor, 1958. 455 pp. Offers and analysis of the balance between military policy and foreign policy.

1294. MACCOBY, M. "The Social Psychology of Deterrence." B. of the Atomic Scientists, 1961, 17: 278-281. A critique of gaming.

1295. McWILLIAMS, W. C. "The Developing Nations and International Order." In W. C. McWilliams (Ed.) *Garrisons and Government; Politics and the Military in New States.* San Francisco: Chandler Publishing Co., 1967. Pp. 303-327.

1296. RAPOPORT, A. "Formal Games as Probing Tools for Investigating Behavior Motivated by Trust and Suspicion." J. of Conflict Resolution, 1963, 7: 570-579.

1297. RUSSETT, B. M. "Calculus of Deterrence." J. of Conflict Resolution, 1963, 7: 97-105. Conditions that make credible large power determination to defend smaller ally.

1298. SCHELLING, T. C. *Arms and Influence.* New Haven: Yale University Press, 1966. ix + 293 pp. Potential military force in international dialogue.

1299. SCHELLING, T. C. "War without Pain, and other Models." World Politics, 1963, 15: 465-487.

1300. SPEIER, H. *Divided Berlin: the Anatomy of Soviet Political Blackmail.* New York: Praeger, 1961. 201 pp.

1301. SPEIER, H. *German Rearmament and Atomic War.* Evanston, Ill.: Row, Peterson, 1957. 272 pp.

1302a. TRUYOL Y SERRA, A. *La teoria de las relaciones internacionales como sociologia* (The theory of international relations as sociology). (2nd Rev. Ed.) Madrid: Instituto de Estudios Politicos, 1963. 65 pp.

1302b. VELLUT, J. L. "Smaller States and the Problem of War and Peace: Some Consequences of the Emergence of Smaller States in Africa." J. of Peace Research, 1967, 3: 252-268.

1303. YOUNG, O. R. *The Politics of Force: Bargaining During International Crises.* Princeton, N.J.: Princeton University Press, 1968. xii + 438 pp. Case studies to generate hypotheses about threats and conflict regulation.

VI.4. See also 1030, 1094, 1104, 1105, 1113, and 1128.

**VI.5. Peace-keeping and conflict regulation**

1304. BOULDING, K. E. "Toward a Theory of Peace." In R. Fisher (Ed.)

*International Conflict and Behavioral Science.* New York: Basic Books, 1964. Pp. 70-87. Vectorial representation of peace as controlled conflict.

1305. BRENNAN, D. G. (Ed.) *Arms Control, Disarmament, and National Security.* New York: Braziller, 1961. 475 pp. Based on Fall 1960 issue of *Daedalus.*

1306. CLANDE, I. L. "United Nations' Use of Military Force." J. of Conflict Resolution, 1963, 7: 117-129.

1307. COSER, L. "Peaceful Settlements and the Dysfunctions of Secrecy." J. of Conflict Resolution, 1963, 7: 246-253.

1308. COTTRELL, F. W. "Research to Establish the Conditions for Peace." J. of Social Issues, 1955, 11 (1): 13-20.

1309. DEUTSCH, M. "Psychological Alternatives to War." J. of Social Issues, 1962, 18 (2): 97-119. Reprinted in Q. Wright, W. M. Evan, & M. Deutsch, *How to Prevent World War III: Some Proposals.* New York: Simon & Schuster, 1962. 460 pp.

1310. EVAN, W. "An International Public Opinion Poll on Disarmament and 'inspection by the people' ": a Study of Attitudes toward Supranationalism." In S. Melman (Ed.) *Inspection for Disarmament.* New York: Columbia University Press, 1958. Pp. 231-250.

1311. FALK, R. A., & MENDLOVITZ, S. H. (Eds.) *The Strategy of World Order: toward a Theory of War Prevention.* (4 vols.) New York: World Law Fund, 1966.

1312. GREHANOV, A. H. "Problemy vojny i mira v sovremennyh uslovijah" (Problems of war and peace under contemporary conditions). Učenye Zapiski (Moskovskij Oblastnoj Pedagogisčeskij Institute) Osnovy Naučz Kommunizm, 1970, 270: 147-169.

1313. HOLSTI, K. J. "Resolving International Conflicts: a Taxonomy of Behavior and Some Figures on Procedures." J. of Conflict Resolution, 1966, 10: 272-296. Practices and probability of each leading to settlement.

1314. JOURNAL OF CONFLICT RESOLUTION. *Weapons Management in World Politics: Proceedings of the International Arms Control Symposium, Dec. 1962.* 1963, 7: 185-661. Special issue edited by J. D. Singer with articles on weapons management and conflict resolution, on various aspects of disarmament, and on the research frontiers in the general area.

1315. LEFEVER, E. W. "The Limits of U.N. Intervention in the Third World." R. of Politics, 1968, 30: 3-18. Role of multistate force in dealing with internal disorder.

1316. NIEZING, J. *Sociology, War and Disarmament.* Rotterdam: Rotterdam University Press, 1970. xii + 131 pp. A collection dealing with peace research.

1317. NIEZING, J. "United Nations' Peace-Keeping Operations as a Politico-Sociological Problem." Mens en Maatschappij, 1966, 41: 259-270.

1318. POOL, I. de S. "Public Opinion and the Control of Armaments." Daedalus, 1960, 89: 984-999.

1319. SOCIAL PROBLEMS. "Threat of War: Policy and Public Opinion." 1963, 11: 1-112. Special issue edited by P. I. Rose and J. Laulicht, with articles by L. Coser, A. Etzioni, C. E. Osgood, and others.

1320. STEGENGA, J. A. *The United Nations Force in Cyprus.* Columbus: Ohio State University Press, 1968. xiii + 227 pp. A case study and evaluation of international peace-keeping.

1321. VAN DOORN, J., & MANS, J. H. "United Nations Forces: on Legitimacy and Effectiveness of International Military Operations." Mens en Maatschappij, 1966, 41: 271-296. A revised version appears in J. van Doorn (Ed.) *Armed Forces and Society.* The Hague & Paris: Mouton, 1968. Pp. 345-377.

1322. WATT, D. C. "Disarmament and Problems of Civil-Military Relations among the Smaller Powers." International Relations, 1964, 2: 651-656. Factors that promote or hinder their participation in the demilitarization of international society.

1323. WIESLANDER, H. *I nedrustningens tecken* (Under the auspices of disarmament). Lund: Gleerup, 1966. 352 pp. Case study of the partial disarmament issue in Sweden, 1925.

1324. WRIGHT, Q. "Causation and Control of War." American Sociological R., 1938, 3: 461-474.

1325. WRIGHT, Q. "Conditions for Successful Disarmament." J. of Conflict Resolution, 1963, 7: 286-292.

VI.5  See also 181, 192, 375, 926, 1021, 1032, 1048, 1093, and 1282.

AUTHOR INDEX


TITLE INDEX


SUBJECT INDEX

# AUTHOR INDEX

(Numbers in parentheses indicate text pages in Part One; numbers not in parentheses indicate serials in Part Two.)

# TITLE INDEX

# SUBJECT INDEX

(All numbers are page numbers, both for text, Part One, and for Bibliography, Part Two.)

## ANNOTATED BIBLIOGRAPHY

# SUBJECT INDEX

KURT LANG received his Ph.D. in 1953 from the University of Chicago. He has taught at the University of Miami, Queens College (CUNY), University of California, and State University of New York at Stony Brook, and is currently on leave in Europe—under a grant from the National Endowment for the Humanities—working on a study of generational change as a transnational phenomenon. His major publications include Collective Dynamics, Television and Politics, and Voting and Nonvoting (all with Gladys Engel Lang). He is the author of several chapters in books devoted to studies of military institutions, as well as the article on the military in the International Encyclopedia of the Social Sciences (1968 edition).